Charles Haddon Spurgeon

Hands Full of Honey

And other sermons preached in 1883

Charles Haddon Spurgeon

Hands Full of Honey
And other sermons preached in 1883

ISBN/EAN: 9783337114572

Printed in Europe, USA, Canada, Australia, Japan

Cover: Foto ©Lupo / pixelio.de

More available books at **www.hansebooks.com**

Hands Full of Honey

And Other Sermons

Preached in 1883

C. H. SPURGEON
Of London

NOTE BY THE AMERICAN PUBLISHERS.

The wide circulation of Mr. Spurgeon's Earlier Sermons, preached a quarter of a century ago, it is believed will give a peculiar interest to these latest discourses of a great preacher still in the vigor of life.

New York, *March,* 1884.

CONTENTS.

I.	HANDS FULL OF HONEY	9
II.	ON LAYING FOUNDATIONS	31
III.	HEREIN IS LOVE	53
IV.	THE BEST WAR-CRY	75
V.	EARNEST EXPOSTULATION	96
VI.	THE BRIDEGROOM'S PARTING WORD	118
VII.	THE TENT DISSOLVED AND THE MANSION ENTERED.	139
VIII.	CHRIST IN YOU	161
IX.	GLORY	183
X.	KNOCK	204
XI.	IMITATORS OF GOD	226
XII.	BUYING WITHOUT MONEY	248
XIII.	THE VOICE FROM THE CLOUD AND THE VOICE OF THE BELOVED	270
XIV.	ACCEPTED OF THE GREAT FATHER	292
XV.	ON HUMBLING OURSELVES BEFORE GOD	312
XVI.	THE LUTHER SERMON AT EXETER-HALL	334
XVII.	BLESSED PROMISES FOR DYING OUTCASTS	356

I.

HANDS FULL OF HONEY.

January 28, 1883.

"And Samson turned aside to see the carcase of the lion: and, behold, there was a swarm of bees and honey in the carcase of the lion. And he took thereof in his hands, and went on eating, and came to his father and mother, and he gave them, and they did eat: but he told not them that he had taken the honey out of the carcase of the lion."—JUDGES xiv. 8, 9.

It was a singular circumstance that a man unarmed should have slain a lion in the prime of its vigor; and yet more strange that a swarm of bees should have taken possession of the dried carcase, and have filled it with their honey. In that country, what with beasts, birds, and insects, and the dry heat, a dead body is soon cleansed from all corruption, and the bones are clean and white: still the killing of the lion, and the finding of the honey, make up a remarkable story. These singular circumstances became afterwards the subject of a riddle; but with that riddle we have no concern at this time. Samson himself is a riddle. He was not only a riddle-maker; but he was himself an enigma very difficult to explain: with his personal character I have at this time little or nothing to do. We are not to-day resting at the house of "Gaius, mine host," where the pilgrims amused themselves with a dish of nuts after dinner; but we are on the march, and must attend to the more important matter of refreshing and inspiring those who are in our company. Neither are we going to discuss difficulties; but as Samson took the honey without being stung, so would we gain instruction without debate. We have in these days so much to do, that we must make practical use of every incident that comes before us in the word of God. My one design is to cheer the desponding and stir up all God's people to greater diligence in his service. I conceive that the text may legitimately be employed for this purpose. By the help of the divine Spirit, even after this lapse of time, we may find honey in the lion.

The particular part of the incident which is recorded in these two verses appears to have been passed over by those who have written upon Samson's life: I suppose it appeared to be too inconsiderable. They are taken up with his festive riddle, but they omit the far more natural and commendable fact of his bringing forth the honey in his hands and presenting it to his father and mother. This is the little scene to which I direct your glances. It seems to me that the Israelitish hero with a slain lion in the background, standing out in the open road with his hands laden with masses of honeycomb and dripping with honey, which he holds out to his parents, makes a fine picture, worthy of the greatest artist. And what a type we have here of our Divine Lord and Master, Jesus, the conqueror of death and hell. He has destroyed the lion that roared upon us and upon him. He has shouted "victory" over all our foes. "It is finished" was his note of triumph; and now he stands in the midst of his church with his hands full of sweetness and consolation, presenting them to those of whom he says, "These are my brother, and sister, and mother." To each one of us who believe in him he gives the luscious food which he has prepared for us by the overthrow of our foes; he bids us come and eat that we may have our lives sweetened and our hearts filled with joy.

To me the comparison seems wonderfully apt and suggestive: I see our triumphant Lord laden with sweetness, holding it forth to all his brethren, and inviting them to share in his joy.

But, beloved, it is written, "As he is, so are we also in this world." All that are true Christians are, in a measure, like the Christ whose name they bear, and it is to his image that we are finally to be conformed. When he shall appear we shall be like him, for we shall see him as he is; and meanwhile, in proportion as we see him now, "we are changed into the same image, from glory to glory, even as by the Spirit of the Lord." The Samson type may well serve as the symbol of every Christian in the world. The believer has been helped by divine grace in his spiritual conflicts, and he has known "the victory which overcometh the world, even our faith." He has thus been made more than a conqueror through him that loved us, and now he stands in the midst of his fellow-men inviting them to Jesus. With the honey in his hands, which he continues still to feast upon, he displays the heavenly sweetness to all that are round about him, saying, "O taste and see that the Lord is good: blessed is the man that trusteth in him."

I have before now met with that popular artist Gustave Doré, and suggested subjects to him. Had he survived among us, and had another opportunity occurred, I would have pressed him to execute a statue of Samson handing out the honey: strength distributing sweetness; and it might have served as a perpetual reminder of what a Christian should be—a Conqueror and a Comforter, slaying lions and distributing honey. The faithful servant of God wrestles with the powers of evil; but with far greater delight he speaks to his friends and companions, saying, "Eat ye that which is good, and let your souls delight themselves in sweetness." Set the statue before your mind's eye, and now let me speak about it.

Three touches may suffice. First, *the believer's life has its conflicts;* secondly, *the believer's life has its sweets;* and, thirdly, *the believer's life leads him to communicate of those sweets to others.* Here is room for profitable meditation.

I. First, then, THE BELIEVER'S LIFE HAS ITS CONFLICTS. To become a Christian is to enlist for a soldier. To become a believer is to enter upon a pilgrimage, and the road is often rough: the hills are steep, the valleys are dark, giants block the way, and robbers lurk in corners. The man who reckons that he can glide into heaven without a struggle has made a great mistake. No cross no crown: no sweat no sweet: no conflict no conquest. These conflicts, if we take the case of Samson as our symbol, *begin early* in the life of the believer. While Samson was a child, the Spirit of the Lord moved him in the camps of Dan—see the last verse of the thirteenth chapter; and as soon as he was on the verge of manhood, he must match himself with a lion. God who intended that his servant should smite the Philistines, and should check their proud oppression of his people Israel, began early to train the hero for his life's conflict. So, when Samson was going to seek a wife, he turned aside into the vineyards of Timnath, and a lion roared upon him. Yes, and the young believer, who as yet has not wrestled with the powers of darkness, will not be long before he hears the roar of the lion, and finds himself in the presence of the great Adversary. Very soon we learn the value of the prayer, "Deliver us from the evil one!" Most of the Lord's servants have been men of war from their youth up. Without are fightings even when within there are no fears. This early combat with the savage beast was intended by God to let him know his strength when under the influence of the Spirit, and to train him for his future combats with Israel's enemies. He that is to smite the Philistines hip and thigh with a great slaughter, until he has laid them heaps on heaps by his single prowess, must begin by rending a lion with his naked hands. He was to learn war in the same school as another and a greater hero, who afterwards said, "Thy servant slew both the lion and the bear, and this uncircumcised Philistine shall be as one of them."

Soldiers are made by war. You cannot train veterans or create victors except by battles. As in the wars of armies so is it in spiritual contests: men must be trained for victory over evil by combat with it. Hence "it is good for a man that he bare the yoke in his youth"; for it will not gall his shoulders in after years. It is assuredly a dangerous thing to be altogether free from trouble: in silken ease the soldier loses his prowess. Look at Solomon, one of the greatest and wisest, and yet, I might say, one of the least and most foolish of men. It was his fatal privilege to sit upon a throne of gold and sun himself in the brilliance of unclouded prosperity, and hence his heart soon went astray, and he fell from his high places. Solomon in his early days had no trouble, for no war was then raging, and no enemy worth notice was then living. His life ran smoothly on, and he was lulled into a dreamy sleep, the sleep of the voluptuous. He had been happier far had he been, like his father, called from his earliest days to trial and conflict; for this might have taught him to stand fast upon the pinnacle of glory whereon the providence of God had placed him. Learn, then, O young brother, that if, like Samson, you are to be a **hero** for Israel, you must early be inured to suffering and daring, in some form or other. When you step aside and seek for meditation in the quiet of the vineyard a young lion may roar upon you; even as in the earliest days of your Lord and Master's public service he was led into the wilderness to be tempted of the devil.

These conflicts, dear friends, may often be *very terrible*. By a young lion is not meant a whelp, but a lion in the fulness of its early strength; not yet slackened in its pace, or curbed in its fury by growing years. Fresh and furious, a young lion is the worst kind of beast that a man can meet with. Let us expect as followers of Christ to meet with strong temptations, fierce persecutions, and severe trials, which will lead to stern conflicts. Do not reckon, thou that art yet putting on thy harness, that thou shalt soon put it off, or that when thou puttest it off it will be quite as bright as it is to-day. It will be dimmed with blood and dust, and battered by many a blow; perhaps thy foe may find a way to pierce it, or at least to wound thee between its joints. I would have every man begin to be a soldier of the cross, but I would at the same time have him count the cost; for it is no child's play, and if he thinks it will be such, he will be grievously disappointed. A young believer will, on a sudden, have a doubt suggested to him of which he never heard before; and it will roar upon him like a young lion; neither will he see all at once how to dispose of it. Or he may be placed in singular circumstances where his duty seems to run counter to the tenderest instincts of his nature; here, too, the young lion will roar upon him. Or, one for whom he has an intense respect may treat him ill because he is a follower of Christ, and the affection and respect which he feels for this person may make his opposition the more grievous: in this also it is with him as when a lion roareth. Or he may suffer a painful bereavement, or sustain a severe loss; or he may have a disease upon him, with consequent pains and depressions, and these may cast the shadow of death upon his spirit; so that again a young lion roars upon him. Brother, sister, let us reckon upon this, and not be dismayed by it, since in all this is the life of our spirit. By such lessons as these we are taught to do service for God, to sympathize with our fellow Christians, and to value the help of our gracious Saviour. By all these we are weaned from earth and made to hunger for that eternal glory which is yet to be revealed, of which we may truly say, " No lion shall be there, neither shall any ravenous beast go up thereon." These present evils are for our future good: their terror is for our teaching. Trials are sent us for much the same reason that the Canaanites were permitted to live in the Holy Land, that Israel might learn war, and be equipped for battles against foreign foes.

These conflicts come early, and they are very terrible; and, moreover, they happen to us *when we are least prepared for them.* Samson was not hunting for wild beasts; he was engaged on a much more tender business. He was walking in the vineyards of Timnath, thinking of anything but lions, and " behold," says the Scripture, "a young lion roared against him." It was a remarkable and startling occurrence. He had left his father and mother and was quite alone; no one was within call to aid him in meeting his furious assailant. Human sympathy is exceedingly precious, but there are points in our spiritual conflict in which we cannot expect to receive it. To each man there are passages in life too narrow for walking two abreast. Upon certain crags we must stand alone. As our constitutions differ, so our trials, which are suited to our constitutions, must differ also. Each individual has a secret with which no friend can intermeddle; for every life has its mystery and its hid treasure. Do not be ashamed, young Christian, if you meet with temptations which appear to you to be quite singular: we have each one thought the same of his trials. You imagine that no one suffers as you do, whereas no temptation hath happened unto you but such as is common to man, and God will with the temptation make a way of escape that you may be able to bear it. Yet for the time being you may have to enter into fellowship with your Lord when he trod the winepress alone, and of the people there was none with him. Is not this for your good? Is not this the way to strength? What kind of piety is that which is dependent upon the friendship of man? What sort of religion is that which cannot stand alone? Beloved, you will have to die alone, and you need therefore grace to cheer you in solitude. The dear wife can attend you weeping to the river's brink, but into the chill stream she cannot go with you; and if you have not a religion which will sustain you in the solitudes of life, of what avail will it be to you in the grim lonesomeness of death? Thus I reckon it to be a happy circumstance that you are called to solitary conflict that you may test your faith, and see of what stuff your hope is made.

The contest was all the worse for Samson, that in addition to being quite alone, "there was nothing in his hand." This is the most remarkable point in the narrative. He had no sword or hunter's spear with which to wound the lordly savage: he had not even a stout staff with which to ward off his attack. Samson stood an unarmed, unarmored man in the presence of a raging beast. So we in our early temptations are apt to think that we have no weapon for the war, and we do not know what to do. We are made to cry out, "I am unprepared! How can I meet this trial? I cannot grasp the enemy to wrestle with him. What am I to do?" Herein will the splendor of faith and glory of God be made manifest, when you shall slay the lion, and yet it shall be said of you "that he had nothing in his hand"—nothing but that which the world sees not and values not.

Now, go one step further, for time forbids our lingering here. I invite you to remember that *it was by the Spirit of God that the victory was won.* We read, "And the Spirit of the Lord came mightily upon him, and he rent him as he would have rent a kid." Let the Holy Spirit help us in our trouble and we need neither company nor weapon; but without him what can we do? Good Bishop Hall says, "If that roaring lion, that goes about continually seeking whom he may devour, find us alone among the vineyards of the Philistines, where is our hope? Not in our heels, he is swifter than we: not in our weapons, we are naturally unarmed: not in our hands, which are weak and languishing; but in the Spirit of God, by whom we can do all things. If God fight in us, who can resist us? There is a stronger lion in us than that against us."

Here is our one necessity,—to be endowed with power from on high: the power of the Holy Ghost. Helped by the Spirit of God, the believer's victory will be complete: the lion shall not be driven away but rent in pieces. Girt with the Spirit's power, our victory shall be as easy as it will be perfect: Samson rent the lion as though it were a little lamb, or a kid of the goats. Well said Paul, "I can do all things through Christ that strengtheneth me." Sin is soon overcome, temptations are readily refused, affliction is joyfully borne, persecution is gladly endured, when the Spirit of glory and of peace resteth upon us. "With God all things are possible;" and as the believer is with God, it cometh to pass that all things are possible to him that believeth.

If we were surrounded by all the devils in hell we need not fear them for an instant if the Lord be on our side. We are mightier than all hell's legions when the Spirit is mightily upon us. If we were to be beaten down by Satan until he had set his foot upon our breast, to press the very life out of us, yet if the Spirit of God helped us we would reach out our hand, and grasp the sword of the Spirit, which is the word of God, and we would repeat the feat of Christian with Apollyon, when he gave the fiend such grievous wounds that he spread his dragon wings and flew away. Wherefore fear not, ye tried ones, but trust in the Spirit of God, and your conflict shall speedily end in victory. Sometimes our conflict is with past sin. We doubtfully enquire, "How can it be forgiven?" The temptation vanishes before a sight of the dying Redeemer. Then inbred lust roars against us, and we overcome it through the blood of the Lamb, for "the blood of Jesus Christ his Son cleanseth us from all sin." Sometimes a raging corruption, or a strong habit, wars upon us, and then we conquer by the might of the sanctifying Spirit of God, who is with us and shall be in us evermore. Or else it is the world which tempts, and our feet have almost gone; but we overcome the world through the victory of faith: and if Satan raises against us the lust of the flesh, the lust of the eye, and the pride of life, all at once, we are still delivered, for the Lord is a wall of fire round about us. The inward life bravely resists all sin, and God's help is given to believers to preserve them from all evil in the moment of urgent need; even as he helped his martyrs and confessors to speak the right word when called unprepared to confront their adversaries. Care not, therefore, oh thou truster in the Lord Jesus, how fierce thine enemy may be this day! As young David slew the lion and the bear, and smote the Philistine too, even so shalt thou go from victory to victory. "Many are the afflictions of the righteous, but the Lord delivereth him out of them all." Wherefore, with a lion-like spirit, meet lions which seek to devour you.

II. Now, then, we come to our second head, which is: THE BELIEVER'S LIFE HAS ITS SWEETS. We are not always killing lions, we are sometimes eating honey. Certain of us do both at a time; we kill lions and yet cease not to eat honey: and truly it has become so sweet a thing to enter into conflict for Christ's sake, that it is a joy to contend earnestly for the faith once delivered to the saints. The same Lord who hath bidden us "quit yourselves like men; be strong," has also said, "Rejoice in the Lord alway; and again I say, rejoice."

The believer's life has its sweets, and these are of the choicest: for what is sweeter than honey? What is more joyful than the joy of a saint? What is more happy than the happiness of a believer? I will not condescend to make a comparison between our joy and the mirth of fools; I will go no further than a contrast. Their mirth is as the crackling of thorns under a pot, which spit fire, and make a noise and a flash, but there is no heat, and they are soon gone out: nothing comes of it, the pot is long in boiling. But the Christian's delight is like a steady coal fire. You have seen the grate full of coals all burning red, and the whole mass of coal has seemed to be one great glowing ruby and everybody who has come into the room out of the cold has delighted to warm his hands, for it gives out a steady heat and warms the body even to its marrow. Such are our joys. I would sooner possess the joy of Christ five minutes than I would revel in the mirth of fools for half a century. There is more bliss in the tear of repentance than in the laughter of gaiety; our holy sorrows are sweeter than the worldling's joys. But, oh, when our joys grow full, divinely full, then are they unspeakably like those above, and heaven begins below. Did you never cry for joy? You say, perhaps, "Not since I was a child." Nor have I; but I have always remained a child as far as divine joy is concerned. I could often cry for joy when I know whom I have believed and am persuaded that he is able to keep that which I have committed to him.

Ours is a joy which will bear thinking over. You can dare to pry into the bottom of it and test its foundation. It is a joy which does not grow stale; you may keep it in your mouth by the year together, and yet it never cloys; you may return to it again, and again, and again, and find it still as fresh as ever. And the best of it is there is no repentance after it. You are never sorry that you were so glad. The world's gay folk are soon sick of their drink; but we are only sorry that we were not gladder still, for our gladness sanctifies. We are not denied any degree of joy to which we can possibly attain, for ours is a healthy, health-giving delight. Christ is the fulness of joy to his people, and we are bidden to enjoy him to the full. Christians have their sweets, and those are as honey and the honeycomb, the best of the best.

Of these joys *there is plenty;* for Samson found, as it were, a living spring of honey, since he discovered a swarm of bees. So abundant was the honey that he could take huge masses of the comb and carry it in his hands, and go away with it, bearing it to others. In the love of Christ, in pardoned sin, in acceptance in the Beloved, in resting in God, in perfectly acquiescing in his will, in the hope of heaven, there is such joy that none can measure it. We have such a living swarm of bees to make honey for us in the precious promises of God, that there is more delight in store than any of us can possibly realize. There is infinitely more of Christ beyond our comprehension than we have as yet been able to comprehend. How blessed to receive of his fulness, to be sweetened with his sweetness, and yet to know that infinite goodness still remains. Perhaps some of you have enjoyed so much of Christ that you could hardly bear any more; but your largest enjoyments are only as tiny shells filled by a single wave of the sea, while all the boundless ocean rolls far beyond your ken. We have exceeding great joy, yea, joy to spare. Our Master's wedding feast is not so scantily furnished that we have to bring in another seat for an extra guest, or murmur to ourselves that we had better not invite at random lest we should be incommoded by too great a crowd. Nay, rather the pillared halls of mercy in which the King doth make his feast are so vast that it will be our life-long business to furnish them with guests, compelling more and more to come in that his house may be filled, and that his royal festival may make glad ten thousand times ten thousand hearts.

Dear friends, if you want to know what are the elements of our joy, I have already hinted at them, but I will for a moment enlarge thereon. *Our joys are often found in the former places of our conflicts.* We gather our honey out of the lions which have been slain for us or by us.

There is, first, our sin. A horrible lion that! But it is a dead lion, for grace has much more abounded over abounding sin. Oh, brothers I have never heard of any dainty in all the catalogue of human joys that could match a sense of pardoned sin. Full forgiveness! Free forgiveness! Eternal forgiveness. See, it sparkles like dew of heaven. To know that God has blotted out my sin is knowledge rich with unutterable bliss. My soul has begun to hear the songs of seraphim when it has heard that note, " I have blotted out thy sins like a cloud, and as a thick cloud thine iniquities." Here is choice honey for you!

The next dead lion is conquered desire. When a wish has arisen in the heart contrary to the mind of God, and you have said—" Down with you! I will pray you down. You used to master me; I fell into a habit and I was soon overcome by you; but I will not again yield to you. By God's grace I will conquer you";—I say, when at last you have obtained the victory such a sweet contentment perfumes your heart that you are filled with joy unspeakable; and you are devoutly grateful to have been helped of the Spirit of God to master your own spirit. Thus you have again eaten spiritual honey.

When you are able to feel in your own soul that you have overcome a strong temptation, the fiercer it was and the more terrible it was the louder has been your song and the more joyful your thanksgiving. To go back to Mr. Bunyan again; when Christian had passed through the Valley of the Shadow of Death during the night, and when he had come entirely out of it and the sun rose, you remember he looked back. (A pause). He was long in taking that look, I warrant you. What thoughts he had while looking back. He could just discern that narrow track with the quagmire on one side and the deep ditch on the other; and he could see the shades out of which the hobgoblins hooted and the fiery eyes glanced forth. He looked back by sunlight and thought within himself, "Ah me! What goodness has been with me! I have gone through all that, and yet I am unharmed!" What a happy survey it was to him! Ah, the joy of having passed through temptation without having defiled one's garments! How must Shadrach, Meshach, and Abednego have felt when they stepped out of the fiery furnace, and were not even singed, neither had the smell of fire passed upon them. Happy men were they to have lived in the centre of the seven-times-heated furnace where everything else was consumed. Here again is "a piece of an honeycomb."

We find honey again from another slain lion; namely, our troubles after we have been enabled to endure them. This is the metal of which our joy-bells are cast. Out of the brass of our trials we make the trumpets of our triumph. He is not the happy man who has seen no trouble; but "blessed is he that endureth temptation, for when he is tried he shall receive a crown of life that fadeth not away."

Death, too. Oh, the honey that is found in dead death. Death is indeed dead. We triumph over him, and are no more afraid of him than little children are of a dead lion. We pluck him by the beard, and say to him, "O death, where is thy sting? O grave, where is thy victory?" We even look forward to the time of our departure with delight, when we shall leave this heavy clay and on spirit wings ascend unto our Father and our God. You see there is rich store of honey for God's people; and we do not hesitate to eat it. Let others say as they will, we are a happy people, happy in Christ, happy in the Holy Spirit, happy in God our Father. So that believers have their sweets.

III. But the third is the point I want to dwell upon: **THE BELIEVER'S LIFE LEADS** HIM TO COMMUNICATE OF THESE SWEETS.

As soon as we have tasted the honey of forgiven sin and perceived the bliss that God has laid up for his people in Christ Jesus, we feel it to be both our duty and our privilege to communicate the good news to others. Here let my ideal statue stand in our midst: the strong man, conqueror of the lion, holding forth his hands full of honey to his parents. We are to be modelled according to this fashion.

And, first, we do this *immediately*. The moment a man is converted, if he would let himself alone, his instincts would lead him to tell his fellows. I know that the moment I came out of that little chapel wherein I found the Saviour, I wanted to pour out my tale of joy. I could have cried with Cennick—

> "Now will I tell to sinners round,
> What a dear Saviour I have found;
> I'll point to thy redeeming blood,
> And say, 'Behold the way to God!'"

I longed to tell how happy my soul was, and what a deliverance I had obtained from the crushing burden of sin. I longed to see all others come and trust my Lord and live! I did not preach a sermon, but I think I could have told out all the gospel at that first hour. Did not you, my friend, feel much the same? Did not your tongue long to be telling of what the Lord had done for you? Perhaps you are one of those proper and retiring people who are greatly gifted at holding their tongues; and therefore you left the feet of Jesus in silence,—silence which angels wondered at. Is that why you have held your tongue ever since? Perhaps if you had begun to speak then you would have continued your testimony to this day. I repeat my assertion that it is the instinct of every newborn soul to communicate the glad tidings which grace has proclaimed in his heart. Just as Samson had no sooner tasted of the honey than he carried a portion of it to his father and mother, so do we hasten to invite our neighbors to Christ. My dear young friend, as soon as ever you know the joy of the Lord, open your mouth in a quiet, humble way, and never allow yourself to be numbered with the deaf and dumb. Let no one stop you from unburdening your heart. Do not follow the bad example of those who have become dumb dogs because of their cowardice at the beginning.

The believer will do this *first to those who are nearest to him*. Samson took the honey to his father and mother who were not far away. With each of us the most natural action would be to tell a brother or a sister or a fellow-workman, or a bosom friend. It will be a great joy to see them eating the honey which is so pleasant to our own palate. It is most natural in a parent at once to wish to tell his children of divine love—have you all done so? You pray for your children, but many of you would be the means of answering your own prayers if you would talk with them one by one. This may appear difficult, but once commenced it will soon grow easy; and, indeed, if it be difficult we should aspire to do it for that very reason. Should we not do many a difficult thing for him who overcame all difficulties for us? At the least, do not deny to your own children the personal testimony of their father or their mother to the surpassing power of grace and the unutterable sweetness of divine love. Tell it to those who are nearest to you.

The believer will do this as best he can. Samson, you see, brought the honey to his father and mother in a rough and ready style, going on eating it as he brought it. If I wished to give honey to my father and mother I should do it up rather daintily: I would at least put it in as respectable a dish as our kitchen could afford: but there were no plates and dishes out there in that Timnath vineyard, and so his own hands were the only salvers upon which Samson could present the delicacy,—"he took thereof in his hands, and came to his father and mother, and he gave them, and they did eat." Perhaps you think, "If I am to speak to any person upon true religion, I should like to do it in poetry." Better do it in prose, for perhaps they will take more notice of your verse than of your subject. Give them the honey *in your hands*, and if there is no dish they cannot take notice of the dish. "Ay, but I should like to do it very properly," says one; "it is a very important matter, I should like to speak most correctly." But my judgment is, that, as you will not be likely to attain to correct speech all in a hurry, and your friends may die while you are learning your grammar and your rhetoric, you had better tell them of Jesus according to your present ability. Tell them there is life in a look at Jesus. Tell them the story simply, as one child talks to another. Carry the honey in your hands, though it drip all round: no hurt will come of the spilling, there are always little ones waiting for such drops. If you were to make the gospel drip about everywhere, and sweeten all things, it would be no waste, but a blessed gain to all around. Therefore, I say to you, tell of Jesus Christ as best you can, and never cease to do so while life lasts.

But then Samson did another thing, and every true believer should do it too: he did not merely tell his parents about the honey, but *he took them some of it*. I do not read, "And he told his father and mother of the honey," but I read, "and he took thereof in his hands." Nothing is so powerful as an exhibition of grace itself to others. Do not talk about it, but carry it in your hands. "I cannot do that," says one. Yes, you can, by your life, your temper, your spirit, your whole bearing. If your hands serve God, if your heart serves God, if your face beams with joy in the service of God, you will carry grace wherever you go, and those who see you will perceive it. You will hardly have need to say, "Come and partake of grace;" for the grace of God in you will be its own invitation and attraction. Let our lives be full of Christ and we shall preach Christ. A holy life is the best of sermons. Soul-winning is wrought by a winning life more surely than by winning words.

Take note, also, that Samson *did this with great modesty*. We have plenty of people about nowadays who could not kill a mouse without publishing it in the Gospel Gazette; but Samson killed a lion and said nothing about it. He holds the honey in his hand for his father and mother—he shows them *that;* but we are specially informed that he told not his father or his mother that he had taken it out of the carcase of the lion. The Holy Spirit finds modesty so rare that he takes care to record it. In telling your own experience be wisely cautious. Say much of what the Lord has done for you, but say little of what you have done for the Lord. You need not make much effort to be brief on that point, for I am afraid that there is not much of it, if all were told. Do not utter a self-glorifying sentence. Let us put Christ to the front, and the joy and blessedness that comes of faith in him; and as for ourselves, we need not speak a word except to lament our sins and shortcomings.

The sum of what I have to say is this,—if we have tasted any joy in Christ, if we have known any consolation of the Spirit, if faith has been to us a real power, and if it has wrought in us peace and rest, let us communicate this blessed discovery to others. If you do not do so, mark you, you will have missed the very object for which God has blessed you. I heard the other day of a Sunday-school address in America which pleased me much. The teacher, speaking to the boys, said, "Boys, here's a watch, what is it for?" The children answered, "To tell the time." "Well," he said, "suppose my watch does not tell the time, what is it good for?" "Good-for-nothing, sir." Then he took out a pencil. "What is this pencil for?" "It is to write with, sir." "Suppose this pencil won't make a mark, what is it good for?" "Good-for-nothing, sir." Then he took out his pocket-knife. "Boys, what is this for?" They were American boys, and so they shouted,—"to whittle with,"—that is to experiment on any substance that came in their way by cutting a notch in it. "But," said he, "suppose it will not cut, what is the knife good for?" "Good-for-nothing, sir." Then the teacher asked, "What is the chief end of man?" and they replied, "To glorify God." "But suppose a man does not glorify God, what is he good for?" "Good-for-nothing, sir." That brings out my point most clearly; there are many professors of whom I will not say that they are good-for-nothing, but methinks if they do not soon stir themselves up to glorify God by proclaiming the sweetness of God's love it will go hard with them. Remember how Jesus said of the savourless salt "henceforth it is good for nothing." What were you converted for? What were you forgiven for? What were you renewed for? What have you been preserved on earth for but to tell to others the glad tidings of salvation and so to glorify God? Do, then, go out with your hands full of the honey of divine love and hold it out to others.

You must assuredly do good by this; you cannot possibly do harm. Samson did not invite his father and mother to see the lion when he was alive and roaring, —he might have done some hurt in that case, by frightening them, or exposing them to injury; but he settled the lion business himself, and when it came to honey he knew that even his mother could not be troubled about *that*; therefore he invited them both to share his gains. When you get into a soul-conflict, do not publish your distress to all your friends, but fight manfully in God's name; but when you possess the joy of Christ and the love of the Spirit, and grace is abundant in your soul, then tell the news to all around. You cannot do any hurt by such a proceeding: grace does good, and no harm, all its days. Even if you blunder over it you will do no mischief. The gospel spilled on the ground is not lost. Good, and only good, must come of making known salvation by Jesus Christ.

It will be much better for you to tell of the sweets of godliness than it will be to make riddles about the doctrine of it. Samson afterwards made a riddle about his lion and the honey; and that riddle ended in fighting and bloodshed. We have known certain Christians spend their lives in making riddles about the honey and the lion, by asking tough doctrinal questions which even angels cannot answer: "Riddle me this," they say, and then it has ended in a fight, and brotherly love has been murdered in the fray. It is much better to bring your hands full of honey to those who are needy, and present it to them that they may eat of it, than it is to cavil and discuss. No hurt can come of telling what the Lord has done for your soul, and it will keep you out of mischief. Therefore, I would stir up all Christian people to continue from day to day exhibiting to needy sinners the blessedness of Christ, that unbelievers may come and eat thereof.

By doing this you will be blessing men far more than Samson could bless his parents; for our honey is honey unto eternity, our sweets are sweets that last to heaven, and are best enjoyed there. Call upon others to taste and see that the Lord is good, and you shall have therein much joy. You shall increase your own pleasure by seeing the pleasure of the Lord prospering in your hand. What bliss awaits useful Christians when they enter into heaven, for they shall be met there by many who have gone before them whom they were the means of turning to Christ. I do often inwardly sing when I perceive that I can scarce go into any town or village but what somebody hunts me up to say to me, "Under God I owe my salvation to your sermons or to your books." What will be the felicities of heaven when we shall meet those who were turned to righteousness by our holding forth the word of life! Our heaven will be seven heavens as we see them there. If you have done nothing but exhibit in your lives the precious results of grace you will have done well. If you have presented to your companions truths that were sweetness itself to you, and tried to say in broken accents "Oh that you knew this peace!" it shall give you joy unspeakable to meet those in glory who were attracted to Christ by such a simple means.

God make you all to be his witnesses in all the circles wherein you move.

II.

ON LAYING FOUNDATIONS.

January 21, 1883.

"And why call ye me, Lord, Lord, and do not the things which I say? Whosoever cometh to me, and heareth my sayings, and doeth them, I will shew you to whom he is like: He is like a man which built an house, and digged deep, and laid the foundation on a rock: and when the flood arose, the stream beat vehemently upon that house, and could not shake it: for it was founded upon a rock. But he that heareth, and doeth not, is like a man that without a foundation built an house upon the earth; against which the stream did beat vehemently, and immediately it fell; and the ruin of that house was great."—LUKE vi. 46-49.

THESE parables describe two classes of hearers; but they say nothing of those who are not hearers. Their position and prospects we must infer from what is said of hearers. Our Lord Jesus Christ has come into the world to tell us of the Father's love, and never man spake as he spake, and yet there are many who refuse to hear him. I do not mean those who are far away, to whom the name of Jesus is well-nigh unknown, but I mean persons in this land, and especially in this great and highly-favored city, who wilfully refuse to hear him whom God has anointed to bring tidings of salvation. Our Lord Jesus is proclaimed, I was about to say, upon the house-tops in this city; for even in their music-halls and theatres Christ is preached to the multitude, and at the corners of our streets his banner is lifted up; and yet there are tens of thousands to whom the preaching of the gospel is as music in the ears of a corpse. They shut their ears and will not hear, though the testimony be concerning God's own Son, and life eternal, and the way to escape from everlasting wrath. To their own best interests, to their eternal benefit, men are dead: nothing will secure their attention to their God. To what, then, are these men like? They may fitly be compared to the man that built no house whatever, and remained homeless by day and shelterless by night. When worldly trouble comes like a storm those persons who will not hear the words of Jesus have no consolation to cheer them; when sickness comes they have no joy of heart to sustain them under its pains; and when death, that most terrible of storms, beats upon them they feel its full fury, but they cannot find a hiding place. They neglect the housing of their souls, and when the hurricane of almighty wrath shall break forth in the world to come they will have no place of refuge. In vain will they call upon the rocks to fall upon them, and the mountains to cover them. They shall be in that day without a shelter from the righteous wrath of the Most High. Alas, that any being who wears the image of man should be found in such a plight! Homeless wanderers in the day of tempest! How my soul grieves for them! Yet, what excuse will those men invent who have refused even to know the way of salvation? What excuse can the tenderest heart make for them? Will they plead that they could not believe? Yet they may not say that they could not hear; and faith cometh by hearing, and hearing by the word of God. Oh my friend, if the word of God comes to you, and you decline to hear it, and therefore do not believe in Jesus, but die in your sins, what is this but soul-suicide? If a man die of a disease when infallible medicine is to be had, must not his death lie at his own door? If a man perish of hunger when bread is all around him and others feed to the full, and he will not have it, will any man pity him? Surely not a drop of pity will be yielded to a lost soul wherewith he may assuage the torment of his conscience, for all holy intelligences will perceive that the sinner chose his own destruction. This shall ever press upon the condemned conscience, "You knew the gospel, but you did not attend to it: you knew that there was salvation, and that Christ was the Saviour, and that pardon was proclaimed to guilty men, but you would not afford time from your farm and from your merchandise, from your pleasures and from your sins, to learn how you could be saved. That which cost God so dear you treated as a trifle. Ah, my dear friends, may none of you belong to the non-hearing class. It is not to such that I shall this morning address myself, and yet I could not enter upon my discourse without a word of loving expostulation with them. Let me part with them by quoting the warning word of the Holy Spirit, "See that ye refuse not him that speaketh. For if they escaped not who refused him that spake on earth, much more shall not we escape, if we turn away from him that speaketh from heaven."

Our earnest attention will now be given to thos who are hearers of the word, and are somewhat affected by it. All hearers are builders of houses for their souls: they are each one doing something to set up a spiritual habitation. Some of these go a considerable distance in this house-building, and even crown the structure by publicly confessing Christ. They say unto him, "Lord, Lord": they meet with his followers, and join with them in reverence to the Master's name; but they do not obey the Lord; they hear him, but they fail to do the things which he says. Hence they are mistaken builders, who fail in the foundation, and make nothing sure except that their house will come down about their ears. Others there are, and we trust they will be found to be many among us, who are building rightly, building for eternity; constructing a dwelling-place with basis of rock, and walls of well-built stone, of which the Lord Christ is both foundation and corner-stone.

I am anxious to speak at this time to those who are just beginning to build for eternity. I am indeed happy to know that there are many such among us. May the Holy Spirit bless this sermon to them.

I. Our first subject will be A COMMON TEMPTATION WITH SPIRITUAL BUILDERS. A common temptation with hearers of the word, according to the two parables before us, is to neglect foundation-work, to get hurriedly over the first part of the business, and run up the building quickly. They are tempted to assume that all is done which is said to be done; to take it for granted that all is right which is hoped to be right; and then to go on piling up the walls as rapidly as possible. The great temptation, I say, with young beginners in religious life, is to scamp the foundation, and treat those things lightly which are of the first importance. The same temptation comes to us throughout the whole of life, but to young beginners it is especially perilous: Satan would have them neglect the fundamental principles upon which their future hope and character are to rest, so that in a future trying hour, from want of a solid foundation, they may yield to evil, and lose the whole of their life-building.

This temptation is all the more dangerous, first, because *these young beginners have no experience.* Even the most experienced child of God is often deceived; how much more the pilgrim who has but just entered the wicket-gate! The tried saint sometimes mistakes that for a virtue which is only a gilded fault, and he fancies that to be genuine which is mere counterfeit; how, then, without any experience whatever, can the mere babe in grace escape deception unless he be graciously preserved? Newly awakened, and rendered serious, earnest hearts get to work in the divine life with much hurry, seizing upon that which first comes to hand, building in heedless haste, without due care and examination. Something must be done, and they do it without asking whether it is according to the teaching of the Lord. They call Jesus "Lord"; but they do what others say rather than what Jesus says. Satan is sure to be at hand at such times that he may lead the young convert to lay in place of gospel repentance a repentance that needs to be repented of, and instead of the faith of God's elect a proud presumption or an idle dream. For that love of God which is the work of the Spirit of God he brings mere natural affection for a minister; and he says, "There, that will do: you must have a house for your soul to dwell in. There are the materials, pile them up." Like children at play upon the beach, the anxious heap up their sand-castles, and please themselves therewith, for they are ignorant of Satan's devices. I am for this cause doubly anxious to save my beloved young friends from the deceiver. The common temptation, is, instead of really repenting, to *talk about* repentance; instead of heartily believing, to *say,* " I believe," without believing; instead of truly loving, to talk of love, without loving; instead of coming to Christ, to speak about coming to Christ, and profess to come to Christ, and yet not to come at all. The character of Talkative in Pilgrim's Progress is ably drawn. I have met the gentleman many times, and can bear witness that John Bunyan was **a photographer** before photography was invented. Christian said of him "He talketh of prayer, of repentance, of faith, and of the new birth; but he knows but only to *talk* of them. I have been in his family, and his house is as empty of religion as the white of an egg is of savor." We have too many such persons around us who are, as to what they say, everything that is to be desired, and yet, by what they are proven to be, mere shams. As tradesmen place dummies in their shops, papered and labelled to look like goods, while yet they are nothing of the sort, so are these men marked and labelled as Christians, but the grace of God is not in them. Oh that you young beginners may be on the alert, that you be not content with the form of godliness, but are made to feel the power of it.

There is this to help the temptation too, that *this plan for the present saves a great deal of trouble.* Your mind is distressed, and you want comfort; well, it will comfort you to say, "Lord, Lord," though you do not the things that Christ says. If you admit the claims of Jesus to be Lord, even though you do not believe on him for salvation, and so neglect the main thing which he commands, yet you will find some ease in the admission. He bids you repent of sin, trust his blood, love his word, and seek after holiness; but it is much easier to admire these things without following after them in your life. To feign repentance and faith is not difficult, but genuine godliness is heart-work, and requires thought, care, sincerity, prayerfulness, and watchfulness. Believe me, real religion is no sport. He that would be saved will find it to be no jesting matter. "The kingdom of heaven suffereth violence"; and he that is easy about the thing, and thinks it is nothing more than the conjuror's "Heigh, presto, done," has made a fatal mistake. "Strive," saith Christ, "to enter into the strait gate." The Spirit striveth in us mightily, and often works us to an agony. The crown of eternal glory is not won without fighting, nor the prize of our high calling received without running; yet by just making a holy profession, and by practicing an outward form, a man imagines that the same result is produced as by seeking the Lord with his whole heart, and believing in the Lord Jesus. If it were so, there would be a fine broad road to heaven, and Satan himself would turn pilgrim. Believe me, dear hearers, this saving of trouble will turn out to be a making of trouble, and, before matters end, the hardest way will turn out to be the easiest way.

This kind of building without foundation has this advantage to back up the temptation,—*it enables a man to run up a religion very quickly.* He makes splendid progress. While the anxious heart is searching after truth in the inward parts, and begging to be renewed by grace, his exulting friend is as happy as he can be in a peace which he has suddenly obtained without question or examination. This rapid grower never asks, "Has my religion changed my conduct? Is my faith attended by a new nature? Does the Spirit of God dwell in me? Am I really what I profess to be, or am I but a bastard professor after all?" No, he puts aside all enquiry as a temptation of the devil. He takes every good thing for granted, and votes that all is gold which glitters. See how fast he goes! The fog is dense, but he steams through it, heedless of danger! He has joined the church: he has commenced work for God: he is boasting of his own attainments: he hints that he is perfect. But is this mushroom building safe? Will it pass muster in the last great survey? Will it stand should a tempest happen? The chimney-shaft is tall, but is it safe? Ay, there's the rub. This is the question which makes an end of much of the boasting which is all around us. It is better to tremble at God's word than boldly to presume. It is better to be fearful, lest after all we may be castaways, than to harden one's forehead with vain confidence. When a man travels upon a wrong road, the faster he runs the further he will go astray. Remember the advice to hasten slowly, and the old proverb which saith, "The more haste the less speed." If you build quickly because you build without a foundation, your time and toil are thrown away.

How common, how deceptive is this temptation! For the young beginner, the man who is just aroused to seek the Lord, will find *a great many to help him in his mistake*, should he neglect the foundation. Kind, good, Christian friends often, without a thought of doing so, help to mislead seeking souls. "Yes," they say, "you are converted," and so perhaps the person would be if all he said was true; but then it is said without feeling; it comes from the lip only, and does not come from the heart; and therefore it is ruinous to encourage him. A kindly assurance from a Christian friend may breed false confidence, if that assurance was mistakenly given. In these days we do not meet with many Christians who err by dealing too severely with converts; the shot strikes the other target. Our forefathers were possibly too suspicious and jealous; but nowadays we nearly all err in the opposite direction: we are so anxious to see everybody brought to Christ, that our wish may tend to delude us into the belief that it is so. We are so willing to cheer and comfort those who seek the Lord, that we may fall into the habit of prophesying smooth things, and thus shun everything which tends to probe and test, lest it should also discourage. Let us beware lest we cry, "Peace, peace," where there is no peace. It will be a sad thing to breed hypocrites when we were looking for converts. I have heard of one who had been into the Enquiry Room a dozen times, and when on another occasion she was invited to go there she said, "I really do not know why I should go, for I have been told that I was saved twelve times already, and I am not a bit better than before they told me so." It would be better to send some home weeping rather than rejoicing. Many a wound needs the lancet more than the plaster. You may be comforted by well-meant assurances of tender friends, and yet that comfort may be all a lie. I therefore warn you against any peace except that which comes from doing that which Jesus commands, or in other words, against any confidence except that which rests in Jesus only, and is attended with repentance, faith, and a life of obedience to your Lord.

No doubt many are encouraged in slight building by the fact that *so many professors are making a fair show, and yet their building is without foundation.* We cannot shut our eyes to the fact that in all churches there are persons who have no depth of spiritual root, and we are afraid no real spiritual life. We cannot root them up, though we fear that they are tares, for we are assured that we should unavoidably root up the wheat with them, and this our Master forbids. There is nothing about their outward conduct which we could lay hold upon as a proof of their being deceivers, and yet a cold chill runs through us when we talk with them, for they have no warmth, and no life, and nothing of the Lord about them. We miss in their conversation that sweet spirituality, that holy unction, that blessed humility, which are sure to be present when men are truly familiar with the Lord, and have entered into living union with him. People of this order mix up with us in our holy convocations, and when they come across the newly-awakened ones, they talk of divine things in such an off-hand and flippant manner that they do serious mischief. They speak about conversion as if it were a mere trifle, a matter as easy as kissing your hand; and so those who are hopeful, and over whom our hearts are yearning, are turned aside by them. Young people are apt to think, "So-and-so is a member of the church, and he is never very precise. If a lukewarm profession satisfies him, why should it not satisfy me!" Ah, my dear friends, but you would not say so in business. If you knew a man was trading without capital and likely to come to bankruptcy, you would not say, "I may do the same." If you saw a man venturing into deep water who could not swim, and you felt sure that he would ultimately sink, you would not follow his example and be drowned too. No, no; let these frothy professors be beacons to you. Get away from Mr. Talkative, lest he make you as hollow a drum as himself. Beware of loose professors, who are as wreckers' lights that lure men upon the rocks. Make sure work for eternity, and bid triflers begone.

Again, there is always at the back of all this an inducement to build without a foundation because *it will not be known, and possibly may not be found out for years.* Foundation-work is quite out of sight, and the house can be got up and be very useful in a great many ways, and it may stand a good while without the underground work; for houses without foundations do not tumble down at once; they will stand for years; nobody knows how long they may keep up, perhaps they may even be inhabited with comfort till the last great flood. Death alone will discover some impostures. Hence, because the ill-founded house will do for the present, and can be used, and may bring immediate comfort, many people consider it economical to leave out the foundation as a needless superfluity. If they are questioned as to their vital godliness they grow angry:—"What business have you to enter into my private business? Why should you meddle with the secrets of my soul?" Ah, dear friend, if we were cruel to you, and wished you to be deceived, we would hold our tongues, or speak to you with the voice of flattery; but as we love you, and as we hope to be blessed in years to come through your true and holy consecration to Christ, we are intensely earnest that you should begin aright. We would have you build that which will not need to be pulled down again, work that will stand when the waters are out and the stream beasts vehemently upon it. I dread that any man should perish without religion, but I dread far more that any man should perish with it, finding his faith to have been false after all. If you do build, build what is worth building: if you must be builders for your souls, and surely you must, or else be shelterless, than take heed on what foundation you build, and be careful what ye build thereon, lest after all you suffer the loss of all your labor in that last tremendous day. How sad it will seem to dwell near the gates of heaven, and spend your lives among those who are to be its future inhabitants, and then for want of sincerity and truth to be shut out of the celestial city. How terrible to find out by experience that there is a back way to the gates of hell even from the gates of heaven. God grant it be not so with one of us here present. O ye builders, care not merely for the present, but build for death, and judgment, and eternity!

This part of our discourse is not only for young people, but for us all—for old as well as young. Depend upon it, there is not one man among us but what has need to search himself, and see whether the foundation of his faith has been truly laid or no.

II. So I advance to the second step, and there we will consider A WISE PRECAUTION WHICH SAFE BUILDERS NEVER FORGET. They dig deep, and never rest till they get a good substantial foundation: they are glad to get to the bottom of all the loose earth and to build on the rock. Let me commend this wise precaution to all of you.

Follow the text and learn to see to your *sincerity*. The Lord Jesus says "Why call ye me, Lord, Lord, and do not the things which I say?" May the Holy Ghost make you true to the core. Be afraid to say a word more than you feel. Never permit yourself to speak as if you had an experience of which you have only read. Let not your outward worship go a step beyond the inward emotion of your soul. If Christ be truly your Lord you will obey him: if he be not your Lord do not call him so. It is a great point in all your religious thoughts, beliefs, words, and acts to have the heart moving in all. It is an awful thing to make a high profession of sanctity, and yet live in the indulgence of secret vice: such persons will listen to my observation and commend me for my faithfulness, and yet continue in their hypocrisy. This is most painful. These men can speak the Jew's language, and yet the tongue of Babylon is more natural to them: they follow Christ, but their hearts are with Belial. Ah, me! My soul is sick at the thought of them. Be true! Be true! If truth will carry you no further than despair, better that you stop in despair than gain a hope by a lie. Do not live on fiction, profession, presumption. Eat ye that which is good, and feed only upon the truth. Remember that when you build with the wood, hay, and stubble of mere notion you are only gathering materials for your own funeral pile in that day when the fire shall devour all lovers and makers of a lie. Be true as steel! Every wise builder for his soul must mind that.

The next thing is *thoroughness.* For observe, according to our Lord, the wise builder digged deep. You cannot do a right thing too well. Dig deep if you do dig a foundation. If it be repentance, let it be an intensely earnest repentance, including a vehement hatred of every form of sin. If you make confession before God, confess with your very soul, and not with your lips only: lay bare your spirit before the glance of Deity. If it be faith that you talk of, believe right up to the hilt. Do not go in for that kind of sceptical believing which is so common nowadays. If thou believest, believe: if thou repentest, repent. In the purging of the soul there is nothing like sweeping out every particle of the old leaven of falsehood; and in bringing in the good things into the heart there is nothing like bringing in everything that Christ prescribes, that of his fulness we may receive, not only grace, but grace for grace, grace upon grace, all the grace that is needed. Be downright in everything. The wise builder dug through the earth, and continued his digging till he reached the rock; and then he dug into the rock, and struck out a trench wherein he might lay his foundation; for he could not be content unless he made sure and thorough work of it. Sincerity and thoroughness are fine building-materials.

Next to that add *self-renunciation;* for that is in the parable. When a man digs a deep foundation he has much earth to throw out. So he that builds for eternity has a great deal to get rid of. Self-trust must go at the beginning; love of sin must follow; worldliness, pride, self-seeking, all sorts of iniquity,—these must be cast aside. There is very much rubbish, and the rubbish must go. You cannot make sure work for eternity without clearing away much which flesh and blood would like to retain. See ye to this, and count the cost.

Then must come *solid principle*. The man who is determined that if he does build he will build securely, digs down to the rock. He says, "I believe in God, he is my helper. I believe in Christ Jesus, and on his atoning sacrifice and living intercession I build my eternal hopes. I also build on the doctrine of grace, for the Lord hath said it,—By grace are ye saved, through faith. I build on Scripture: nothing but the warrant of the word will do for me." What God has said is a rock: what man teaches is mere shifting sand. What a blessed thing it is to get down to the eternal principles of divine verity! You that pick up your religion from your mothers and fathers; you that follow it because it happened to be in the family; what are you worth in the day of trouble? You are blown down like a booth, or a hut of boughs. But you that know what you believe, and why you believe it, you who, when you put your foot down, know what you are standing upon, and are persuaded that you have firm rock beneath you; you are the men who will stand fast when mere pretenders are hurled out of their place. Oh, my dear seeking friends, fix upon true principles, and be not content with falsehood.

These truthful principles must be *firmly adhered to*. Bind your building to the rock. A house will not stand merely because it is *on* the rock; you must get its foundation into the rock. The house must take a grip of the rock, and the rock must grasp the house. The more you can get the house to be a bit of the rock, and the rock, as it were, to grow up into the house, the more secure you are. It is of no use saying, "Yes, I confide in Christ, in grace, in revelation," unless your very life enters into these things, and they enter into you. Hypocrites, Job says, are stolen away in the night; so easily are they removed. The inventor of some new notion comes along, cracks up his novel wares, and silly souls are at once taken in by him. Christ may go, grace may go, and the Bible may go, too: their new master has them wholly in his power. We want not such unsubstantial men; we care not for these speculating builders whose carcases are all around us. We have had enough of castles in the air; we need true men, who will stand fast like the mountains while errors, like clouds, blow over them. Remember the huge shaft at Bradford, and how many were slain by its fall, and let it teach you to hold hard to foundation truths, and never depart from them.

The man in the second parable did not build as he should; what may I say of him? I will say three words. First, he was a man who had *nothing out of sight:* you could see all his house when you looked at it. If you can see all a man's religion at a glance he has no religion worth having. Godliness lies most in secret prayer, private devotion, and inward grace. The wise builder had the most costly part of his house buried in the ground; but the other man showed all that he had above ground. He is a poor tradesman who has no stock but that which he puts into the window. He will not last long who has no capital. He cannot long stand who has no backbone within. Beware of a religion of show.

Next, this man had *nothing to hold to.* He built a house, but it stood upon the loose soil: he easily dug into that, and stuck up his house; but his walls had no holdfast. Beware of a religion without holdfasts. But if I get a grip upon a doctrine they call me a bigot. Let them do so. Bigotry is a hateful thing, and yet that which is now abused as bigotry is a great virtue, and greatly needed in these frivolous times. I have been inclined lately to start a new denomination, and call it "the Church of the Bigoted." Everybody is getting to be so oily, so plastic, so untrue, that we need a race of hard-shells to teach us how to believe. Those old-fashioned people who in former ages believed something, and thought the opposite of it to be false, were truer folk than the present time-servers. I should like to ask the divines of the broad school whether any doctrine is worth a man's dying for it. They would have to reply, "Well, of course, if a man had to go to the stake or change his opinions, the proper way would be to state them with much diffidence, and to be extremely respectful to the opposite school." But suppose he is required to deny the truth? "Well, there is much to be said on each side, and probably the negative may have a measure of truth in it as well as the positive. At any rate, it cannot be a prudent thing to incur the odium of being burned, and so it might be preferable to leave the matter an open question for the time being." Yes, and as these gentlemen always find it unpleasant to be unpopular, they soften down the hard threatenings of Scripture as to the world to come, and put a color upon every doctrine to which worldly-wise men object. The teachers of doubt are very doubtful teachers. A man must have something to hold to, or he will neither bless himself nor others. Bring all the ships into the pool; but do not moor or anchor one of them; let each one be free! Wait you for a stormy night, and they will dash against each other, and great mischief will come of this freedom. Perfect love and charity will not come through our being all unmoored, but by each having his proper moorings and keeping to them in the name of

God. You must have something to hold to; but the builder in the parable had not, and so he perished.

The foolish builder had *nothing to resist outward circumstances*. On summer days his house was a favorite resort, and was considered to be quite as good as his neighbor's in all respects. Frequently he rubbed his hands and said, "I do not see but what my house is quite as good his, and perhaps a little better: the fact is, I had a few pounds to spare which I did not bury in the ground as he did, and with it I have bought many a little ornament, so that my habitation has a finer look than his building." So it seemed; but when the torrent came raging down the mountain side, his building, having nothing wherewith to resist the violence of the flood, fell down at once, and not a trace of it remained, when the storm had ceased. Thus do men fail because they offer no resistance to forces which drive them into sin; the great current of evil finds in them victims, and not opponents.

III. Thirdly, we will now gather from our text A SET OF ARGUMENTS, URGING US TO TAKE CARE OF THE FOUNDATION. I will glance over these arguments, wishing much that I had time to enforce them. The first is this. We ought to build with a good foundation at the beginning, because otherwise *we shall not build well in any other part of the house*. Bad work in the foundation influences all the rest of the courses. In the Revised Version at the end of the forty-eighth verse instead of "For it was founded upon a rock," we read, "Because it had been well builded." The house was built well at the bottom, and that led the workmen to put in good work all the way up, so that all through "it had been well builded." The other man built badly underground, and did the same up to the roof. When you get into the habit of slovenly work in secret the tendency is to be slovenly in public too. If the underground part of our religion is not firmly laid upon Christ, then in the upper part there will be rotten work, half-baked bricks, mud instead of mortar, and a general scamping of everything. When a great Grecian artist was fashioning an image for the temple he was diligently carving the back part of the goddess, and one said to him, "You need not finish that part of the statue, because it is to be built into the wall." He replied, "The gods can see in the wall." He had a right idea of what is due to God. That part of my religion which no man can see should be as perfect as if it were to be observed by all. The day shall declare it. When Christ shall come everything shall be made known, and published before the universe. Therefore see to it that it be fit to be thus made known.

See, again, that we ought to have good foundations when we *look at the situation whereon the house is to be built.* It is clear from this parable that both these houses were built in places not far from a river, or where streams might be expected to come. Certain parts of the South of France are marvellously like Palestine, and perhaps at the present moment they are more like what the Holy Land was in Christ's day than the Holy Land now is. When I reached Cannes last year I found that there had been a flood in the town. This flood did not come by reason of a river being swollen, but through a deluge of rain. A waterspout seems to have burst upon the hill-side, tearing up earth, and rocks, and stones, and then hurrying down to the sea. It rushed across the railway station and poured down the street which led to it, drowning several persons in its progress. When I was there a large hotel—I should think five stories high—was shored up with timber, and was evidently doomed; for when this stream rushed down the narrow street it undermined the lower courses of the building, and as there were no foundations at all able to bear such a test the whole erection was rendered unsafe. The Saviour had some such case in his mind's eye. A torrent of water would come tearing down the side of the mountain, and if a house was built on the mere earth, it would be carried away directly, but if it were fastened into the rock so that it became part and parcel of it, then the flood might rush all around it, but it would not shake the walls. Beloved builder of a house for your soul, your house is so situated that one of these days there must come great pressure upon it. "How do you know?" Well, I know that the house wherein my soul lives is pitched just where winds blow, and waves rise, and storms beat. Where is yours? Do you live in a snug corner? Yes, but one of these times you will find that the snug corner will be no more shielded than the open riverside; for God so orders providence that every man has his test sooner or later. It may be that you think yourself past temptation, but the idea is a delusion, as time will show. Perhaps from the very fact that you seem quite out of the way, a peculiar temptation may befall you. Therefore, I do pray you, because of the exposed condition of your life's building, build upon a good foundation.

The next argument is, build deep, because of the *ruin which will result from a bad foundation.* The foolish builder's house was without a foundation. Notice that word, "*without a foundation.*" Write down the expression and see whether they apply to you or not. What happened to this house without a foundation? The stream beat vehemently on it. The river's bed had long been dry, but suddenly it was flooded, and the torrent rolled with tremendous power. Perhaps it was persecution, perhaps it was prosperity, perhaps it was trouble, perhaps it was temptation, perhaps it was prevalent scepticism, perhaps it was death; but, anyhow, the flood beat vehemently upon that house; and now we read the next word,—"And *immediately it fell.*" It did not stand a prolonged assault, it was captured at once. "Immediately it fell." What! in a minute, all that fair profession gone? "Immediately it fell." Why, that is the man I shook hands with the other Sunday, and called him "Brother," and he has been seen drunk! or he has been in the frivolous assembly, using unhallowed language! or he has become an utter doubter all on a sudden! It is sorrowful work burying our friends, but it is much more sorrowful work to lose them in this fashion: and yet so they vanish. They are gone: even as Job saith "the east wind carrieth him away and he departeth." "Immediately" they fall, and yet we thought so highly of them, and they thought so highly of themselves. "Immediately it fell"; their profession could not endure trial, and all because it had no foundation.

Then it is added, "And the ruin of that house was great." The house came down with a crash, and it was the man's all. The man was an eminent professor, and hence his ruin was all the more notable. It was a great fall because it could never be built up again. When a man dies a hypocrite certainly there is no hope of restitution for him. By the stream the very debris of the ruined house was swept away; nothing was left. Oh, men, if you lose a battle you may fight again and win another; if you fail in business you may start again in trade and realize a fortune; but if you lose your souls the loss is irretrievable. Once lost, lost for ever. There will be no second opportunity. Do not deceive yourselves about that. Therefore, dig deep, and lay every stone most firmly upon the foundation of rock.

For lastly, and perhaps this will be the best argument, *observe the effect of this good, sure building,* this deep building. We read that when the flood beat upon the wise man's house "*it could not shake it.*" That is very beautiful. Not only could it not carry it away, but "it could not shake it." I see the man: he lost his money and became poor, but he did not give up his faith: "It could not shake it." He was ridiculed and slandered, and many of his former friends gave him the cold shoulder; but "It could not shake it." He went to Jesus under his great trial and he was sustained: "It could not shake it." He was very sick and his spirit was depressed within him, but still he held his confidence in Christ: "It could not shake it." He was near to die; he knew that he must soon depart out of this world, but all the pains of death and the certainty of dissolution could not shake him. He died as he lived, firm as a rock, rejoicing as much as ever, nay, rejoicing more, because he was nearer to the kingdom and to the fruition of all his hopes. "It could not shake it." It is a grand thing to have a faith which cannot be shaken. I saw one day a number of beech trees which had formed a wood: they had all fallen to the ground through a storm. The fact was they leaned upon one another to a great extent, and the thickness of the wood prevented each tree from getting a firm hold of the soil. They kept each other up and also constrained each other to grow up tall and thin, to the neglect of root-growth. When the tempest forced down the first few trees the others readily followed one after the other. Close to that same spot I saw another tree in the open, bravely defying the blast, in solitary strength. The hurricane had beaten upon it, but it had endured all its force unsheltered. That lone, brave tree seemed to be better rooted than before the storm. I thought, "Is it not so with professors?" They often hold together, and help each other to grow up, but if they have not firm personal roothold, when a storm arises they fall in rows. A minister dies, or certain leaders are taken away, and over go the members by departure from the faith and from holiness. I would have you be self-contained, growing each man into Christ for himself, rooted and grounded in love and faith and every holy grace. Then when the worst storm that ever blew on mortal man shall come, it will be said of your faith, "It could not shake it." I beseech you who are now seeking Christ to take care that you build well, that you may stand long in our Zion, steadfast and unmovable. God grant it for Christ's sake. Amen.

III.

"HEREIN IS LOVE."

February 18, 1883.

"Herein is love, not that we loved God, but that he loved us, and sent his Son to be the propitiation for our sins. Beloved, if God so loved us, we ought also to love one another."—1 JOHN iv. 10, 11.

The law commands love; indeed, all its precepts are summed up in that one word "love." More widely read it runs thus: "Thou shalt love the Lord thy God with all thy heart, and with all thy soul, and with all thy strength, and with all thy mind; and thy neighbor as thyself": yet all this amounts only to "Thou shalt love."

But the law by reason of our depravity never produced love. We were commanded to love, but we did no such thing. The spirit that is in us is selfish, and it lusteth to envy and to enmity. Whence come wars and fightings among us? Come they not from our lusts? Since the Fall man has become man's bitterest foe upon the earth, and the world is full of hating, slandering, struggling, fighting, wounding, and slaying: all that law can do is to show the wrong of enmity, and threaten punishment; but it cannot supply an unregenerate heart with the fountain of love. Man remains unloving and unlovable till the gospel takes him in hand and by grace accomplishes that which the law could not do, in that it was weak through the flesh. Love is winning many hearts to the kingdom of God, and its reign shall extend till love shall rule over the whole earth, and so the kingdom of God shall be set up among men, and God shall dwell among them. At the present moment love is the distinguishing mark of the people of God. Jesus said, " By this shall all men know that ye are my disciples, if ye have love one to another"; and John said, " We know that we have passed from death unto life, because we love the brethren." The man whose spirit is selfish has not the spirit of Christ, and " if any man have not the spirit of Christ he is none of his." The man whose spirit is that of envy and contention is evidently no follower of the lowly and loving Jesus, and those who do not follow Jesus are none of his.

They that are Christ's are filled with his love. " Every one that loveth is born of God, and knoweth God. He that loveth not knoweth not God; for God is love." God is the centre of the believer's love; the saints are an inner circle specially beloved, and all mankind are embraced within the circumference of the ring of love. " He that dwelleth in love dwelleth in God, and God in him"; and he alone is a child of God whose spirit is kindly and affectionate, and who seeks, wherever he is, to promote peace, goodwill towards men.

The saints begin with love to God. That must ever hold the highest place; for God is the best and noblest being, and we owe him all our hearts. Then comes, for Jesus' sake, love to all who are in Christ. There is a peculiarly near and dear relationship existing between one child of God and all the rest. Loving him that begat, we love all them that are begotten of him. Should not a child love his brothers with a tender, peculiar affection? This principle of love, once implanted, induces in the heart of the converted man a love towards all mankind. Not that he can take any complacency in the wicked; God himself cannot do that; his holiness abhors all iniquity. The love desired is not the love of complacency, but the love of benevolence; so that we wish well, and to the utmost of our power would do well, unto all those that dwell upon the face of the earth. In this holy charity, this unselfish love, be ye imitators of God as dear children. Our heavenly Father is kind to the unthankful and to the evil, and so must we be; desiring that even the most abandoned may yet be rescued and made right and good. Love desires to create that which is lovable even in the most unlovable of mankind, and God helping the effort, she suceeds.

I hear one say, "This is a vast idea. Are we to love at this rate? Where is the love to come from? Our hearts are narrow, men are unworthy, provocations are numerous, another spirit is abroad in the world: where is this love to come from?—this flood of love which is to cover the tops of the mountains of man's unworthiness?" Hast thou entered into the springs of the sea? or hast thou walked in search of the depths? Yes, by the leadings of God's Spirit we will search out the springs of the sea of love. Only in one place shall we find love enough for our supreme purpose, which is also the purpose of the Lord himself. There is one shoreless ocean into which we may be baptized, and out of which we may be filled until we overflow. Where is the unfailing motive of love? For love is tried, and hardly put to it to hold her own. Can we find a motive that will never fail even toward the most provoking of mankind? Can we find an argument for affection which shall help us in times of ingratitude, when base returns threaten to freeze the very heart of charity? Yes, there is such a motive; there is a force by which even impossibilities of love can be accomplished, and we shall be supplied with a perpetual constraint moving the heart to ceaseless charity.

Come with me, then, in the first place, to notice *the infinite spring of love*—"Herein is love, not that we loved God, but that God loved us;" secondly, let us observe *the marvellous outflow of that love*—"God sent his Son to be the propitiation for our sins;" and then, thirdly, let us notice *the overflow of that love in us*, when it fills our hearts and runs over to others—"Beloved, if God so loved us, we ought also to love one another."

I.—First, THE INFINITE SPRING OF LOVE. Our text has two words upon which I would place an emphasis—"*not*" and "*but*."

The first is "*not*." "Herein is love, not"—"not that we loved God." Very naturally many conclude that this means "not that we loved God first." That is not exactly the truth taught here, but still it is a weighty truth, and is mentioned in this same chapter in express words—"We love him because he first loved us" (verse nineteen). The cause of love in the universe is not that man loved God first. No being in existence could love God before God loved him; for the existence of such a being is due to God's previous love. His plans of love were all laid and many of them carried out before we were born; and when we were born we none of us loved God first so as to seek after God before he sought after us, so as to desire reconciliation with God before he desired reconciliation with us. No; whatever may be said about freewill as a theory, it is never found as a matter of fact that any man, left to himself, ever woos his God, or pines after friendship with his Maker. If he repents of sin it is because the Spirit of God has first visited him and shown him his sin; if he desires restoration it is because he has first of all been taught to dread the wrath of God and to long for holiness.

> "No sinner can be beforehand with thee;
> Thy grace is most sovereign, most rich, and most free."

We inscribe a negative in black capital letters upon the idea that man's love can ever be prior to the love of God. That is quite out of the question.

"Not that we loved God." Take a second sense—that is, not that any man did love God at all by nature, whether first or second; not that we, any one of us, ever did or ever could have an affection towards God while we remained in our state by nature. Instead of loving God, man is indifferent to God. "No God," saith the fool in his heart, and by nature we are all such fools. It is the sinner's wish that there were no God. We are atheistical by nature, and if our brain does not yield to atheism, yet our heart does. We wish that we could sin according to our own will, and that we were in no danger of being called to account for it. God is not in all our thoughts, or if he does enter there it is as a terror and a dread. Nay, worse than that: man is at enmity with God by wicked works. The holiness which God admires man hath no liking for; the sin which God abominates has about it sweetness and fascination for the unrenewed heart; so that man's ways are contrary to the ways of God. Man is perverse; he cannot walk with God, for they are not agreed; he is all evil, and God is all goodness, and therefore no love to God exists in the natural heart of man. He may say that he loves God, but then it is a god of his own inventing, and not Jehovah, the God of the Bible, the only living and true God. A just God and a Saviour the natural mind cannot endure: the carnal mind is enmity against God, and is not reconciled to God, neither indeed can be. The unregenerate heart is, as to love, a broken cistern which can hold no water. In our natural state, there is none that doeth good, no not one; so is there also none that loveth God, no, not one.

We come nearer to John's meaning when we look at this negative as applying to those who do love God. "Not that we loved God,"—that is, that our love to God, even when it does exist, and even when it influences our lives, is not worthy to be mentioned as a fountain of supply for love. The apostle points us away from it to something far more vast, and then he cries, "Herein is love." I am looking for "the springs of the sea," and you point me to a little pool amid the rocks which has been filled by the flowing tide. I am glad to see that pool: how bright! how blue! how like the sea from whence it came! But do not point to this as the source of the great waterfloods: for if you do I shall smile at your childish ignorance, and point you to yon great rolling main which tosses its waves on high. What is your little pool to the vast Atlantic? Do you point me to the love in the believer's heart, and say, "Herein is love!" You make me smile. I know that there is love in that true heart; but who can mention it in the presence of the great rolling ocean of the love of God, without bottom and without shore? The word *not* is not only upon my lip but in my heart as I think of the two things, "Nor that we loved God, but that God loved us." What poor love ours is at its very best when compared with the love wherewith God loves us!

Let me use another figure. If we had to enlighten the world, a child might point us to a bright mirror reflecting the sun, and he might cry, "Herein is light!" You and I would say, "Poor child, that is but borrowed brightness; the light is not there, but yonder, in the sun:

the love of saints is nothing more that the reflection of the love of God. We *have* love, but God *is* love. When I think of the love of certain saints to Christ, I am charmed with it; for it is a fruit of the Spirit not to be despised. When I think of Paul the Apostle counting all things but loss for Christ; when I think of our missionaries going one after another into malarious parts of the African coast, and dying for Christ; and when I read the Book of Martyrs, and see confessors standing on the fagots, burning quick to the death, still bearing witness to their Lord and Master,—I do rejoice in the love of saints to their Lord. Yet this is but a streamlet; the unfathomable deep, the eternal source from which all love proceeds, infinitely exceeds all human affection, and it is found in God, and in God alone. "Herein is love, not that we loved God, but that God loved us."

Let us contrast our love to God with his love to us. Dear brethren, we do love God, and we may well do so, since he is infinitely lovable. When the mind is once enlightened it sees everything that is lovable about God. He is so good, so gracious, so perfect that he commands our admiring affection. The spouse in the Song, when she thought of her beloved, mentioned all manner of beauties, and then cried, "Yea, he is altogether lovely." It is natural, therefore, that one who sees God should love him. But, now, think of God's love to us: is it not incomparably greater, since there was nothing lovely in us whatever, and yet he loved us? In us there is by nature nothing to attract the affection of a holy God, but quite the reverse; and yet he loved us. Herein, indeed, is love!

When we love God it is an honor to us; it exalts a man to be allowed to love a Being so glorious. A philosopher once wrote that for a man to speak of being the friend of God was too daring, and in the reverence of this thoughtful heathen there was much to admire; for indeed there is an infinite difference between the glorious God and the sinful creature man. Though God in condescension allows us to call him friend, and Jesus says, "Ye are my friends!" yet this is beyond reason, and is a sweet revelation of the Holy Spirit. What an uplifting there is in it for us! On the other hand, God's love to us can add nothing to him; it gives, but receives not. Divine love can have no recompense. That he, the Infinite, should stoop to love the finite: that he the infinitely pure should love the guilty, this is a vast condescension. See, moreover, what it involved; for this love rendered it necessary that in the person of his dear Son God should be "despised and rejected of men," should make himself of no reputation, and should even be numbered with the transgressors. "Herein is love!"

When we love God we are gainers by the deed. He that loves God does in the most effectual manner love himself. We are filled with riches when we abound in love to God; it is our wealth, our health, our might, and our delight. But God gains nothing by loving us. I hardly like to set the two in contrast, for our love is so poor and pitiable a thing as compared with the immeasurable love of God.

It is our duty to love God; we are bound to do it. As his creatures we ought to love our Creator; as preserved by his care we are under obligation to love him for his goodness: we owe him so much that our utmost love is a mere acknowledgment of our debt. But God loved us to whom he owed nothing at all; for whatever might have been the claims of a creature upon his Creator, we had forfeited them all by our rebellion. Sinful men had no rights towards God except the right of being punished. Yet the Lord manifested boundless love to our race, which was only worthy to be destroyed. Oh words! How ye fail me! I cannot utter my heart by these poor lips of clay. Oh God, how infinite was thy love which was given without any obligation on thy part, freely and unsought, and all because thou willest to love—yea, thou dost love because thou art love. There was no cause, no constraint, no claim why thou shouldest love mankind, except that thine own heart led thee so to do. What is man that thou art mindful of him? "Herein is love, not that we loved God, but that God loved us."

I have thus pointed out the well-head of love: let us draw from it, and from none other. If you go into the world and say, "I am to love my fellow-men because I love God," the motive is good, but it is questionable, limited, and variable. How much better to argue—I am to love my fellow-men because God loves me. When my love grows cold towards God, and when by reason of my infirmity and imperfection I am led even to question whether I do love God at all, then my argument and my impulse would fail me if it came from my own love to God; but if I love the fallen because God loved me, then I have an unchanging motive, and unquestionable argument, and a forcible impulse not to be resisted: hence the apostle cried, "The love of Christ constraineth us." It is always well for a Christian to have the strongest motive, and to rely upon the most potent and perpetual force, and hence the apostle bids us look to divine love, and not to our own. "Herein is love," saith he, "not that we loved God, but that God loved us." So far the "not."

Let us turn to the "but." "*But* that he loved us." I have nothing new to say, nor do I wish to say anything new; but I should like you to meditate on each one of these words:—"*He loved us.*" Three words, but what weight of meaning! "*He*," who is infinitely holy and cannot endure iniquity,—"*He* loved us"; "*He*," whose glory is the astonishment of the greatest of intelligent beings,—"He loved us." "*He*," whom the heaven of heavens cannot contain, "loved us." "He" who is God all-sufficient, and needs nothing of us, neither can indeed receive anything at our hands,—"He loved us." What joy lies sleeping here! Oh, that we could wake it up! What hope, too, for hopeless sinners, because "God loved us." If a man could know that he was loved of all his fellow-men, if he could have it for certain that he was loved by all the angels, doted on by cherubim and seraphim, yet these were but so many drops, and all put together could not compare with the main ocean contained in the fact that "*God* loved us."

Now ring that second silver bell: "He *loved* us." I do not think that the apostle is here so much speaking of God's special love to his own elect as of his love to men in general. He saw our race ruined in the fall, and he could not bear that man should be destroyed. Lord, what is man that thou dost visit him in love? Yet he did so visit him. The Lord's love made him lament man's revolt, and cry, "I have nourished and brought up children, and they have rebelled against me"; whereupon he bade heaven and earth witness to his grief. He saw that sin had brought men into wretchedness and misery, and would destroy them for ever; and he would not have it so. He loved them with the love of pity, with the love of sweet and strong benevolence, and he declared it with an oath: "As I live, saith the Lord, I have no pleasure in the death of him that dieth, but that he turn unto me and live." "Herein is love." But if you and I be reconciled to God we can lay the emphasis, each one for himself, upon this word *love*, and view it as special, effectual, electing love. Let each believer say, "He loved *me*, and gave himself for *me*." Then what force is in my text: "He *loved* us": it is not enough that he pitied us, or spared us, or helped us; but "he *loved* us." It has often made me rise from my seat to think that God loves me! I could not sit still and hear the thrilling truth. Such knowledge is too wonderful for me: it is high, I cannot attain unto it. It is sweet to be loved even by a dog; it is sweet to be loved by a babe; it is sweet to be loved by a friend; it is sweet to be loved by God's people; but, oh! to be loved of God, and to know it!—this is paradise. Would a man want any other heaven than to know for certain that he enjoyed the love of God?

Note the third word. "He loved *us*,"—"us,"—the most insignificant of beings. There is an anthill somewhere; it is no matter to you where it is. It teems with ants. Stir the nest, and they swarm in armies. Think of one of them. No; you do not need to know anything about him! His business is no concern of yours; so let him go. But that ant, after all, is more considerable to you than you are to God. "All the inhabitants of the earth are reputed as nothing." What are you even in this great city!—one man, one woman in London, in England, in the population of the world,—what a cipher you are! Yet what is the population of this world compared with the universe? I suppose that all these stars which we see at night, all the countless worlds within our range of vision, are but as a little dust in a lone corner of God's great house. The whole solar system, and all the systems of worlds we have ever thought of, are but as a drop of a bucket compared with the boundless sea of creation; and even that is as nothing compared to the infinite God: and yet "He loved *us*"—the insignificant creatures of an hour. What is more, he loved us though in our insignificance we dared to rebel against him. We boasted against him; we cried, "Who is Jehovah?" We lifted up our hand to fight with him. Ridiculous rebellion! Absurd warfare! Had he but glanced at us and annihilated us, it would have been as much as we could merit at his hands; but to think that he should love us,—*love us*, mark you, when we were in rebellion against him. This is marvellous.

Observe that the previous verse speaks of us as being dead in sin. "In this was manifested the love of God toward us, because that God sent his only-begotten Son into the world, that we might live through him." Then we were dead, dead to all goodness, or thought or power, of goodness, criminals shut up in the condemned cell; and yet God loved us with a great love even when we were dead in trespasses and sins. Child of God, God's love to you to-day is wonderful; but think of his love to you when you were far gone in rebellion against him. When not a throb of holy, spiritual life could be found in your entire being; yet he loved you and sent his Son that you might live through him. Moreover, he loved us when we were steeped in sin. Does not our text tell us so? for he sent his Son to be the propitiation for our sins, and this implies that we needed to be reconciled. Our righteous Judge was angry with us; his righteous wrath smoked against our evil, and yet even then "He loved us." He was wroth with us as a Judge, but yet he loved us: he **was** determined to punish, and yet resolved to save.

This is a world of wonders! I am utterly beaten by

my text. I confess myself mastered by my theme. But who among us can measure the unfathomable? "Herein is love," that God freely, out of the spontaneous motion of his own heart, should love us. This is the argument for love; this is the inexhaustible fountain out of which all love must come. If we desire love, may we come and fill our vessels here and bear it out to others. Love springing from our own bosoms is flat, feeble and scant; but the love of God is a great deep, for ever fresh and full and flowing. Here are those springs of the sea of which we spake: " Herein is love!"

II. I want your attention a little longer while I speak as best I can upon THE MARVELLOUS OUTFLOW OF THAT LOVE. "Herein is love, not that we loved God, but that he loved us, and sent his Son to be the propitiation for our sins." Beloved, the love of God is seen in creation: he that studies the mechanism of the human frame and of its surroundings will see much of divine kindness therein. The love of God is to be seen in providence: he that watches the loving hand of God in daily life will not need to look far before he sees tokens of a Father's care. But if you want to know when the great deep of God's love was broken up, and arose in the fulness of its strength to prevail over all; if you would see it revealed in a deluge, like Noah's flood, you must wait till you see Jesus born at Bethlehem and crucified on Calvary; for his mission to men is the divinest manifestation of love.

Consider every word: "He sent his Son." God "*sent.*" Love caused that mission. If there was to be reconciliation between God and man, man ought to have sent to God; the offender ought to be the first to apply for forgiveness; the weaker should apply to the greater for help; the poor man should ask of him who distributes alms; but "Herein is love" that God "sent." He was first to send an embassy of peace. To-day "we are ambassadors for Christ, as though God did beseech you by us: we pray you in Christ's stead, be ye reconciled to God." Oh, the wonder of this, that God should not wait till rebellious men had sent to his throne for terms of reconciliation, but should commence negotiations himself!

Moreover, God sent such an One: he "sent *his Son*." If men send an embassy to a great power they select some great one of their nation to wait upon the potent prince; but if they are dealing with a petty principality they think a subordinate person quite sufficient for such a business. Admire, then, the true love of the infinitely gracious God, that when he sent an embassy to men he did not commission an angel nor even the brightest spirit before his throne; but he sent his Son,—oh, the love of God to men! He sent his equal Son to rebels who would not receive him, would not hear him, but spat upon him, scourged him, stripped him, slew him! Yes, "he spared not his own Son, but freely delivered him up for us all." He knew what would come of that sending of him, and yet he sent him.

> "Jesus, commission'd from above,
>   Descends to men below,
> And shows from whence the springs of love
>   In endless currents flow.
>
> "He, whom the boundless heaven adores,
>   Whom angels long to see,
> Quitted with joy those blissful shores,
>   Ambassador to me!
>
> "To me, a worm, a sinful clod,
>   A rebel all forlorn:
> A foe, a traitor, to my God,
>   And of a traitor born."

Note further, not only the grandeur of the ambassador, but the tenderness of the relationship existing between him and the offended God. "He sent his Son." The previous verse says, "His only-begotten Son." We cannot speak of God except after the manner of men, for God in all his glory is incomprehensible; but speaking after the manner of men, what must it have cost Jehovah to take his only Son from his bosom to die? Christ is the Father's self; in essence they are one: there is but one God. We do not understand the mystery of the Trinity in unity, but we believe it. It was God himself who came hither in the person of his dear Son: he underwent all: for we are "the flock of God which he hath purchased with his own blood." Remember Abraham with the knife unsheathed, and wonder as you see him obey the voice which says, "Take now thy son, thine only son, Isaac, whom thou lovest, and offer him for a sacrifice." Remember yet again that the Lord actually did what Abraham in obedience willed to do: he gave up his Son! "It pleased the Father to bruise him; he hath put him to grief." Christ's death was in fact God in human form suffering for human sin; God incarnate bleeding because of our transgressions. Are we not now carried away with the streams of love? I speak my best, my brethren; but if my words were what they ought to be they would set your souls on fire. Is not all heaven still astounded at the death of the Only-begotten? It has not recovered from its amazement that the heir of all things should bow his head to death. How can I fitly tell you how much God loved the world when he gave his Only-begotten to die that sinners might live!

Go a step further. "God sent his Son *to be a propitiation*," that is, to be not only a reconciler, but the reconciliation. His sacrifice of himself was the atonement through which mercy is rendered possible in consistency with justice. I have heard men say with scorn that God required a sacrifice before he would be reconciled, as if that were wrong on the part of the Judge of all. But let me whisper in their ears: God required it, it is true, for he is just and holy; but God found it himself. Remember that—Jehovah found the ransom which he demanded. It was himself, his own Son, one with himself, that became the propitiation and the reconciliation. It was not that God the Father was unkind, and could not be placated unless he smote his Son; but that God the Father was so kind that he could not be unjust, so supremely loving that he must devise a way by which men could be justly saved. An unjust salvation would have been none at all. The Lord found the reconciliation—I will not say in the sufferings of Christ, though that is true: I will not say in the death of Christ, though that is true; but I will put it in Scriptural words, and here we have it in 1 John ii. 2: "He"—that is, Jesus himself—"is the propitiation for our sins." The sent one in himself, as well as in all that he did and all that he suffered, is the reconciliation between God and man. "Herein is love!" for in order that there might be peace and love between man and God, God finds the sin-offering, becomes himself the atonement, that love might reign supreme.

What seems to me the most wonderful thing of all is that the Lord Jesus should deal, not only with our sorrow, but with our sin; for "he is the propitiation for our *sins*." That God should deal with us as to our virtues, if we had any; that he should deal with us as to our love, if we had any, might not seem so difficult; but that he should send his Son to dwell with us as sinners—ay, and to come into contact with our sins, and thus to take the sword, not only by its hilt, but by its blade, and plunge it into his own heart, and die because of it, this is a miracle of miracles. O friends, Christ never gave himself for our righteousness, but he laid down his life for our sins. He viewed us as sinners when he came to save us. "Jesus Christ came into the world to save sinners." If I had not found Christ till this very minute, I hope I should find him now as my mind drinks in this doctrine. By God's Spirit there seems to me to be such a window opened that even despair may see the light, for if the thing which God sent his Son to deal with was the sin of man, then I, even though I am nothing but a mass of loathsomeness and sin, may yet enjoy the infinite love of God. Oh, guilty ones, hear these words, which are more sweet than music, and fuller of delight than all poetry; for even the harps of angels never rise to higher measures than these which I do so poorly and simply rehearse in your ears,—even these glad tidings, that God who made the heavens and the earth, whom ye have offended, wills not that you die, but loves you so greatly that he opens up a road of reconciliation through the body of his own dear Son. There was no other way by which you could be reconciled to God, for had he reconciled you to a part of himself and not to his justice, you had not been in very truth at all reconciled to God. It is now to God completely just, holy, whose anger burns against sin; it is to him that you are reconciled by faith in Christ Jesus, through the laying down of his life for men. Oh that God would bless this to all who hear the glad tidings!

III. We come at last to think of the CONSEQUENT OUTFLOW OF LOVE FROM US,—" Beloved, if God so loved us, we ought also to love one another." Our love then to one another is simply God's love to us, flowing into us, and flowing out again. That is all it is. "Herein is love, not that we loved God, but that God loved us," and then we love others. You have seen a noble fountain in a continental city adorning a public square. See how the water leaps into the air; and then it falls into a circular basin which fills and pours out its fulness into another lower down, and this again floods a third. Hear the merry plash as the waters fall in showers and cataracts from basin to basin! If you stand at the lower basin and look upon it and say, "Herein is water;" that is true, and will be true of the next higher one, and so forth; but if you would express the truth as to where the water really is, you may have to look far away, perhaps upon a mountain's side, for there is a vast reservoir from which pipes are laid to bring these waters and force them to their height that they may descend so beautifully. Thus the love we have to our fellow-creatures drops from us like the descending silvery cataract from the full basin, but the first source of it is the immeasurable love of God which is hidden away in his very essence, which never changes, and never can be diminished. Herein is love! If you and I desire to love our fellow Christians and to love the fallen race of man, we must be joined on to the aqueduct which conducts love from this eternal source, or else we shall soon fail in love.

Observe, brethren, then, that as the love of God is the source of all true love in us, so a sense of that love stimulates us. Whenever you feel that you love God you overflow with love to all God's people; I am sure you do. It is when you get to doubt the love of God that you grow hard and cold; but when you are fired with the love of a dying Saviour who gave himself for you, you feel as if you loved every beggar in the street, and you long to bring every harlot to Christ's dear feet; you cannot help it. Man, if Christ baptizes your heart into his love, you will be covered with it, and filled with it.

Your love will respect the same persons as God's love does, and for the same reasons. God loves men; so will you; God loves them when there is no good in them, and you will love them in the same way. Sometimes the wickedness of men kindles in the heart of a true Christian a stronger affection for them. The deeper down they are the more they want a Saviour. Did not our Moravian brethren feel when they went out as missionaries that they would prefer to go first to the most barbarous tribes?—for they said, "The more degraded they are the more they need a Saviour." And should not the missionary spirit make believers feel, if men are sunk until they are as low as brutes, and as savage as devils, that this is the stronger reason for our being eager to bring them to Christ? I hope that abominable spirit which used to come in among Christian people has been kicked away to its father the devil, where it ought to be: I mean the spirit which despises the poor and the fallen. When I have heard people say, "What is the good of looking after such riff-raff?" I have been saddened. The church of God feels that the souls of the meanest are precious,— that to save the most foul, the most ignorant, the most degraded, the most brutalized man or woman that ever lives is an object worthy of the effort of the whole church, since God thought it worthy of the death of Jesus Christ, that he might bring sinners dead in sin to live unto himself.

Brothers and sisters, **we shall not have** grasped the **truth** unless we feel that our **love to men** must be practical, because God's love to **us was so.** His love **did not lie pent up** like the waters in the secret caverns of **the earth, but** it welled **up like the** waters in **the days** of Noah, when we read that the fountains of the great deep were broken up. In the gift of the Lord Jesus we behold the reality of divine love. When we see the poor we must not say, " Be ye warmed; be ye filled; I am sorry for you"; but we must let our love relieve them from our stores. If we see the ignorant we must not say, "Dear me, the church is neglecting the masses; the church must wake up": but we must bestir ourselves and struggle ourselves to win sinners. If there be any near you who are degraded, do not say, "I wish somebody would go after them." No; go after them yourself. We have each one a mission: let that mission be fulfilled.

Our love ought to follow the love of God in one point, namely, in always seeking to produce reconciliation. It was to this end that God sent his Son. Has anybody offended you? Seek reconciliation. "Oh, but I am the offended party." So was God, and he went straight away and sought reconciliation. Brother, do the same. "Oh, but I have been insulted." Just so: so was God: all the wrong was towards him, yet he sent. "Oh, but the party is so unworthy." So are you; but "God loved you and sent his Son." Go you and write according to that copy. I do not mean that this love is to come out of your own heart originally, but I do mean that it is to flow out of your heart because God has made it to flow into it. You are one of those basins of the fountain; love has poured into you from above, let it run over to those who are below. Go forth at once, and try and make reconciliation, not only between yourself and your friend, but between every man and God. Let that be your object. Christ has become man's reconciliation, and we are to try and bring this reconciliation near to every poor sinner that comes in our way. We are to tell him that God in Christ is reconciled; we are to say to him, "He is the propitiation for our sins, and not for ours only, but for the sins of the whole world." Mark that word! It tallies with that other, "Behold the Lamb of God, which taketh away the sin of the world." God is now able to deal on gospel terms with the whole race. We need never think that we shall meet with men to whom God will not consent to be reconciled. The propitiation is such that whosoever comes to God shall be received through it. God is always within to receive every soul that comes to him by Jesus Christ. "God so loved the world, that he gave his only-begotten Son, that whosoever believeth in him should not perish, but have everlasting life." Your work and mine is reconciliation, and everything that tends that way.

When we have done all, what then? We shall have nothing whereof to glory. Suppose a man should become so loving that he gave himself wholly up for his fellow-creatures, and actually died for them, would he have anything to boast of? Read my text over again. "Beloved, if God so loved us, we *ought* also to love one another"; so that if you get to the highest point of self-sacrifice you will never be able to boast, for you have only then done what it was your duty to have done. Thus you see the highest grade of Christianity excludes all idea of salvation by works, for when we come up to its utmost pitch, if we give our body to be burned for love, yet still we have done no more than it was our duty to have done, considering the tremendous obligations under which the love of God has laid us.

If you had to manage waterworks for the distribution of water all over this city, and there was a certain pipe into which you poured water, and none ever came out at the other end, do you know what you would do? You would take it out and say, "This does not suit my purpose: I want a pipe that will give out as well as receive." That is exactly what the Lord desires of us. Do not selfishly say, "I want to sit down and enjoy the love of God. I shall never say a word to anybody about Christ. I will never give a poor creature so much as a brass farthing; but I want to sit down and be solaced with the love of God." If you think thus, you are a pipe plugged up; you are of no use; you will have to be taken out of the system of the church; for the system of love-supply for the world requires open pipes, through which love divine may freely flow. May the Lord clear you and fill you, so that out of you there may continually flow rivers of living water. Amen.

IV.

THE BEST WAR-CRY.

March 4, 1883.

"The Lord his God is with him, and the shout of a king is among them."—NUMBERS xxiii. 21.

It was a singular spectacle to see the king of Moab and his lords climbing to the tops of the craggy rocks, accompanied by that strange being, the Eastern prophet Balaam. They are seeking to look upon Israel with the evil eye, and flash down curses upon her tents in the plain beneath. You see them gazing down from the mountains upon the encampment in the wilderness below, even as vultures from aloft spy out their prey. They watch with keen and cruel eyes. Cunning and malice are in their countenances. How Balak longs to crush the nation which he fears! They are secretly endeavoring by spell and enchantment to bring evil upon the people whom Jehovah has chosen and led into the wilderness. You see them offering their seven bullocks and their seven rams upon the seven altars which they have set up upon Pisgah's rocks; and Balaam retires to wait until the afflatus shall come upon him, and he shall be able to prophesy. In all probability Moses knew nothing about this at the time; and certainly the people below knew nothing of the foul conspiracy. There lay the tribes in the valley, unaware that mischief was brewing, and quite unable to meet the dark design even if they had been aware of it. What a mercy it was for them that they were guarded by a Watcher, and a holy one, whose eyes can never slumber. How true it is—"I the Lord do keep it; I will water it every moment: lest any hurt it, I will keep it night and day." The Lord's eyes are fixed upon Balaam the hireling, and Balak the Son of Zippor: in vain do they weave the enchantment and work the divination; they shall be utterly ashamed and confounded. They were baffled in their machinations, and utterly defeated in their schemes, and that for one single reason: it is written, "JEHOVAH SHAMMAH—the Lord is there." God's presence in the midst of his people is as a wall of fire round about them, and a glory in their midst. The Lord is their light and their salvation, whom shall they fear?

At this present time God has a people, a remnant according to the election of grace, who still dwell like sheep in the midst of wolves. When, as a part of the Lord's church, we look at our surroundings, we see much that might cause us alarm; for never, either day or night, is Satan quiet. Like a roaring lion he goeth about, seeking whom he may devour: he plots in secret his crafty devices: if it were possible he would deceive even the very elect. This prince of darkness has on earth many most diligent servants, compassing sea and land to make proselytes, laying out all their strength, and using all their craft and cunning if by any means they may destroy the kingdom of God, and blot out the truth from under heaven. It is saddest of all to see certain men who know the truth in some degree, as Balaam did, entering into league with the adversary against the true Israel. These combine their arts, and use all possible means that the gospel of the grace of God, and the church that holds it, may utterly be destroyed. If the church be not destroyed it will be no thanks to her enemies, for they would swallow her up quick. When we look upon the signs of the times our heart grows heavy; for iniquity abounds, the love of many waxes cold, many false spirits have gone abroad into the earth, and some whom we looked upon as helpers are proving themselves to be of another order. What then? Are we dismayed? By no means, for that same God who was in the midst of the church in the wilderness is in the church of these last days. Again shall her adversaries be defeated. Still will he defend her, for the Lord has built his church upon a rock, and the gates of hell shall not prevail against her. The reason of her safety is this:—

"God in the midst of her doth dwell;
Nothing shall her remove;
The Lord to her a helper shall,
And that right early, prove."

Our text declares the grand safeguard of the church of God, ensuring her against every peril known and unknown, earthly or Satanic;—"Jehovah his God is with him, and the shout of a king is among them."

May the Holy Spirit help me while I try to speak first upon *God's presence with his people;* secondly, upon *the results of that presence;* and, thirdly, upon *how, by the grace of God, that presence may be preserved continually amongst us.*

I. First, let me speak a little upon GOD'S PRESENCE AMONG HIS PEOPLE. It is *an extraordinary presence,* for God's ordinary and usual presence is everywhere. Whither shall we flee from his presence? He is in the highest heaven and in the lowest hell: the hand of the Lord is upon the high hills, and his power is in all deep places. This knowledge is too high and wonderful for us: yet everywhere is God, for in him we live and move and have our being. Still there is a peculiar presence; for God was among his people in the wilderness as he was not among the Moabites and the Edomites their foes, and God is in his church as he is not in the world. It is a peculiar promise of the covenant that God will dwell with his people and walk among them. By the gift of the Holy Spirit the Lord is with us and in us at this hour. He saith of his church, "Here will I dwell, for I have desired it." This is much more than God's being about us; it includes the favor of God towards us, his consideration of us, his working with us. An active nearness to bless is the presence of which we speak.

Here we may say with great reverence that God is with his people *in the entireness of his nature*. The Father is with us, for the Father himself loveth us. Like as a father pitieth his children, so the Lord pitieth them that fear him. He is near to us, supplying our needs, guiding our steps, helping us in time, and tutoring us for eternity. God is where his children are, hearing every groan of their sorrow, marking every tear of their distress. The Father is in the midst of his family, acting a father's part towards them. "Lord, thou hast been our dwelling-place in all generations." He is never far from any into whose breasts he has put the spirit of adoption whereby we cry, "Abba, Father!" Come, ye children of God, rejoice in this: your heavenly Father has come unto you, and abides with you. We have also the presence of the divine Son of God. Said he not to his apostles, "Lo, I am with you alway, even unto the end of the world"? Have we not this for our joy whenever we come together, that we meet in his name, and that he still says, "Peace be unto you," and manifests himself unto us as he doth not unto the world. Many of you know most delightfully what it is to have fellowship with God, for "truly our fellowship is with the Father, and with his Son Jesus Christ"; and this fellowship were not ours if we were not made nigh by his precious blood. Very near are we to the heart of Christ; he dwells with us; yea, he is one with us. Peculiarly this presence relates to the Holy Ghost. It is he who represents the Lord Jesus who has gone from us. We have a double portion of Christ's spirit, because we see him now that he is taken up; even as Elisha had a double portion of Elijah's spirit, according to the prophet's saying, "If thou see me when I am taken from thee, it shall be so unto thee"; that is, a double portion of my spirit shall rest upon thee. It was expedient that our Lord and Master should go, that the Spirit might be given. That Spirit once outpoured at Pentecost has never been withdrawn. He is still in the midst of this dispensation, working, guiding, quickening, comforting, exercising all the blessed office of the Paraclete, and being for us and in us God's advocate, pleading for the truth, and for us. Yes, dear friends, the Father, the Son, and the Holy Spirit are in the midst of the true church of God when that church is in a right and healthy state; and if the triune God be gone away from the church, then her banners must trail in the dust, for her warriors have lost their strength. This is the glory of the church of God—to have the grace of the Lord Jesus Christ, and the love of God the Father, and the communion of the Holy Ghost to be her never-failing benediction. What a glory to have Father, Son, and Holy Spirit manifesting the Godhead in the midst of our assemblies, and blessing each one of us.

For God to dwell with us: what *a condescending presence* this is! And will God in very truth dwell among men? If the heaven of heavens cannot contain him, will he abide among his people? He will! He will! Glory be to his name! "Know ye not that your bodies are the temples of the Holy Ghost?" God dwelleth in us. Wonderful word! Who can fathom the depth of this grace? The mystery of the incarnation is equalled by the mystery of the indwelling. That God the Holy Ghost shall dwell in our bodies is as extraordinary as that God the Son should inhabit that body which was born of the blessed virgin. Strange, strange is this, that the Creator should dwell in his creatures, that the Infinite should tabernacle in finite beings. Yet so it is, for he has said, "Certainly I will be with thee."

What *an awe* this imparts to every true church of God! You may go in and out of certain assemblies, and you may say, "Here we have beauty! here we have adornment, musical, ecclesiastical, architectural, oratorical, and the like!" but to my mind there is no worship like that which proceeds from a man when he feels—the Lord is here. What a hush comes over the soul! Here is the place for the bated breath, the unsandalled foot, and the prostrate spirit. Now are we on holy ground. When the Lord descends in the majesty of his infinite love to deal with the hearts of men, then it is with us as it was in Solomon's temple when the priests could not stand to minister by reason of the glory that filled the place. Man is set aside, for God is there. In such a case the most fluent think it better to be silent; for there is at times more expressiveness in absolute silence than in the fittest words. "How dreadful is this place! this is none other but the house of God, and this is the gate of heaven." For why? Because Jacob had said, "Surely the Lord is in this place." We regard the lowliest assemblies of the most illiterate people with solemn reverence if God be there: we regard the largest assemblies of the wealthiest and most renowned with utter indifference if God be not there.

This is the one *necessary* of the church: the Lord God

must be in the midst of her, or she is nothing. If God be there, peace will be within her walls, and prosperity within her palaces; but if the Lord be not there woe unto the men that speak in his name, for they shall cry in bitterness, "Who hath believed our report?" Woe unto the waiting people, for they shall go away empty! Woe unto the sinners in a forsaken Zion, for them comes no salvation! The presence of God makes the Church to be a joyful, happy, solemn place: this brings glory to his name and peace to his people; but without it, all faces are pale, all hearts are heavy.

Brethren, this presence of God is *clearly discerned* by the gracious, though others may not know it. Yet methinks even the ungracious in a measure perceive it,—coming into the assembly they are struck with a secret something, they know not what; and if they do not immediately join in the worship of the present God, yet a deep impression is made upon them beyond any that could be caused by the sound of human speech, or by the grandeur of outward show. They feel awed, and retire abashed. Certainly the devil knows where God is,—none better than he. He hates the camp of which Jehovah is the leader; against it he doubles his enmity, multiplies his plots, and exercises all his power. He knows where his kingdom finds its bravest assailants, and he therefore attacks their head-quarters, even as did Balaam and Balak of old.

Let us look at Balaam for a moment. May we never run in the way of Balaam for a reward; but let us stand in his way for a moment that he may be our beacon. This man had sold himself for gold, and though he knew God and spoke under inspiration, yet he knew him not in his heart, but was willing to curse God's people for hire. He was thwarted in his design because God was there.

It is worth our while to see what kind of a God Jehovah is in Balaam's estimation. He describes our God in verse nineteen,—"God is not a man that he should lie; neither the son of man that he should repent: hath he said, and shall he not do it? or hath he spoken, and shall he not make it good?" Balaam perceived that the God who was in the midst of his people is not a changeable God, not a false God, not one who promises and forgets, or promises and eats his words, or promises what he cannot and will not perform. The God of Israel is faithful and true, immutable, unchanging: every one of his promises shall be fulfilled: none of his words shall fall to the ground. "Hath he said, and shall he not do it?—hath he spoken, and shall it not come to pass?" What a joy it is to have such a God as this among us,—a promise-making and a promise-keeping God; a God at work for his people, as he has declared he would be; a God comforting and cheering his people, and fulfilling in their experience that which his word had led them to expect. This God is our God for ever and ever; he shall be our guide even unto death.

My dear friends, we sometimes hear men talk of the failure of the church. We are afraid that some churches do fail. Wherever failure occurs, the bottom of it is the absence of the Lord of hosts, for he cannot fail. I heard one, speaking of the district in which he lives, say, "We are a religious people; almost all the people attend a place of worship, but," he added, "I am bound to add that of spiritual life we have few traces. One church has given up its prayer-meetings; another feels that its entertainments are more important than its worship, and another is notorious for worldliness." This is a testimony as terrible as it is common. The worst thing that can be said of any Christian community is this: "Thou hast a name to live and art dead." "Thou art neither cold nor hot." Our Lord Jesus says, "I would thou wert cold or hot. So then because thou art lukewarm, and neither cold nor hot, I will spew thee out of my mouth." A church without life and zeal makes Christ sick; he cannot bear it. He can put up with downright godlessness sooner than with a profession of religion out of which the life and the power are gone, since it has cooled down into lukewarmness. This, then, we should pray for continually—the presence of God in the midst of his people.

> "Great Shepherd of thine Israel
> Who didst between the cherubs dwell,
> And ledd'st the tribes, thy chosen sheep,
> Safe through the desert and the deep:
>
> Thy church is in the desert now;
> Shine from on high, and guide us through;
> Turn us to thee, thy love restore;
> We shall be saved, and sigh no more."

II. To whet your desire for this let me pass on to the second head of my subject, which is briefly to describe THE RESULTS OF THIS DIVINE PRESENCE. Some of these results are *mentioned in the context*. One of the first is *leading*—"God brought them out of Egypt" (verse 22). The best critics give us another rendering: "God is bringing them out of Egypt." When God is in the midst of his people he is leading them, so that we may cheerfully sing that song, "He leadeth me; he leadeth me," and go on with David to word it, "He leadeth me beside the still waters." We want no other leader in the church when we have God; for his eye and arm will guide his people. I am always afraid of having human rules in a church, and equally fearful of being governed by human precedents. I am afraid of power being vested in one, or two, or twenty men; the power must be in the Lord himself. That church which has

God in the midst of it rules itself, and goes right without any other guidance but that which comes of the Holy Spirit's working. Such a church keeps together without aiming at uniformity, and goes on to victory even though it makes no noise. That movement is right which is led by God, and that is sure to be all wrong which is led in the best possible way if God be absent. Organization is all very well, but I sometimes feel inclined to join with Zwingle in the battle when he said, "In the name of the Holy Trinity let all loose:" for when everybody is free, if God be present everybody is bound to do the right. When each man moves according to the divine instinct in him there will be little need of regulations: all is order where God rules. Just as the atoms of matter obey the present power of God, so do separate believers obey the one great impelling influence. Oh, for God to be in the church to lead it: and it shall be rightly guided. Do not fall in love with this particular system or that, my brother; do not cry up this scheme of working or that! Get the Spirit of God, and almost any shape that spiritual life takes will be a form of energy suitable for the particular emergency. God never leads his people wrongly. It is for them to follow the fiery, cloudy pillar; though it lead them through the sea, they shall traverse it dry-shod; though it lead them through a desert, they shall be fed; though it bring them into a thirsty land, they shall drink to the full of water from the rock. We must have the Lord with us to guide us into our promised rest.

The next blessing is *strength*. "He hath as it were the strength of an unicorn" (verse 22). It is generally agreed that the creature here meant is an extinct species of urus or ox, most nearly represented by the buffalo of the present period. This gives us the sentence,—"He hath as it were the strength of a buffalo." When God is in a church, what rugged strength, what massive force, what irresistible energy is sure to be there! And how untamable is the living force! You cannot yoke this buffalo to everybody's plough: it has its own free way of living, and it acts after its own style. When the Lord is with a church her power is not in numbers, though very speedily she will increase; her power is not wealth, though God will take care that the money comes when it is needed: her power lies in God, and that power becomes irresistible, untamable, unconquerable. Force and energy are with the Lord. I do fear me that what many bodies of Christian people need is this force. Examine yonder religious body: it is huge, but it lacks muscle; it is a fine-looking organization, but soul, sinew, backbone are wanting. Where God is there is sure to be life-force. When the Spirit of God descended upon the first saints they began to speak with wondrous power; and though they were persecuted, they were not subdued. No bit could be put into their mouths to hold them in, for they went everywhere preaching the word. Of the true Israel it shall be said—his strength is as the strength of the buffalo: it cannot be controlled or conquered.

The next result is *safety*. "Surely there is no enchantment against Jacob, neither is there any divination against Israel." The presence of God quietly baffles all the attempts of the evil one. I have noticed, dear brethren, in this church, where we have had God's presence in a great measure, that all around us people have gone off to this opinion and to the other fancy, yet our members as a rule have stood firm. Persons say to me, "Do you not sometimes answer the scepticisms of the day?" I answer, No. They do not come in my way. "Do not modern opinions trouble your church?" They have not done so. Why? because God is there, and spiritual life in vigorous exercise does not fall a victim to disease. A gracious atmosphere does not agree with modern doubt. When people fall into that evil they go where the thing is indulged, or at least where it is combated; where in some way or other they can develop their love of novelty and foster the notion of their own wisdom. Infidelity, Socinianism, and modern thought can make no headway where the Spirit is at work. Enchantment does not lie against Israel, and divination does not touch Jacob. If a church will keep to truth, keep to God, and do its own work, it can live like a lamb in the midst of wolves without being torn in pieces. Have God with you, and not only the evil of doctrinal error but every other shall be kept far from you. There was even when Christ was in the Church a Judas in the midst of it; and even in the apostles' days there were some that went out from them because they were not of them, for if they had been of them doubtless they would have continued with them; hence we may not expect to be without false brethren. But the true safety of the church is not a creed, not an enactment for expelling those who violate the creed; the presence of God alone can protect his people against the cunning assaults of their foes.

Upon these words "there is no enchantment against Jacob, no divination against Israel," suffer a few sentences. There are still a few foolish people in the world who believe in witchcraft and spells, but ye, beloved, if you love the Lord, throw such nonsense to the winds. Do you not hear people talk about this being lucky and that unlucky? This notion is heathenish and unchristian. Never utter such nonsense. But even if there were such things as witchcraft and divination, if this house were full of devils and the air swarmed with invisible sprites of an evil sort, yet if we be the people of God, surely there is no enchantment against us. Divination cannot touch a child of God: the evil one is chained. Wherefore be of good courage: if God be for us, who can be against us?

Further than that, God gives to his people the next blessing, that is of his so *working among them* as to make them a wonder, and cause out-siders to raise enquiries about them. "According to this time it shall be said of Jacob and of Israel, What hath God wrought?" Is not that a singular thing? Here is Balaam with his seven altars, and seven bullocks, and seven rams, and here is Balak, and they are all going to compass some dreadful evil against Israel. The prophet is a man of great skill in the occult arts: and what does God say? In effect he says,—From this hour in which you try to curse them I will bless them more than ever, until I will make them say, and their enemies say, "What hath God wrought?" Brethren, there is another question, "What hath Israel wrought?" I am glad that Israel's work is not my subject just now, because I should make a very wretched sermon out of it; we have better music in the words, "What hath God wrought?" Let me tell, not what *I* have done, but what God has done; not what human nature is, but what God's nature is, and what the grace of God will work in the midst of his people. If God be with us we shall be signs and wonders, until those about us shall say, "What is this that God is doing?" Yes, in you, poor Jacob, wrestling, halting on your thigh, men shall see marvels and cry, "What hath God wrought?" Much more shall it be so with you, my brother Israel, you who have prevailed and won the blessing; you are as a prince with God, and you shall make men enquire, "What hath God wrought?"

When God is with his people he will give them *power of a destructive kind.* Do not be frightened. Here is the text for it: "Behold, the people shall rise up as a great lion, and lift up himself as a young lion"—that is, as a lion in the fulness of his vigor,—"he shall not lie down until he eat of the prey, and drink the blood of the slain." God has put into his church, when he is in it, a most wonderful, destructive power as against spiritual wickedness. A healthy church kills error, and tears in pieces evil. Not so very long ago our nation tolerated slavery in our colonies. Philanthropists endeavored to destroy slavery; but when was it utterly abolished? It was when Wilberforce roused the church of God, and when the church of God addressed herself to the conflict, then she tore the evil thing to pieces. I have been amused with what Wilberforce said the day after they passed the Act of Emancipation. He merrily said to a friend when it was all done, "Is there not something else we can abolish?" That was said playfully, but it shows the spirit of the church of God. She lives in conflict and victory; her mission is to destroy everything that is bad in the land. See the fierce devil of intemperance how it devours men! Earnest friends have been laboring against it, and they have done something for which we are grateful, but if ever intemperance is put down, it will be when the entire church of God shall arouse herself to protest against it. When the strong lion rises up the giant of drunkenness shall fall before him. "He shall not lie down until he eat of the prey, and drink the blood of the slain." I augur for the world the best results from a fully aroused church. If God be in her there is no evil which she cannot overcome. This crowded London of ours sometimes appals me,—the iniquity which reigns and rages in the lower districts, the general indifference and the growing atheism of the people,—these are something terrible; but let not the people of God be dismayed. If the Lord be in the midst of us we shall do with this as our sires have done with other evils: we shall rise up in strength, and not lie down till the evil is destroyed. For the destructions, mark you, of God's people, are not the destructions of men and women; they consist in the overthrow of sin, the tearing in pieces of systems of iniquity. This it is which God shall help his church to do, he being in the midst of her.

Once more: the results of God's presence are to be seen, not only in the context, but in other matters which we have personally experienced and hope to experience more fully still. Note them. When God is in a church there is a *holy awe* upon the hearts of his people; there is also a childlike trustfulness and hopefulness, and consequent courage and joy. When the Lord is in the midst of his people the ordinances of his house are exceeding sweet; baptism and the Lord's Supper become divinely painted pictures of our burial in Christ, and of our life through him; the preaching of the word drops as dew and distils as the rain; the meetings for prayer are fresh and fervent; we want to stay in them hour after hour, we feel it such a happy thing to be there. The very house wherein we meet grows beautiful to us; we love the place where our Lord is wont to meet with us. Then work for Christ is easy, nay, delightful; God's people never want urging on, they are eager for the fray, when the Lord is with them. Then, too, suffering for Christ becomes pleasant, yea, any kind of suffering is easily borne.

> "I can do all things, or can bear
> All sufferings, if my Lord be there:
> Sweet pleasures mingle with the pains,
> While his left hand my head sustains."

Then prayer grows abundant all over the church, both in private and in public. Then life is made vigorous; the feeblest becomes as David, and David like the angel of the Lord. Then love is fervent; unity is unbroken; truth is esteemed, and the living of truth in the life is sought after by all the people of God. Then effort is successful; the church enlarges the bounds of her tent, for she breaks forth on the right hand and on the left. Then her seed inherits the Gentiles, and the desolate places are inhabited. Then God gives unto her the holy energy with which she vanquishes nations. When God is with her she becomes like a sheaf of fire in the midst of the stubble, and consumes her adversaries round about. "Fair as the moon, clear as the sun, and terrible as an army with banners," is a church which has God in her midst.

But now notice one thing in my text, and with that I close this description. Where God is, we are told, "*The shout of a king is among them.*" What is the shout of a king? When great commanders are known to have come into a camp what a thrill of joy it causes among their trusty warriors. When the soldiers have been much dejected it has been whispered in their tents—

"The king has come to marshal us,
 All in his armor dressed,"

and from that moment every man has cheered up. At the sight of the king as he comes riding into the camp the host raises a great shout. What means it? It is a shout of loyal love—they are glad to welcome their leader. So is it with us when we sing—

"The King himself comes near,"

we are all as glad as glad can be. Those who cannot come out to see their prince, because they are lying on their sick beds in hospital, clap their hands, while even the little children in their mothers' arms join in the general joy. "The king is come," say they, and his presence kindles their enthusiasm till they make the hills ring again. You know how the stern Ironsides felt when Cromwell came along; every man was a hero when he led the way. They were ready for any adventure, no matter how difficult, as long as their great chief was there. That enthusiasm which was inspired by Alexander, and by Napoleon, and by other great commanders, is the earthly image of the spiritual fervor felt by the church when the Lord Jesus is in her midst.

What next? When the King comes and they have received him with enthusiasm, he cries, "Now is the hour of battle;" and at once a shout goes up from his warriors who are eager for the fight. When a clan of Highlanders was led to the battle by their chief he had only to show them the enemy and with one tremendous shout they leaped upon them like lions. It is so with the people of God. When God is with us then are we strong, resolute, determined. The charge of the servants of God is as the rush of a hurricane against a bowing wall and a tottering fence. In God is our confidence of victory. With God present no man's heart fails him; no doubt enters the host. "Be strong, and quit yourselves like men," is the word that is passed round, for their king's eye makes them brave and the presence of his majesty secures them triumph. My brethren, let us cry to God, entreating him to be among us. This it is that you want in your Sunday-schools, in your mission halls, in your street preaching, in your tract distributing; it is this that I want beyond everything when I have to speak to you in this vast house. If I could hear the sound of my Master's feet behind me I would speak though I were lying upon the borders of the grave; but if God be gone I am bereft of power. What is the use of words without the Spirit? We might as well mutter to the whistling winds as preach to men without the Lord. O God, if thou be with us then the shout of a King is among us, but without thee we pine away.

III. Thirdly, let us look at a very important point, and a very practical one too: What can be done for THE SECURING AND PRESERVING OF THE PRESENCE OF GOD WITH THE CHURCH? This is a matter that would require several sermons to discuss it fully; but I notice that there is *something even in the conformation of a church* to secure this. God is very tolerant, and he bears with many mistakes in his servants and yet blesses them; but depend upon it, unless a church is formed at the very outset upon scriptural principles and in God's own way sooner or later all the mistakes of her constitution will turn out to be sources of weakness. Christ loves to dwell in a house which is built according to his own plans, and not according to the whims and fancies of men. The church ought not to set up as her authority the decrees of men, either living or dead; her ruler is Christ. Associations formed otherwise than according to Scripture must fail in the long run. I wish Christians would believe this. Chillingworth said, "The Bible, and the Bible alone, is the religion of Protestants." That is not true. Certain Protestants have tacked many other things to the Bible; and they are suffering as the result of their folly, for they cannot keep their church from becoming Popish. Of course they cannot: they have admitted a little leaven of Popery, and it will leaven the whole lump. The dry rot in one part of the house will spread throughout the whole fabric sooner or later. Let us be careful to build on the foundation of Christ, and then let every man take heed how he build thereon; for even if the foundation is good, yet if he build with hay and stubble the fire will cause him grievous loss.

But next, God will only dwell with a church which is *full of life*. The living God will not inhabit a dead church. Hence the necessity of having really regenerated people as members of the church. We cannot secure this in every case with all our watching: tares will grow among the wheat. But if the admission of unregenerate men is usual, and there are no restrictions, then the Lord will be grieved and leave us. God dwelleth not in temples made with hands: he has nothing to do with bricks and mortar; he dwells in living souls. Remember that text: "God is not the God of the dead, but of the living," and it bears this sense among others, that he is not the God of a church made up of unconverted people. Oh that we may all live unto God, and may that life be past all question.

That being supposed, we next notice that to have God among us we must be *full of faith*. Unbelief gives forth such a noxious vapor that Jesus himself could not stop where it was. His strength was paralyzed:—"He could not do mighty works there because of their unbelief." Faith creates an atmosphere in which the Spirit of God can work: meanwhile the Spirit of God himself creates that faith, so that it is all of his own working from first to last. Brothers, sisters, do you believe your God? Do you believe up to the hilt? Alas, too many only believe a little! But do you believe his every word? Do you believe his grandest promises? Is he a real God to you, making his words into facts every day of your lives? If so, then the Lord is among us as in the holy place

Faith builds a pavilion in which her king delights to sit enthroned.

With that must come *prayer*. Prayer is the breath of faith. I do not believe God will ever be long with a church that does not pray: and I feel certain that when meetings for prayer, when family prayer, when private prayer, when any form of prayer comes to be at a discount, the Lord will leave the people to learn their weakness. Want of prayer cuts the sinews of the church for practical working; she is lame, feeble, impotent, if prayer be gone. If anything be the matter with the lungs we fear consumption: prayer-meetings are the lungs of the church, and anything the matter there means consumption to the church, or at best a gradual decline, attended with general debility. Oh, my brothers, if we want to have God with us, pass the watchword round, "Let us pray." Let us pray after the fashion of the widow who was importunate and would not be repulsed; remember, it is written, "Men ought always to pray, and not to faint." Where prayer is fervent God is present.

Supposing there is this faith and prayer, we shall also need *holiness of life*. You know what Balaam did when he found he could not curse the people. Satanic was his advice. He bade the king of Moab seduce the men of Israel by the women of Moab that were fair to look upon; these were to fascinate them by their beauty, and then to invite them to their idolatrous rites, which rites were orgies of lust: he hoped that the lewdness of the people would grieve the Lord and cause him to leave them and then Moab could smite them. He sadly succeeded. If it had not been for Phineas who in holy wrath drove his javelin right through a man and woman in the very act of sin, sparing none in the vehemence of his zeal, Israel had been quite undone. So in a church. The devil will work hard to lead one into licentiousness, another into drunkenness, a third into dishonesty, and others into worldliness. If he can only get the goodly Babylonish garment and the wedge of gold buried in an Achan's tent, then Israel will be chased before her adversaries. God cannot dwell in an unclean church. A holy God abhors the very garments spotted by the flesh. Be ye holy as Christ is holy. Do not take up with this German-silver electrotype holiness, which is so much boasted of nowadays. Do not be deluded into self-righteousness, but seek after real holiness; and if you do find it you will never boast about it: your life will speak, but your lips will never dare to say, "See how holy I am." Real holiness dwells with humility, and makes men aspire after that which yet lies beyond them. Be holy, upright, just, straight, true, pure, chaste, devout. God send us this behavior, and then we shall keep him among us as long as we live.

Lastly, when we have reached to that, let us have *practical consecration*. God will not dwell in a house which does not belong to him. No, the first thing with any one of us is to answer this question:—Dost thou give thyself up to Christ, body, soul, and spirit, to live for him and to die for him? Wilt thou give him all that thou hast of talent and ability, and substance, and time, and life itself? Where there is a church made up of consecrated people, there God will remain, and there he will make a heaven below, and there the shout of a king shall be heard, and there his strength shall be revealed, and there his glory shall be seen even as it is beheld on high. The Lord send us this, for Jesus' sake. Amen and Amen.

V.

EARNEST EXPOSTULATION.

April 1, 1883.

"Or despisest thou the riches of his goodness and forbearance and longsuffering; not knowing that the goodness of God leadeth thee to repentance."—ROMANS ii. 4.

THE apostle is intensely personal in his address. This verse is not spoken to us all in the mass, but to some one in particular. The apostle fixes his eyes upon a single person, and speaks to him as "Thee" and "Thou." "Despisest *thou* the riches of his goodness and forbearance and longsuffering; not knowing that the goodness of God leadeth *thee* to repentance?" It should ever be the intent of the preacher to convey his message to each hearer in his own separate individuality. It is always a very happy sign when a man begins to think of himself as an individual, and when the expostulations and invitations of the Gospel are seen by him to be directed to himself personally. I will give nothing for that indirect, essay-like preaching which is as the sheet lightning of summer, dazzling for the moment, and flaming over a broad expanse, but altogether harmless, since no bolt is launched from it, and its ineffectual fires leave no trace behind. I will give nothing for that kind of hearing which consists in the word being heard by everybody in general and by no one in particular. It is when the preacher can "Thee" and "Thou" his hearers that he is likely to do them good. When each man is made to say, "This is for me," then the power of God is present in the word. One personal, intentional touch of the hem of Christ's garment conveys more blessing than all the pressure of the crowd that thronged about the Master. The laying of his healing hand upon the individual who was suffering had more virtue in it than all those heavenly addresses which fell from his lips upon minds that did not receive the truth for themselves. I do pray that we may come to personal dealings with the Lord each one for himself, and that the Spirit of God may convince each man and woman, according as the case may stand before the living God. O my hearer, *thou* art now to be lovingly spoken with: I speak not to *you* as unto many, but unto *thee*, as one by thyself.

Observe that the apostle singled out an individual who had condemned others for transgressions, in which he himself indulged. This man owned so much spiritual light that he knew right from wrong, and he diligently used his knowledge to judge others, condemning them for their transgressions. As for himself, he preferred the shade, where no fierce light might beat on his own conscience and disturb his unholy peace. His judgment was spared the pain of dealing with his home offences by being set to work upon the faults of others. He had a candle, but he did not place it on the table to light his own room; he held it out at the front door to inspect therewith his neighbors who passed by. Ho! my good friend, my sermon is for thee. Paul looks this man in the face and says, "Therefore thou art inexcusable, O man, whoever thou art, that judgest: for wherein thou judgest another thou condemnest thyself; for thou that judgest doest the same things:" and then he pointedly says to him: "Thinkest thou this, O man, that judgest them which do such things, and doest the same, that thou shalt escape the judgment of God?" Well did the apostle aim that piercing arrow; it hits the centre of the target and strikes a folly common to mankind. The poet of the night-watches wrote,—

"All men think all men mortal but themselves."

As truly might I say, "All men think all men guilty but themselves." The punishment which is due to sin the guilty reckon to be surely impending upon others, but they scarce believe that it can ever fall upon themselves. A personal doom for themselves is an idea which they will not harbor: if the dread thought should light upon them they shake it off as men shake snow-flakes from their cloaks. The thought of personal guilt, judgment, and condemnation is inconvenient; it breeds too much trouble within, and so they refuse it lodging. Vain men go maundering on their way, whispering of peace and safety; doting as if God had passed an act of amnesty and oblivion for them, and had made for them an exception to all the rules of justice, and all the manner of his courts. Do men indeed believe that they alone shall go unpunished? No man will subscribe to that notion when it is written down in black and white, and yet the mass of men live as if this were true; I mean the mass of men who have sufficient light to condemn sin in others. They start back from the fact of their own guiltiness and condemnation, and go on in their ungodliness as if there were no great white throne for them, no last assize, no judge, no word of condemnation, and no hell of wrath. Alas, poor madmen, thus to dream! O Spirit of Truth, save them from this fatal infatuation.

Sin is always on the downward grade, so that when a man proceeds a certain length he inevitably goes beyond it. The person addressed by the apostle first thought to escape judgment, and then he came to think lightly of the goodness, forbearance, and longsuffering of God. He thinks he shall escape in the future, and because of that he despises the present goodness and longsuffering of the Most High. Of course he does. If he does not believe in the terrors of the world to come for himself, he naturally reckons it to be a small thing to have been spared their immediate experience. Barren tree as he is, he does not believe that he will ever be cut down, and therefore he feels no gratitude to the dresser of the vineyard for pleading, "Let it alone yet another year, till I dig about it, and dung it." I wish, as God shall help me, to drive hard at the consciences of men upon this matter. I would be to you, my careless friend, what Jonah was to Nineveh: I would warn you, and bestir you to repentance. Oh that the Holy Ghost would make this sermon effectual for the arousing of every unsaved soul that shall hear or read it!

I. First, let me speak this morning to thee, O unregenerate, impenitent man, concerning THE GOODNESS OF GOD WHICH THOU HAST EXPERIENCED. Thou hast known the goodness, and forbearance, and longsuffering of God. According to the text, "riches" of these have been spent upon unconverted, ungodly men, and upon thee as one of them. Let me speak with thee first, O man, and remind thee how favored thou hast been of God by being made a partaker of "the richness of his *goodness*." In many cases this is true of temporal things. Men may be without the fear of God, and yet, for all that, God may be pleased to prosper their endeavors in business. They succeed almost beyond their expectation— I mean some of them; probably the description applies to thee. They rise from the lowest position, and accumulate about them the comforts and luxuries of life. Though they have no religion, they have wit, and prudence, and thrift, and so they compete with others, and God permits them to be winners in the race for wealth. Moreover, he allows them to enjoy good health, vigor of mind, and strength of constitution: they are happy in the wife of their youth, and their children are about them. Theirs is an envied lot. Death seems for awhile forbidden to knock at their door, even though he has been ravaging the neighborhood; even sickness does not molest their household. They are not in trouble as other men, neither are they plagued like other men. Abraham had to prepare a Machpelah, and David mourned over his sons; but these have had to make scant provision for family sepulchre: a hedge has in very deed been set about them and all that they have. I know that it is thus with many who do not love God, and have never yielded to the entreaties of his grace. They love not the hand which enriches them, they praise not the Lord who daily loadeth them with benefits. How is it that men can receive such kindness, and yield no return? O sirs, you are to-day blessed with all that need requires; but I pray you remember that you might have been in the depths of poverty. An illness would have lost you your situation; or a slight turn in trade would have left you bankrupt. You are well to-day; but you might have been tossing to and fro upon a bed of sickness, you might have been in a hospital, about to lose a limb. Shall not God be praised for health and freedom from pain? You might have been shut up in yonder asylum, in the agonies of madness. A thousand ills have been kept from you; you have been exceedingly favored by the goodness of the Most High. Is it not so? And truly it is a wonderful thing that God should give his bread to those that lift up their heel against him, that he should cause his light to shine upon those who never perceive his goodness therein, that he should multiply his mercies upon ungodly men who only multiply their rebellions against him, and turn the gifts of his love into instruments of transgression.

Furthermore, this goodness of God has not only come to you in a temporal form, O impenitent man, but it has also visited you in a spiritual manner. Myriads of our fellowmen have never had an opportunity of knowing Christ. The missionary's foot has never trodden the cities wherein they dwell, and so they die in the dark. Multitudes are going downward, downward; but they do not know the upward road: their minds have never been enlightened by the teachings of God's word, and hence they sin with less grievousness of fault. You are placed in the very focus of Christian light, and yet you follow evil! Will you not think of this? Time was when a man would have to work for years to earn enough money to buy a Bible. There were times when he could not have earned one even with that toil: now the word of God lies upon your table, you have a copy of it in almost every room of your house; is not this a boon from God? This is the land of the open Bible, and the land of the preached word of God: in this you prove the richness of God's goodness. Do you despise this wealth of mercy? Possibly you have enjoyed the further privilege of sitting under a ministry which has been particularly plain and earnest: you have not had sermons preached *before* you, they have been preached *at* you: the minister has seized upon you and tugged at your conscience, as though he would force you to the Saviour. With cries and entreaties you have been invited to your heavenly Father, and yet you have not come. Is this a small thing?

What is more, you have been favored with a tender conscience. When you do wrong you know it, and smart for it. What mean those wakeful nights after you have yielded to a temptation? What means that miserable feeling of shame? that fever of unrest? You find it hard to stifle the inward monitor, and difficult to resist the Spirit of God. Your road to perdition is made peculiarly hard; do you mean to follow it at all costs, and go over hedge and ditch to hell?

You have not only been aroused by conscience, but the good Spirit has striven with you, and you have been almost persuaded to be a Christian. Such has been the blessed work of the Spirit upon your heart that you have at times been melted down, and ready to be moulded by grace. A strange softness has come over you, and if you had not gathered up all your evil strength, and if the devil had not helped you to resist, you had by this time dropped into the Saviour's arms. Oh, the riches of the goodness of God to have thus wooed you, and pressed his love upon you! You have scarcely had a stripe, or a frown, or an ill word from God; his ways have been all kindness, and gentleness, and longsuffering from the first day of your memory even until now. "Despisest thou the riches of his goodness?" O man, answer this, I implore thee.

The apostle then dwells upon the riches of "*forbearance.*" Forbearance comes in when men having offended, God withholds the punishment that is due to them; when men, having been invited to mercy, have refused it, and yet God continues to stretch out his hands, and invite them to come to him. Patient endurance of offences and insults has been manifested by God to many of you, who now hear these words of warning. The Lord knows to whom I speak and may he make you, also, know that I am speaking to you, even to you. Some men have gone back to the very sin of which for awhile they repented: they have suffered for their folly, but have turned again to it with suicidal determination. They are desperately set on their own ruin, and nothing can save them. The burnt child has run to the fire again; the singed moth has plunged again into the flame of the candle: who can pity such self-inflicted miseries? They are given over to perdition, for they will not be warned. They have returned to the haunt of vice, though they seemed to have been snatched from the deep ditch of its filthiness. They have wantonly and wilfully returned to their cups, though the poison of former draughts is yet burning in their veins. Yet, despite this folly, God shows forbearance towards them. They have grievously provoked him when they have done despite to his word, and have even turned to laughter the solemnities of his worship, against their own consciences, and to their own confusion: yet when his hand has been lifted up he has withdrawn it in mercy. See how God has always tempered his providence with kindness to them. He laid them low so that they were sore sick, but at the voice of their moaning he restored them. They trembled on the brink of death, yet he permitted them to recover strength; and now, despite their vows of amendment, here they are, callous and careless, unmindful of the mercy which gave them a reprieve.

Did you ever think what is included in the riches of forbearance. There are quick tempered individuals who only need to be a little provoked, and hard words and blows come quick and furious: but, oh, the forbearance of God when he is provoked to his face by ungodly men! By men, I mean, who hear his word, and yet refuse it! They slight his love, and yet he perseveres in it. Justice lays its hand on the sword, but mercy holds it back in its scabbard. Well might each spared one say,—

> "O unexhausted Grace,
>   O Love unspeakable!
> I am not gone to my own place;
>   I am not yet in hell!
> Earth doth not open yet,
>   My soul to swallow up.
> And, hanging o'er the burning pit,
>   I still am forced to hope."

Our apostle adds to goodness and forbearance the riches of "*longsuffering.*" We draw a distinction between forbearance and longsuffering. Forbearance has to do with the magnitude of sin; longsuffering with the multiplicity of it: forbearance has to do with present provocation; longsuffering relates to that provocation repeated, and continued for a length of time. Oh, how long doth God suffer the ill manners of men! Forty years long was he grieved with that generation whose carcases fell in the wilderness. Has it come to forty years yet with you, dear hearer? Possibly it may have passed even that time, and a half-century of provocation may have gone into eternity to bear witness against you. What if I should even have to say that sixty and seventy years have continued to heap up the loads of their transgressions, until the Lord saith, "I am pressed down under your sins; as a cart that is full of sheaves I am pressed down under you." Yet for all that, here you are on praying ground and pleading terms with God; here you are where yet the Saviour reigns upon the throne of grace; here you are where mercy is to be had for the asking, where free grace and dying love ring out their charming bells of invitation to joy and peace! Oh, the riches of his goodness, and forbearance, and longsuffering. Threefold is the claim: will you not regard it? Can you continue to despise it!

I should like to set all this in a striking light if I could, and therefore I would remind you of who and what that God is who has exhibited this goodness, forbearance, and longsuffering to men. Remember how *great* he is. When men insult a great prince the offence is thought to be highly heinous. If any one should openly insult our own beloved Queen, and continue to do so, all the nation would be clamorous to have the impertinence ended speedily. We cannot bear that a beloved ruler should be publicly insulted. And what think you of the sin which provokes God? which to his face defies him? and in his very courts resists him? Shall this always be forborne with? Is there not a limit to longsuffering? *Goodness* also adds another item to the provocation; for we naturally say, "Why should one so good be treated so cruelly?" If God were a tyrant, if he were unrighteous or unkind, it were not so much amiss that men stood out against him; but when his very name is love, and when he manifests the bowels of a Father towards his wandering children it is shameful that he should be so wantonly provoked. Those words of Jesus were extremely touching when he pointed to his miracles, and asked, "For which of these things do you stone me?" When I think of God I may well say—for which of his deeds do you provoke him? Every morning he draws the curtain and glads the earth with light, and gives *you* eyes to see it; he sends his rain upon the ground to bring forth bread for man, and he gives *you* life to eat thereof—is this a ground for revolting from him? Every single minute of our life is cheered with the tender kindness of God, and every spot is gladdened with his love. I wonder that the Lord does not sweep away the moral nuisance of a guilty race from off the face of earth. Man's sin must have been terribly offensive to God from day to day, and yet still he shows kindness, love, forbearance. This adds an excessive venom to man's disobedience. How can he grieve such goodness? How can divine goodness fail to resent such base ingratitude?

Think also of God's *knowledge:* for he knows all the transgressions of men. "What the eye does not see the heart does not rue," is a truthful proverb; but every transgression is committed in the very presence of God, so that penitent David cried, "Against thee, thee only have I sinned, and done this evil in thy sight." Transgression is committed in the sight of God, from whose eyes nothing is hidden. Remember also, that the Lord never can forget; before his eyes all things stand out in clear light not only the things of to-day, but all the transgressions of a life. Yet for all this he doth forbear. With evil reeking before his face, he is slow to anger, and waiteth that he may be gracious.

All this while, remember, the Lord is great in *power*. Some are patient because they are powerless; they bear and forbear because they cannot well help themselves; but it is not so with God. Had he but willed it, you had been swept into hell; only a word from him and the impenitent had fallen in the wilderness, and their spirits would have passed into the realms of endless woe. In a moment the Lord could have eased him of his adversary; he could have stopped that flippant tongue, and closed that lustful eye in an instant. That wicked heart would have failed to beat if God had withdrawn his power, and that rebellious breath would have ceased also. Had it not been for longsuffering you unbelievers would long since have known what it is to fall into the hands of an angry God. Will you continue to grieve the God who so patiently bears with you.

Be it never forgotten that sin is to God much more intolerable than it is to us. He is of purer eyes than to behold iniquity. Things which we call little sins are great and grievous evils to him: they do, as it were, touch the apple of his eye. "Oh, do not," he says, "do not this abominable thing that I hate!" His Spirit is grieved and vexed with every idle word and every sensual thought; and hence it is a wonder of wonders that a God so sensitive of sin, a God so able to avenge himself of his adversaries, a God who knows the abundance of human evil, and marks it all, should nevertheless exhibit riches of goodness and forbearance and longsuffering: yet this is what you, my ungodly hearer, have been experiencing many a long year. Here let us pause; and oh that each one who is still unsaved would sing most sincerely the words of Watts,

> "Lord, we have long abused thy love,
>   Too long indulged our sin,
> Our aching hearts e'en bleed to see
>   What rebels we have been.
>
> "No more, ye lusts, shall ye command,
>   No more will we obey;
> Stretch out, O God, thy conq'ring hand,
>   And drive thy foes away."

II. Come with me, friend, and let me speak to thee of THE SIN OF WHICH THOU ART SUSPECTED. Hear me, unconverted sinner: the sin of which thou art suspected is this,—"Despisest thou the riches of his goodness and forbearance and longsuffering?" The Lord's goodness ought to be admired and to be adored, and dost thou despise it? His goodness ought to be wondered at and told as a marvel in the ears of others, and dost thou despise it! That I might rake thy conscience a little, lend me thine ear.

Some despise God's goodness, forbearance, and longsuffering, because they *never even gave a thought to it*. God has given you life to keep you in being, and he has indulged you with his kindness, but it has not yet occurred to you that this patience is at all remarkable or worthy of the smallest thanks. You have been a drunkard, have you? a swearer? a Sabbath breaker? a lover of sinful pleasure? Perhaps not quite so; but still you have forgotten God altogether, and yet he has abounded in goodness to you: is not this a great wrong? The Lord saith, "Hear, O heavens, and give ear, O earth: I have nourished and brought up children, and they have rebelled against me. The ox knoweth his owner, and the ass his master's crib: but these my creatures do not know, my favored ones do not consider." Why, you have no such forbearance with others as God has had with you. You would not keep a dog if it never followed at your heel, but snarled at you: you would not even keep a potter's vessel if it held no water, and was of no service to you; you would break it in pieces, and throw it on the dunghill. As for yourself, you are fearfully and wonderfully made, both as to your body and as to your soul, and yet you have been of no service to your Maker, nor even thought of being of service to him. Still, he has spared you all these years, and it has never occurred to you that there has been any wonderful forbearance in it. Assuredly, O man, thou despisest the long-suffering of thy God.

Others have, perhaps, thought of it, but *have never seriously meditated thereon.* When we offend a man, if we are right-minded, we not only note the fact with regret, but we sit down and weigh the matter, and seek to rectify it; for we would not be unjust to any person, and if we felt that we had been acting unfairly it would press upon our minds until we could make amends. But are there not some of you who have never given half an hour's consideration to your relation to your God? He has spared you all this while, and yet it has never occurred to you to enter into your chamber and sit down and consider your conduct towards him. It would seem to be too much trouble even to think of your Creator. His longsuffering leads you to repentance, but you have not repented: in fact, you have not thought it worth your while to consider the question at all: you have thought it far more important to enquire, "What shall I eat and what shall I drink?" Bread and broadcloth have shut out the thought of God. Ah me, you will stand at his judgment bar before long—and then? Perhaps ere this week is finished you may have to answer, not to me, but unto him that sits upon the throne; therefore I do implore you now, for the first time give this matter thought. Despise no longer the goodness and longsuffering of God.

This longsuffering is despised, further, by those who have *imagined that God does not take any great account of what they do.* So long as they do not go into gross and open sin, and offend the laws of their country, they do not believe that it is of any consequence whether they love God or not, whether they do righteousness or not, whether they are sober and temperate, or drunken and wanton: whether they are clean in heart by God's Spirit, or defiled in soul and life. Thou thinkest that God is altogether such an one as thyself, and that he will wink at thy transgression and cover up thy sin; but thou shalt not find it so. That base thought proves that thou despisest his longsuffering.

Some even get to think that the warnings of love are so much wind, and *that the threatenings of God will never be fulfilled.* They have gone on for many years without being punished, and instead of drawing the conclusion that the longer the blow is in falling the heavier it will be when it does come, they imagine that because it is long delayed the judgment will never come at all; and so they sport and trifle between the jaws of death and hell. They hear warnings as if they were all moonshine, and fancy that this holy Book, with its threatenings, is but a bugbear to keep fools quiet. If thou thinkest so, sir, then indeed thou hast despised the goodness and forbearance and longsuffering of God. Do you imagine that this forbearance will last for ever? Do you dream that at least it will continue with you for many years? I know your secret thoughts: you see other men die suddenly, but your secret thought is that you will have long space and ample time: you hear of one struck down with paralysis, and another carried off by apoplexy, but you flatter yourselves that you will have plenty of leisure to think about these things. Oh, how can you be so secure? How can you thus tempt the Lord? False prophets in these evil days play into men's hands and hold out the hope that you may go into the next world wrong, and yet be set right in the end. This is a vile flattery of your wicked hearts; but yet remember that even according to their maunderings centuries may elapse before this fancied restoration may occur. A sensible man would not like to run the risk of even a year of agony Half-an-hour of acute pain is dreaded by most people. Can it be that the very men who start back from the dentist's door, afraid of the pinch which extricates an aching tooth, will run the risk of years of misery? Take the future of the impenitent even on this footing, it is a thing to be dreaded, and by every means avoided. I say, these flattering prophets themselves, if rightly understood, give you little enough of hope; but what will come to you if the old doctrine proves to be true and you go away into everlasting fire in hell, as the Scripture puts it? Will you live an hour in jeopardy of such a doom? Will you so despise the longsuffering and forbearance of the Lord?

I will not enlarge and use many words, for I am myself weary of words: I want to persuade you even with tears. My whole soul would attract you to your God, your Father. I would come to close quarters with you, and say, Do you not think that, even though you fall into no doctrinal error, and indulge no hazy hope as to either restitution or annihilation, yet still it is a dreadful despising of God's mercy when you keep on playing with God, and saying to his grace, "Go thy way for this time; when I have a more convenient season I will send for thee"? The more gentle God is the more you procrastinate, and the more in tenderness he speaks of pardon the more you transgress. Is this generous? Is it right? Is it wise? Can it be a fit and proper thing to do? Oh, my dear hearer, why will you act thus shamefully? Some of you delight to come and hear me preach, and drink in all I have to say, and you will even commend me for being earnest with your souls; and yet, after all, you will not decide for God, for Christ, for heaven. You are between good and evil, neither cold nor hot. I would ye were either cold or hot; I could even wish that ye either thought this word of mine to be false, or else that, believing it to be true, you at once acted upon it. How can you incur the double guilt of offending God and of knowing that it is an evil thing to do so? You reject Christ, and yet admit that he ought to be received by you! You speak well of a gospel which you will not accept for yourselves! You believe great things of a Saviour whom you will not have to be your Saviour! Jesus himself says, "If I tell you the truth, why do you not believe me?"

"Despisest thou the longsuffering of God?" Dare you do it? I tremble as I think of a man despising God's goodness. Is not this practical blasphemy? Darest thou do it? Oh, if thou hast done it hitherto, do it no more. Ere yon sun goes down again, say within thy heart, "I will be a despiser of God's goodness no longer; I will arise and go unto my Father, and I will say unto him,—Father, I have sinned. I will not rest until in the precious blood he has washed my sins away."

III. In closing this sermon I desire to remind thee, O ungodly man, of THE KNOWLEDGE OF WHICH THOU ART FORGETFUL. Read my text:—"Despisest thou the riches of his goodness and forbearance and longsuffering; *not knowing that the goodness of God leadeth thee to repentance?*" Now there are many here who know as a matter of doctrine that the goodness of God leads them to repentance, and yet they do not know it as a practical truth affecting their lives: indeed, they so act that it is not true to them at all. Yet, if they do not know this they are wilfully ignorant; not willing to retain in their minds a fact so disagreeable to them. None are so blind as those who will not see: but he who does not see, and yet hath eyes, has a criminality about his blindness which is not found in that of those who have no sight. Dear hearer, whether you know this truth or not, I would remind you that God's patience with you is meant to lead you to repentance. "How?" say you. Why, first by *giving you an opportunity to repent.* These years, which are now coming to a considerable number with you, have been given you in order that you might turn to God. By the time you were twenty-one you had sinned quite enough; perhaps you had even then begun to mislead other youths, and to instruct in evil those under your influence. Why did not God take you away at once? It might have been for the benefit of the world if he had done so; but yet you were spared till you were thirty. Did not each year of your lengthened life prove that the Lord was saying, "I will spare him, for perhaps he will yet amend and think upon his God. I will give him more light, and increase his comforts; I will give him better teaching, better preaching; peradventure he will repent." Yet you have not done so. Have you lived to be forty, and are you where you were when you were twenty? Are you still out of Christ? Then you are worse than you were; for you have sinned more deeply and you have provoked the Lord more terribly. You have now had space enough. What more do you need? When the child has offended, you say, "Child, unless you beg pardon at once, I must punish you": would you give a boy so many minutes to repent in as God has given you years? I think not. If a servant is continually robbing you; if he is careless, slothful, disobedient, you say to him, "I have passed over your faults several times, but one of these days I shall discharge you. I cannot always put up with this slovenliness, this blundering, this idleness: one of these times you will have to go." Have you not so spoken to your female servant, and thought it kind on your part to give her another chance? The Lord has said the same to you; yet here you are, a living but impenitent man; spared, but spared only to multiply your transgressions. This know, that his forbearance gives you an opportunity to repent; do not turn it into an occasion for hardening your heart.

But next, the Lord in this is pleased to give *a suggestion to you to repent*. It seems to me that every morning when a man wakes up still impenitent, and finds himself out of hell, the sunlight seems to say, "I shine on thee yet another day, as that in this day thou mayst repent." When your bed receives you at night I think it seems to say, "I will give you another night's rest, that you may live to turn from your sins and trust in Jesus." Every mouthful of bread that comes to the table says, "I have to support your body that still you may have space for repentance." Every time you open the Bible the pages say, "We speak with you that you may repent." Every time you hear a sermon, if it be such a sermon as God would have us preach, it pleads with you to turn unto the Lord and live. Surely the time past of your life may suffice you to have wrought the will of the Gentiles. "The times of your ignorance God winked at, but now commandeth men everywhere to repent." Do not life and death, and heaven and hell, call upon you so to do? Thus you have in God's goodness space for repentance, and a suggestion to repent.

But something more is here; for I want you to notice that the text does not say, "The goodness of God *calleth* thee to repentance," but "*leadeth* thee." This is a much stronger word. God calls to repentance by the gospel; God *leads to repentance* by his goodness. It is as though he plucked at your sleeve and said, "Come this way." His goodness lays its gentle hand on you, drawing you with cords of love and bands of a man. God's forbearance cries, "Why wilt thou hate me? What wrong have I done thee? I have spared thee; I have spared thy wife and children to thee; I have raised thee up from the bed of sickness; I have loaded thy board; I have filled thy wardrobe; I have done thee a thousand good turns; wherefore dost thou disobey? Turn unto thy God and Father, and live in Christ Jesus."

If, on the other hand, you have not received rich temporal favors, yet the Lord still leads you to repentance by a rougher hand; as when the prodigal fain would have filled his belly with husks, but could not, and the pangs of hunger came upon him; those pains were a powerful message from the Father to lead him to the home where there was bread enough and to spare. "The goodness of God leadeth thee to repentance." Oh, that thou wouldest yield to its sweet leadings, and follow as a child follows the guidance of a nurse. Let thy crosses lead thee to the cross; let thy joys lead thee to find joy in Christ.

Do you not think that all this should *encourage you to repent*, since God himself leads you that way? If God leads you to repentance he does not mean to cast you away. If he bids you repent, then he is willing to accept your repentance, and to be reconciled to you. If he bids you change your mind, it is because his own mind is love. Repentance implies a radical change in your view of things, and in your estimate of matters; it is a change in your purposes, a change in your thoughts and in your conduct. If the Lord leads you that way he will help you in it. Follow his gracious leading till his divine Spirit shall lead you with still greater power and still greater efficacy, till at last you find that he has wrought in you both repentance and faith, and you are saved in the Lord with an everlasting salvation. If "the goodness of God leadeth thee to repentance," then be sure of this, that the goodness of God will receive thee when thou dost repent, and thou shalt live in his sight as his well-beloved and forgiven child.

I close now, but I am sorry so to do, for I have not pleaded one-half as I could have wished. Yet what more can I say? I will put it to yourselves. If you were in God's stead, could you bear to be treated as you have treated him? If you were all goodness and tenderness, and had borne with a creature now for thirty or forty years, how would you bear to see that creature still stand out, and even draw an inference from your gentleness to encourage him in his rebellion? Would you not say, "Well, if my longsuffering makes him think little of sin, I will change my hand. If tenderness cannot win him, I must leave him; if even my love does not affect him, I will let him alone. He is given unto his evil ways—I will cease from him, and see what his end will be"? O Lord, say not so, say not so unto any one in this house, but of thy great mercy make this day to be as the beginning of life to many. O that hearts may be touched with pity for their slighted Saviour, that they may seek his face! Here is the way of salvation: "Believe in the Lord Jesus Christ, and thou shalt be saved." You know how the Master bade us put it. "Go ye into all the world and preach the gospel to every creature: he that believeth and is baptized shall be saved." First, we are to preach faith, whereby we lay hold on Christ; then baptism, whereby we confess that faith, and own that we are dead and buried with Christ that we may live with him in newness of life. Those are the two points he bids us set before you, and I do set them before you. Weary, but not quite wearied out, O impenitent man, I plead with thee! Though thou hast so often been pleaded with in vain, once more I speak with thee in Christ's stead, and say—Repent of thy sin, look to thy Saviour, and confess thy faith in his own appointed way. I verily believe that if I had been pleading with some of you to save the life of a dog I should have prevailed with you a great while ago. And will you not care about the saving of your own souls? Oh, strange infatuation—that men will not consent to be themselves saved; but foolishly, madly, hold out against the mercy of God which leads them to repentance. God bless you, beloved, and may none of you despise his goodness, and forbearance, and longsuffering.

VI.

THE BRIDEGROOM'S PARTING WORD.

April 15, 1883.

"Thou that dwellest in the gardens, the companions hearken to thy voice: cause me to hear it."—Solomon's Song viii. 13.

The Song is almost ended: the bride and bridegroom have come to their last stanzas, and they are about to part for a while. They utter their adieux and the bridegroom says to his beloved, "Thou that dwellest in the gardens, the companions hearken to thy voice: cause me to hear it." In other words—when I am far away from thee, fill thou this garden with my name, and let thy heart commune with me. She promptly replies, and it is her last word till he cometh, "Make haste, my beloved, and be thou like to a roe or to a young hart upon the mountains of spices." These farewell words of the Well-beloved are very precious to his chosen bride. Last words are always noticed: the last words of those who loved us dearly are much valued; the last words of one who loved us to the death are worthy of a deathless memory. The last words of the Lord in this canticle remind me of the commission which the Master gave to his disciples or ever he was taken up: when he said to them, "Go ye into all the world, and preach the gospel to every creature." Then, scattering benedictions with both his hands, he ascended into the glory, and "a cloud received him out of their sight." As the sermon progresses you will see why I say this, and you will detect a striking likeness between the commission connected with the ascension and the present adieu, wherein the spiritual Solomon saith to his espoused Solyma, "Thou that dwellest in the gardens, the companions hearken to thy voice: cause me to hear it."

1. We will get to our text at once, without further preface, and we notice in it, first of all, AN APPOINTED RESIDENCE. The bridegroom, speaking of his bride, says, "Thou that dwellest in the gardens." The Hebrew is in the feminine, and hence we are bound to regard it as the word of the Bridegroom to his bride. It is the mystical word of the church's Lord to his elect one. He calls her "Inhabitress of the gardens"—that is the word. So then, dear friends, we who make up the church of God are here addressed this morning under that term, "Thou that inhabitest the gardens."

This title is given to believers here on earth, first, by way of *distinction*—distinction from the Lord himself. He whom we love dwelleth in the ivory palaces, wherein they make him glad: he is gone up into his Father's throne, and has left these gardens down below. He came down awhile that he might look upon his garden, that he might see how the vines flourished, and gather lilies; but he has now returned to his Father and our Father. He watered the soil of his garden with his bloody sweat in Gethsemane, and made it to bear fruit unto life by being himself laid to sleep in the tomb of Joseph of Arimathea: but all this lowly work is over now. He does not dwell in the gardens as to his corporeal presence; his dwelling-place is on the throne. Jesus has not taken us up with him; he will come another time to do that; but now he leaves us among the seeds and flowers and growing plants to do the King's work until he comes.

He was a visitor here, and the visit cost him dear; but he is gone back unto the place whence he came out, having finished the work which his Father gave him: our life-work is *not* finished, and hence we must tarry awhile below, and be known as inhabitants of the gardens.

It is expedient that we should be here, even as it is expedient that he should *not* be here. God's glory is to come of our sojourn here, else he would have taken us away long ago. He said to his Father, "I pray not that thou shouldest take them out of the world, but that thou shouldest keep them from the evil." He himself is an inhabitant of the palaces, for there he best accomplishes the eternal purposes of love; but his church is the inhabitress of the gardens, for there she best fulfills the decrees of the Most High. Here she must abide awhile until all the will of the Lord shall be accomplished in her and by her, and then she also shall be taken up, and shall dwell with her Lord above. The title is given by way of distinction, and marks the difference between her condition and that of her Lord.

Next, it is given by way of *enjoyment*. She dwells in the gardens, which are places of delight. Once you and I pined in the wilderness, and sighed after God from a barren land. We trusted in man, and made flesh our arm, and then we were like the heath in the desert, which seeth not when good cometh. All around us was the wilderness of this world, a howling wilderness of danger, and need, and disorder. We said of the world at its very best, "Vanity of vanities, all is vanity." Do you remember how you roamed, seeking rest and finding none? Your way was the path of darkness which leadeth unto death. Then you were poor and needy, and sought water and there was none, and your tongue cleaved unto the roof of your mouth for thirst. Then came the Lord that bought you, and he sought you until he brought you into the gardens of his love, where he satisfied you with the river of the water of life, and filled you with the fruits of his Spirit, and now you dwell in a goodly land: "The fountain of Jacob shall be upon a land of corn and wine; also his heavens shall drop down dew." Your portion is with the Lord's saints, yea, with himself; and what can be a better portion? Is it not as the garden of the Lord? You dwell where the great Husbandman spends his care upon you and takes a pleasure in you. You dwell where the infinite skill and tenderness and wisdom of God manifest themselves in the training of the plants which his own right hand has planted; you dwell in the church of God, which is laid out in due order, and hedged about and guarded by heavenly power; and you are, therefore, most fitly said to dwell in the gardens. Be thankful: it is a place of enjoyment for you: awake and sing, for the lines have fallen unto you in pleasant places. Just as Adam was put into the garden of Eden for his own happiness, so are you put into the garden of the church for your comfort. It is not a perfect paradise of bliss, but it has many points of likeness to paradise: for God himself doth walk therein, the river of God doth water it, and the tree of life is there unguarded by the flaming sword. Is it not written, "I the Lord do keep it: I will water it every moment; lest any hurt it, I will keep it night and day"? See, beloved, although you are distinguished from your Lord by being here while he is there, yet you are made partakers of his joy, and are not as those who are banished into a salt land to die in desolation. The Lord's joy is in his people, and you are made to have a joy in them also: the excellent of the earth, in whom is all your delight, are made to be the comrades of your sojourning.

The title is also used by way of *employment* as well as enjoyment. Adam was not put in the garden that he might simply walk through its borders, and admire its flowers, and taste its fruits; but he was placed there to keep it and to dress it. There was sufficient to be done to prevent his stagnating from want of occupation. He had not to toil sufficiently to make him wipe the sweat from his brow, for that came of the curse: " In the sweat of thy face shalt thou eat bread:" but still he was not permitted to be idle, for that might have been a worse curse. Even for a perfect man unbroken leisure would not be a blessing. It is essential even to an unfallen creature that he should have work to do—fit work and honorable, seeing it is done by a creature for the great Benefactor who had created him. If we had not our daily tasks to fulfil, rest would corrode into rust, and recreation would soon gender corruption. You and I are set in the garden of the church because there is work for us to do which will be beneficial to others and to ourselves also. Some have to take the broad axe and hew down mighty trees of error; others of a feebler sort can with a child's hand train the tendril of a climbing plant, or drop into its place a tiny seed. One may plant and another may water: one may sow and another gather fruit. One may cut up weeds and another prune vines. God hath work in his church for us all to do, and he has left us here that we may do it. Our Lord Jesus would not keep a single saint out of heaven if there were not a needs-be for his being here in the lowlands, to trim these gardens of herbs, and watch these beds of spices. Would he deny his well-beloved the palm branch and the crown if it were not better for us to be holding the pruning-hook and the spade? A school-book wherewith to teach the little children may be for a while more to our true advantage than a golden harp. To turn over the pages of Scripture wherewith to instruct the people of God may be more profitable to us than to hear the song of seraphim. I say, the Master's love to his own which prompts him to pray, "I will that they also whom thou hast given me be with me where I am, that they may behold my glory," would long ago have drawn all the blood-bought up to himself above, had it not been the fact that it is in infinite wisdom seen to be better that they should abide in the flesh. Ye are the lights of the world, ye are the salt of the earth: shall the light and the salt be at once withdrawn? Ye are to be as a dew from the Lord in this dry and thirsty land; would ye be at once exhaled? Brothers, have you found out what you have to do in these gardens? Sisters, have you found out the plants for which you are to care? If not, arouse yourselves and let not a moment pass till you have discovered your duty and your place. Speak unto him who is the Lord of all true servants, and say to him, "Show me what thou wouldest have me to do. Point out, I pray thee, the place wherein I may serve thee." Would you have it said of you that you were a wicked and slothful servant? Shall it be told that you dwelt in the gardens, and allowed the grass to grow up to your ankles, and suffered the thorns and the thistles to multiply until your land became as the sluggard's vineyard, pointed at as a disgrace and a warning to all that passed by? "O thou that dwellest in the gardens!" The title sets forth employment constant and engrossing.

Dear friends, it means also *eminence*. I know many Christian people who do not feel that they dwell in the gardens. They reside in a certain town or village where the gospel may be preached, but not in demonstration of the Spirit and in power. A little gospel is made to go a long way with some preachers. In some ministries there is no life or power, no unction or savor. The people who meet under such preaching are cold of heart and dull in spirit; the prayer-meetings are forgotten; communion of saints has well-nigh died out; and there is a general deadness as to Christian effort. Believe me, it is a dreadful thing when Christian people have almost to dread their Sabbath days; and I have known this to be the case. When you are called to hard toil through the six days of the week you want a good spiritual meal on the Sabbath, and if you get it, you find therein a blessed compensation and refreshment. Is it not a heavenly joy to sit still on the one day of rest, and to be fed with the finest of the wheat? I have known men made capable of bearing great trials—personal, relative, pecuniary, and the like—because they have looked backward upon one Sabbatic feast, and then forward to another. They have said in their hour of trouble,—"Patience, my heart; the Lord's day is coming, when I shall drink and forget my misery. I shall go and sit with God's people, and I shall have fellowship with the Father and with the Son, and my soul shall be satisfied as with marrow and fatness, till I praise the Lord with joyful lips." But what a sorry case to dread the Sunday, and to mutter, "I shall get nothing next Sunday any more than I did last Sunday except some dry philosophical essay, or a heap of the childish toys and fireworks of oratory, or the same dull mumbling of a mechanical orthodoxy." Oh, brethren and sisters, my text is scarcely meant for those who dwell in such deserts, but it speaks with emphasis to those who dwell where sweet spiritual fruits are plentiful, where odors and perfumes load the air, where the land floweth with milk and honey. **If any of you** happen **to** dwell where Christ is **set** forth evidently crucified among you, and where your hearts do leap for very joy because the King **himself** comes **near to** feast his saints and make them **glad in** his presence, then **it is to you that my text** hath **a voice** and a call: "Thou **that dwellest in the gardens, in the choicest places of all** Immanuel's land, **let me hear thy voice."**

Yet one more word. The title here employed is not only for **eminence** but for *permanence*. **"O tho that** *dwellest* in the gardens." **If you are only permitted to** enjoy sound gospel teaching now and again, and then are forced **to cry, "It** may be another twelve months before I shall be again **fed** on royal dainties." Then **you are in a** trying case, and **you need to cry to** God **for help: but blessed are** those **who dwell in the good land, and** daily fill their homers **with heavenly manna.** "Blessed are they that **dwell in thy house: they will be still** praising thee." No **spot on** earth **is so dear to the** Christian as that whereon he meets **his Lord. I can** understand why the Jew asked **of a** certain town **that** was recommended **to** him as good for business, **"Is there a** synagogue there?" Being **a** devout man, **and finding** that there **was no** synagogue, he said he **would rather remain where trade was** dull, but where **he could go with his** brethren **to worship. Is it not so with us? How my heart has** longed **for these blessed assemblies! Give me a crust and a** full gospel **rather than all riches and a barren ministry.** The **profitable hearing of the word is** the greatest enjoyment **upon earth to godly men.** It would be banishmen**t to go where every** week's business turned into **a mint of money if one** were also compelled **to be a** member of **an unhappy, quarrelsome, or** inactive church. **Our** greatest joy is in thee, O Jerusalem! Let our tongue cleave to the roof of our mouth if we prefer thee not above our greatest joy!

> "How charming is the place
>   Where my Redeemer God
> Unveils the beauties of his face,
>   And sheds his love abroad.
>
> "Not the fair palaces,
>   To which the great resort,
> Are once to be compared with this,
>   Where Jesus holds his court."

Beloved, if you dwell in the gardens you have a double privilege, not only of being found in a fat and fertile place, but in living there continually. You might well forego a thousand comforts for the sake of this one delight, for under the gospel your soul is made to drink of wines on the lees well refined.

This, then, is my first head—appointed residence:—"Thou that dwellest in the gardens." Is not this a choice abode for the Lord's beloved? I leave you to judge how far this describes yourselves. If it be your case, then listen to what the Bridegroom has to say to you.

II. Secondly, let us note the RECORDED CONVERSE: "Thou that dwellest in the gardens, the companions hearken to thy voice." She was in the gardens, but she was not quiet there, and why should she be? God gives us tongues on purpose that they should be used. As he made birds to sing, and stars to shine, and rivers to flow, so has he made men and women to converse with one another to his glory. Our tongue is the glory of our frame, and there would be no glory in its being for ever dumb. The monks of La Trappe, who maintain perpetual silence, do no more than the rocks among which they labor. When God makes bells he means to ring them. It may be thought to be a desirable thing that some should speak less, but it is still more desirable that they should speak better. When the tongue indites a good matter, it is no fault if it be nimble as the pen of a ready writer. It is not the quantity, it is the quality of what we say that ought to be considered.

Now, observe that evidently the spouse held with her companions *frequent intercourse*,—"The companions hearken to thy voice." She frequently conversed with them. I hope it is so among those of you who dwell in this part of Christ's garden. It should be so: "Then they that feared the Lord spake often one to another;" they had not now and then a crack, now and then the passing of the time of day, but they held frequent converse. Heaven will consist largely in the communion of saints, and if we would enjoy heaven below we must carry out the words of the creed in our practice,—"I believe in the communion of saints." Let us show that we do believe in it. Some persons sit still in their pews till the time to go, and then walk down the aisle in majestic isolation, as if they were animated statues. Do children thus come in and out of their father's house with never a word for their brothers and sisters? I know professors who float through life like icebergs from whom it is safest to keep clear: surely these partake not of the spirit of Christ. It is well when such icebergs are drawn into the gulf stream of divine love and melt away into Christ and his people. There should be among those who are children of the common Father a mutual love, and they should show this by frequent commerce in their precious things, making a sacred barter with one another. I like to hear them making sacred exchanges: one mentioning his trials, another quoting his deliverances; one telling how God has answered prayer, and another recording how the word of God has come to him with power. Such converse ought to be as usual as the talk of children of one family.

And next, it should be *willing and influential;* for if you notice, it is put here: "Thou that dwellest in the gardens, the companions *hearken* to thy voice." They do not merely hear it, and say to themselves, "I wish she would be quiet," but they hearken, they lend an ear, they listen gladly. I know some Christians whose lips feed many. I could mention brethren and sisters who drop pearls from their lips whenever they speak. We have still among us Chrysostoms, or men of golden mouths; you cannot be with them for half an hour without being enriched. Their anointing is manifest, for it spreads to all around them. When the Spirit of God makes our communications sweet, then the more of them the better. I like to get sometimes under the shadow of God's best people, the fathers in Israel, and to hear what they have to say to the honor of the name of the Lord. We who are young men feel gladdened by the testimonies of the ancients; and as for the babes in grace, they look up to the gray-beards and gather strength from their words of experience and grace. If there are any here whose language is such that others delight to listen to it, it is to such that my text is especially addressed; and when I come to open up the latter part of it I want you that have the honeyed tongues, I want you who are listened to with pleasure, to notice how the Beloved says to you, "The companions hearken to thy voice: cause me to hear it." Give thy Lord a share of thy sweet utterances: let thy Saviour's ear be charmed as well as thy companion's ears. Come, speak to him as well as to thy brethren, and if there be music in thy voice let that music be for the Well-beloved as well as for thy fellow-servants. This is the very heart of the matter. I cannot help alluding to it even before we have fairly reached that part of the text. The converse of the bride in the gardens was constant, and it was greatly esteemed by those who enjoyed it.

I gather from the text, rather by implication than otherwise, that the converse was *commendable;* for the bridegroom does not say to the spouse, "Thou that dwellest in the gardens, thy companions hear too much of thy voice." No; he evidently mentions the fact with approval, because he draws an argument from it why he also should hear that self-same voice. Brothers, I leave it to yourselves to judge whether your communications with one another are always such as they should be. Are they always worthy of you? What communications have ye had this morning? Can I make a guess? "Nice and fresh this morning." "Quite a change in the weather." Is not this the style? How often we instruct each other about what we all know! When it rains so as to soak our garments we gravely tell each other that it is very wet. Yes, and if the sun shines we are all eager to communicate the wonderful information that it is warm. Dear me, what instructors of our generation we are! Could we not contrive to change the subject? Is it because we have nothing to say of love, and grace, and truth that we meet and part without learning or teaching anything? Perhaps so. I wish we had a little more small change of heavenly converse: we have our crowns and sovereigns for the pulpit, we need groats and pence for common talk, all stamped with the image and superscription of the King of heaven. O Holy Spirit enrich us after this sort. May our communications be such that if Jesus himself were near we might not be ashamed for him to hear our voices. Brethren, make your conversation such that it may be commended by Christ himself.

These communications were, no doubt, *very beneficial.* As iron sharpeneth iron, so does a man's countenance his friend. Oh, what a comfort it is to drop in upon a cheerful person when you yourself are heavy! What a ballast it puts into your ship, when you are a little too merry, to meet with one in sore travail who bids you share his burden and emulate his faith. We are all the better, believe me, when our Lord can praise us, because the companions hearken to our voices.

In fact, our communications with one another ought to be *preparatory* to higher communications still. The converse of saints on earth should be a rehearsal of their everlasting communion in heaven. We should begin here to be to one another what we hope to be to one another world without end. And is it not pleasant to rise from communion with your brethren into communion with the Bridegroom?—to have such talk to one another that at last we perceive that truly our fellowship is with the Father and with his Son Jesus Christ? We thought that we only communed with our brethren; but, lo! we see that the Lord himself is here; do not our hearts burn within us? We two are talking of him, and now we see that he himself is here, opening to us the Scriptures, and opening our hearts to receive those Scriptures in the power of them. Beloved, let us try if we cannot make it so, that as we dwell together as church members, and work together in one common vineyard, we may be always making our fellowship with each other a grand staircase of fellowship with the King himself. Let us so talk that we may expect to meet Jesus while we are talking. How sweet to hear and see the Master in the servant, the Bridegroom in the bridegroom's friend, the Head in the members, the Shepherd in the sheep, the Christ in every Christian! Thus may we rise upon the wings of hallowed intercourse with holy ones to yet more hallowed intercourse with the Holy One of Israel.

Thus have we meditated upon two things: we have noted the appointed residence and the recorded converse. We know what we are talking about.

III. Now comes the pith of the text: INVITED FELLOWSHIP—"The companions hear thy voice: cause me to hear it." It is beautiful to hear the Beloved say in effect, "I am going away from you, and you see me no more; but I shall see you: do not forget me. Though you will not hear my voice with your bodily ears, I shall hear your voices: therefore speak to me. Unseen I shall feed among the lilies; unperceived I shall walk the garden in the cool of the day: when you are talking to others do not forget me. Sometimes turn aside, and when you have shut to the door, and no eye can see, nor ear can hear, then let me hear thy voice: it has music in it to my heart, for I died to give you life. Let me hear the voice of your prayer, and praise, and love."

Now, I note concerning this invitation, first of all, that it is very *loving and condescending* to us that the Lord should wish to hear our voice. I do not wonder that some of you love to hear my voice, because the Holy Spirit has blessed it to your conversion: but what good has Jesus ever derived from any of us? Is it not marvellous that he, the infinitely blessed, should want to hear our voices when all that he hath heard from us has been begging, sighing, and a few poor broken hymns? You do not want to hear a beggar's voice, do you? I expect if the man you have helped a score of times should be to-morrow morning at your door, you would say, "Dear, dear; there is that man again." Might not the Well-beloved say the same of you? "There she is again: come on the same errand. Come to confess some new faults, or to ask fresh favors." But instead of being tired of us our Lord says, "Let me hear thy voice." O loving Bridegroom! Must he not love us very truly to ask us to speak with him? See, he asks as though he begged it of us as a favor, "Let me hear thy voice. Thy companions hearken: let me take a share in their intercourse: they find thy voice pleasant, let it be a pleasure also to me. Come, do not deny me, thy heart's best beloved! Do not be silent unto me! Come, speak to me with thine own sweet mouth."

It is condescending and gracious, and yet how *natural* it is! How like to Christ! Love ever seeks the company of that which it loves. What would a husband say if his wife was seen to be chatty and cheerful to everybody else, but never spoke to him? I cannot suppose such a case: it would make too sorrowful a household. I should pity the poor, broken-hearted man who should be forced to say, "My beloved, others hear thy voice, and admire it, wilt thou not speak to me, thy husband?" O believer, will you let the Lord Jesus, as it were with tears in his eyes, say to you, "You talk to everybody but to me: you lay yourself out to please everybody but me: you are a charming companion to everybody but to me?" Oh, our Beloved, how ill have we treated thee! How much have we slighted thee! In looking back, I fear there are many of us who must feel as if this gentle word of the Lord had also a sharp side to it. I do remember my faults this day. The text goes like a dagger to my soul, for I have spoken all day long to others, and have had scarce a word for him whom my soul loveth. Let us mend our converse, and henceforth show our Lord a truer love.

We may truly add, that this invitation to fellowship is a *blessed and profitable* request. We shall find it so if we carry it out, especially those of us who are called by God to use our voices for him among the crowds of our companions. I address some brothers and sisters here who are preachers and teachers. What a relief it is, when you have been letting the companions hear your voice, to stop a bit and let Jesus hear it! What a rest to leave the congregation for the closet, to get away from where they criticise you to one who delights in you. What a relief, I say. And what a help to our hearts! Jesus gives us sweet returns if we commune with him, and such as speakers greatly need. The apostles said that they would give themselves to the word of God and to prayer. Yes, we must put those two things together. We shall never fitly handle the word of God without prayer. When we pray we are taught how to speak the word to others. Salvation and supplication are a blessed pair. Put the two together, so that, when you speak to others about salvation, you do it after having baptized your own soul into supplication. "The companions hear thy voice: cause me to hear it: before thou speakest with them speak to me: whilst thou art still speaking with them still speak with me; and when thy speaking to men is done, return unto thy rest and again speak with me."

This invitation is *a many-sided one*; for when the bridegroom says, "Cause me to hear it," he means that she should speak to him in all sorts of ways. Frequently we should be heard in praise. If thou hast been praising the Lord in the audience of others, turn aside and praise him to his face. Sing thy song to thy Beloved himself. Get into a quiet place and sing where only he can hear. I wish we had more of that kind of music which does not care for other audience than God. Oh, my God, my heart shall find *thee*, and every string shall have its attribute to sing, while my whole being shall extol *thee*, my Lord! The blessed Virgin had none with her but Elizabeth when she sang, "My soul doth magnify the Lord, and my spirit doth rejoice in God my Saviour." Oh, let the Lord hear your voice! Get up early to be alone with him. So let it be with all your complaints and petitions; let them be for Jesus only. Too often we fill our fellow creature's ear with the sad tale of all our care. Why not tell the Lord about it, and have done with it? We should employ our time far more profitably if, instead of murmuring in the tent, we enquired in the Temple.

Speak with Jesus Christ, dear friends, in little broken sentences, by way of frequent ejaculation. The best of Christian fellowship may be carried on in single syllables. When in the middle of business you can whisper, "My Lord and my God!" You can dart a glance upward, heave a sigh, or let fall a tear, and so will Jesus hear your voice! When nobody observes the motion of your lips you may be saying, "My Beloved, be near me now!" This is the kind of fellowship which your Saviour asks of you. He says, "The companions hear thy voice: cause me to hear it. Be sure that when thou speakest with others thou dost also speak with me!"

This is such a blessed invitation that I think, dear friends, we ought to avail ourselves of it at once. Come, what say you? The best Beloved asks us to speak with him, what shall we say at once? Think for an instant! What shall I say? Perhaps I have the start of you, because I have my word ready. Here it is:—"Make haste my beloved, and be thou like to a roe or to a young hart upon the mountains of spices." "Why," say you, "that is what the Church said in the last verse of the Song." Exactly so, and that is what we may wisely say at this moment. We cannot improve upon it. "Come quickly; even so, come quickly, Lord Jesus." Often and often, then, when you are about your business, say, "Come, Lord Jesus! Come quickly!" It is a sweet frame of mind to be in to be willing to invite Christ to come; and whenever you cannot do so let it be a warning to you that you are in dangerous waters. I can imagine a man in business calling himself a Christian about to engage in a doubtful transaction: how is he to discern the danger? Let him ask the Lord Jesus Christ to come while he is doing it. "Oh dear no"; cries one, "I had rather he should not come until that matter had been finished and forgotten." Then be you sure that you are moving in the wrong direction. Suppose you think of going to a certain place of amusement about which you have a question, it is easy to decide it thus:—When you take your seat your first thing should be to bow you head and ask for a blessing, and then say, "Lord, here I sit waiting for thine appearing." "Oh," say you, "I should not want the Lord to come there." Of course you would not. Then do not go where you could not wish your Lord to find you. My text may thus be a monitor to you, to keep you from the paths of the destroyer. Jesus says, "Let me hear thy voice," and let thy voice utter these desires,—"Even so, come quickly; come, Lord Jesus!"

Alas, time reproves me; I must hasten on.

IV. I have a fourth head, which shall be very briefly handled. I find according to the Hebrew that the text has in it a REQUESTED TESTIMONY. According to learned interpreters the Hebrew runs thus: "*Cause to hear me.*" Now, that may mean what I have said, "Cause me to hear;" but it may also mean, "Cause them to hear me." Now hearken; you that are in Christ's garden: make those who dwell in that garden with you to hear from you much about him. In the church every one has a right to talk about the Head of the church. Some of our brethren in this Tabernacle kindly undertake to speak to individuals about their souls, and now and then they receive very sharp rebuffs. What right has he to put such a question? How dare he intrude with personal remarks? What! Is the man poaching? No: these are the Lord's preserves; and the Lord's gamekeepers have a right to do as they are bidden by him. They are not poaching in this place, for they are on the Master's own land. Anywhere inside these four walls we may speak to anybody about Christ, and no man may forbid you. Speak lovingly and tenderly and prudently; but certainly the law of the house is that here we may speak about the Lord of the house. There are some other things you may not talk about, but about the Lord Jesus you may speak as much as you will. In the garden, at any rate, if not in the wild wilderness, let the Rose of Sharon be sweetly spoken of. Let his name be as ointment poured forth in all the church of God.

Again, you, according to the text, are one that can make people hear, so that "the companions hearken to thy voice;" then make them to hear of Jesus. You have the gift of speech: use it for Christ crucified. I always feel regret when a powerful speaker espouses any other cause but that of my Lord. Time was when I used to wish that Milton had been a preacher, and instead of writing a poem had proclaimed the gospel to the multitude. I know better now, for I perceive that God doth not use learning and eloquence so much as knowledge of Christ and plain speech; but still I am jealous of any man who can speak well that he should not give my Lord the use of his tongue. Well-trained tongues are rare things, and they should be all consecrated to Christ's glory. If you can speak to the companions—make them hear about Christ: if you can speak well, make them to hear attractive words about Christ.

If you do not speak about Christ to strangers, do speak to your *companions*. They will hearken to you; therefore let them hearken to the word of the Lord. I have heard of men who called themselves Christians who yet never spoke to their children about their souls, never spoke to their servants nor to their workpeople about Jesus and his love. This is to murder souls. If tongues can bless and do not, then they in effect curse men by their silence. If you have a voice, make the name of Jesus to be sounded out all around you. Many are the voices that strike upon the ear: the world is full of din, even to distraction, yet the name which is above all other names is scarcely heard. I pray you, my brethren, you that are like silver bells, ring out that name o'er hill and dale. As with a clarion, trumpet forth the saving name of Jesus till the deaf hear the sound thereof. Whatever is left out of your testimony, be sure that Christ crucified is first and last in it. Love Christ and live Christ; think of Christ and speak of Christ. When people go away from hearing you preach, may they have to say, "He kept to his subject: he knew nothing but Jesus." It is ill when a man has to say of preachers, "They have taken away my Lord, and I know not where they have laid him." Yet in certain sermons you meet with a little about everything except the one thing. They offer us what we do not need; but the need of the soul is not supplied. Oh, my brethren, cause Christ to be heard. Hammer on that anvil always: if you make no music but that of the harmonious blacksmith it will suffice. Ring it out with sturdy blows—"Jesus, Jesus, Jesus crucified." Hammer away at that. "Now you are on the right string, man," said the Duke of Argyle, when the preacher came to speak upon the Lord Jesus. . It needed no duke to certify that. Harp on that string. Make Jesus to be as commonly known as now he is commonly unknown. So may God bless you as long as you dwell in these gardens, till the day break and the shadows flee away. Amen.

VII.

THE TENT DISSOLVED AND THE MANSION ENTERED.

May 6, 1883.

"For we know that if our earthly house of this tabernacle were dissolved, we have a building of God, an house not made with hands, eternal in the heavens."—2 CORINTHIANS v. 1.

PAUL ranks among the bravest of the brave. We note also with admiration how the hero of so many dangers and conflicts, who could glow and burn with fervor, was yet among the calmest and quietest of spirits. He had learned to live beyond those present circumstances which worry and disturb; he had stolen a march upon the shadows of time, and entered into possession of the realities of eternity. He looked not on the things which are seen, but he set his whole regard on the things which are not seen; and by this means he entered into a deep and joyful peace which made him strong, resolute, steadfast, immovable. I would to God that we had all acquired Paul's art of being "always confident,"—his habit of having the inward man renewed day by day. The most of us are far too like the insect of the summer hour, which sports away its life of moments among the flowers, and lo! all is over. Are we not too apt to live in the immediate present which is revealed by the senses? The ox projects no thought upward or beyond: to stand in the cool brook or lie down in the fat pasturage is its all in all: even thus is it with the mass of men, their souls are tethered to their bodies, imprisoned within the circumstances of the day. If we could be completely delivered from the thraldom of things seen and felt, and could feel the full influence of the invisible and the eternal, how much of heaven we might enjoy before the celestial shores are reached!

Paul's life was rough and stormy, yet who might not desire it? Had there been no life to come, he would have been of all men the most miserable, for he was one of the poorest, most persecuted, most despised, most slandered, most wearied, and most suffering of mortals: and yet if I had to put my finger upon happy lives I should not hesitate to select among the foremost the life of the Apostle Paul, for whom to live was Christ. It is also to be specially noted as to his happiness that he had a reason for it. My text begins with the word, "For." Paul is always argumentative, the leaning of his mind is in that direction; hence, if he is cast down he has a reason for it, and if he is calm he can show just cause for his peace. Some religionists are deliriously happy, but they cannot tell you why. They can sing and shout and dance, but they can give no reason for their excitement. They see an enthusiastic crowd, and they catch the infection: their religion is purely emotional; I am not going to condemn it, yet show I unto you a more excellent way. The joy which is not created by substantial causes is mere froth and foam, and soon vanishes away. Unless you can tell why you are happy you will not long be happy. If you have no principle at the back of your passion your passion will burn down to a black ash, and you will look in vain for a living spark. Some professors have not enough emotion, their hearts are too small, though I cannot say that their heads are too large; but there are others whose hearts are their main force, who are soon on fire, blazing away like shavings and brushwood when first the flame lights upon them; but their brains are an uncertain quantity, never sufficient to manage the furnace of their emotions. It was not so with Paul: he was a well-balanced man. If able to defy the present and rejoice in prospect of the future, he had a solid reason for so doing. I like a man who is fervent and enthusiastic, and yet in his fervor is as reasonable as if he were some cool logician. Let the heart be like a fiery, high-mettled steed, but take care that it is curbed and managed by discretion. An instructed Christian man is rational even in his ecstasies: ready to give a reason for the hope that is in him, when that hope seems to rise above all reason. He is glad, gladdest of the glad, but he knows the why and the wherefore of his gladness; and so he can bear the cruel test to which the world exposes spiritual joy. The true believer's peace can answer the cavils of men or devils; it can justify itself in its opposition to all appearances. This is a house built upon a foundation, a tree which has a firmly settled root, a star fixed in its sphere; and thus it is infinitely superior to the house upon the sand, the tree plucked up, the fleeting vapor of mere emotion. May God, the Holy Spirit, instruct us so that we may know the truth out of which solid happiness is sure to grow!

I see in the text before us, first of all, *a catastrophe which Paul saw to be very possible*—" If our earthly house of this tabernacle were dissolved"; secondly, *the provision which he surely knew to be made* should that catastrophe occur—" We have a building of God, a house not made with hands, eternal in the heavens"; and thirdly, I shall dwell for a minute or two upon *the value of this knowledge to Paul and to the rest of us in our present trying condition.*

I. First, then, consider THE CATASTROPHE WHICH PAUL

saw to be very possible: "If our earthly house of this tabernacle were dissolved."

He did not fear that he himself would be dissolved: he had not the slightest fear about that. The catastrophe which he looked forward to is known among us by the name of "death"; but he calls it the dissolving of the earthly house of his tabernacle; the taking down of his tent-house body. He does not say, "If I were to be destroyed," or "If I were to be annihilated"; he knows no supposition of that character; he feels assured that he himself is perfectly safe. There is latent within the text an element of deep quiet as to his real self. "*We* know that if *our* earthly house of this tabernacle were dissolved, *we* have a building of God." The "we" is all unharmed and unmoved; if our house were dissolved *we* should not be undone; if we were to lose this earthly tent we have "a building of God, eternal in the heavens." The real man, the essential self, is out of harm's way; and all that he talks about is the falling to pieces of a certain tabernacle or tent in which for the present he is lodging. Many people are in a great fright about the future, yet here is Paul viewing the worst thing that could happen to him with such complacency that he likens it to nothing worse than the pulling down of a tent in which he was making shift to reside for a little season. He was afraid of nothing beyond that, and if that happened he had expectations which reconciled him to the event, and even helped him to anticipate it with joy.

Paul was not absolutely sure that his body would be dissolved. He hoped that he might be alive and remain at the coming of the Lord, and then he would be changed and be for ever with the Lord, without passing through death. Still, he was willing to leave this in the Lord's hands, and when he saw it to be possible that he should be numbered among the blessed dead who die in the Lord he did not shrink from the prospect, but bravely found a metaphor which set forth the little fear which he entertained concerning it.

The apostle perceived that the body in which he lived *was frail in itself*. Paul was accustomed to make tents. I do not suppose he ever manufactured any very large or sumptuous ones—probably he did not own capital enough for that, but he was a tent worker and mender. The use of tents was common enough among the Roman people in Paul's day. The gentry delighted in bright pavilions which they could set up at pleasure, and the commoner folk found pleasure in spending a part of their time under canvas. Whilst he was sitting writing this letter it is most likely that Paul had a tent or two to repair lying near his hand, and this suggested to him the language of the verse before us. When a tent is newly placed it is but a frail structure, very far removed from the substantiality of a house; in that respect it is exactly like this feeble corporeal frame of ours, which is crushed before the moth. Paul felt that his body would not need any great force to overthrow it; it was like the tent which the Midianite saw in his dream, which only needed to be struck by a barley cake, and lo! it lay along. A house of solid masonry may need a crowbar and a pick to start its stones from their places, but feebler tools will soon overturn a tent and make a ruin of it. The body is liable to dissolution from causes so minute as to be imperceptible—a breath of foul air, an atom of poisonous matter, a trifle, a mere nothing, may end this mortal life. I hope that you and I duly remember the frailty of our bodies. We are not so foolish as to think that because we are in robust health to-day we must necessarily live to old age. We have had among ourselves lately abundant evidence that those who appear to be the healthiest are often the first to be taken away, while feeble persons linger on among us, whose lives are a continued wonder and a perpetual struggle. When we think of the brittle ware whereof our bodies are made it is not strange that they should soon be broken. Is it not a wonderful thing that we continue to live? much more wonderful than that we should die? Dr. Watts has wisely said—

> "Our life contains a thousand springs,
> And dies if one be gone;
> Strange! that a harp of thousand strings
> Should keep in tune so long."

Some small affair interferes with a minute valve or organ of secretion, mischief is engendered by it, the whole current of life is hindered, and by-and-by death ensues. It is a very delicate process by which dust remains animated; a thousand things can stay that process, and then our body is dissolved. Paul, therefore, because he saw his body to be frail as a bubble, looked forward to the time when the earthly house of his soul would be dissolved.

When he was writing this epistle *he had many signs about him that his body would be dissolved.* His many labors were telling upon him; he was worn down with fatigue, he was spent in his Master's service. He was so full of the heavenly fire that he could never rest: after he had evangelized one city he was forced to hasten to another; if he was driven out of one village he hurried to the next, for he was eager to deliver the message of salvation. He wore himself out with labor, and he felt, therefore, that the day would come when his body would give way under the intense excitement of his life-agony. In addition to this he endured cold and hunger, and nakedness, and sickness, and infirmities brought upon him by his missionary self-sacrifice. He had a hard time of it as to physical endurance, and I should think there was scarcely a limb of the man that did not suffer in consequence of the imprisonments, scourgings, stonings, and other hardships which he had suffered. He felt that one of these days in all probability the house of his tent would come down through the violence of his persecutors. Once he most touchingly spoke of himself as "such an one as Paul the Aged;" and aged men cannot get away from the consciousness that their body is failing. Certain crumbling portions warn the old man that the house is dilapidated; the thatch which has grown thin or blanched tells its tale. There are signs about the aged which warn them that their earthly house was not built to stand for ever; it is a tabernacle or tent set up for a temporary purpose, and it shows signs of waxing old, and being ready to pass away. Hence, then, Paul was led to feel that both from the natural frailty of the body, and also from the injuries which it had already sustained, there was before him the evident probability that the earthly house of his tabernacle would be dissolved.

Besides, Paul's frail body had been *subject to exceeding great perils*. I saw the other day an encampment of gipsies out upon the common; many of this wandering race were sitting under a coarse covering sustained by sticks, I should exaggerate if I called them poles; and I could not help feeling that such an abode was all very well on a warm day, but not at all desirable when the east-wind was blowing, or a shower of sleet was driving along, or a deluge of rain descending. The apostle's body was a tent which was subjected to great stress of weather. God had not screened him; though one of the most precious men that ever lived, yet he was exposed to more danger than almost any other of the Lord's servants. Here is his own account of the matter:— "Thrice was I beaten with rods, once was I stoned, thrice I suffered shipwreck, a night and a day I have been in the deep; in journeyings often, in perils of waters, in perils of robbers, in perils by mine own countrymen, in perils by the heathen, in perils in the city, in perils in the wilderness, in perils in the sea, in perils among false brethren; in weariness and painfulness, in watchings often, in hunger and thirst, in fastings often, in cold and nakedness." Well might he reckon that ere long his poor shepherd's shanty would give way under such rude blasts.

Besides, Paul knew that so *many others whom he had known and loved had already died*, and he gathered from this that he would himself die. There used to sit in this house a brother who has often assured me that he should not die, and that if any Christian man did die, it was because he grieved the Lord. I am sorry to say that I have missed that brother for many months: I hope he has not yet disproved his own theory; but I am sure that he will do so sooner or later unless our Lord should hasten his advent. Whenever I meet with an enthusiast who boasts that he shall never die, I find it best to let him wait and see. One fine old Irish clergyman has frequently sought to instruct me in the art of being immortal, and he has been grieved and angry because I never set much store by the long life which he offered me. Though an old man, he assured me that he should never die; he expected in a short time to throw out all the infirmities of his years in the form of a rash, and then he should be as vigorous as ever. Alas! the good rector is buried, and his crazy brain is at rest. It is appointed unto men once to die. I should have thought that since so many of the excellent of the earth have fallen asleep, nobody would ever have been so mad as to raise a question about its being the common lot. Our crowded cemeteries supply ten thousand arguments why each one of us may expect to die in due time. This earthly house of our tabernacle will be dissolved; all things unite to warrant the belief.

Now, brethren, this was all that Paul did expect on the sad side; and truly it is not much. Is it? Certain Swiss peasants not very long ago were feeding their flocks on one of the lofty upland valleys. On one side of the pasturage stood a number of *châlets*, or wooden huts, in which they were accustomed to live during the summer, poor shelters which were left as soon as the winter set in. One day they heard a strange rumbling up in the lofty Alps, and they understood what it meant; it meant that a mass of rock or snow or ice had fallen, and would soon come crushing down in the form of an avalanche. In a brief space their fears were realized, for they saw a tremendous mass come rushing from above, bearing destruction in its course. What did it destroy? Only the old, crazy *châlets;* that was all. Every man of the shepherds was safe, and untouched: the event was rather to them a matter which caused a Te Deum to be sung in the village church below than a subject for mourning and sorrow. They said, "The avalanche is terrible, but it has not slain the aged mother, nor crushed the babe in its cradle: it has injured none of us, but only buried a few hovels which we can soon rebuild." Their case is a picture of ours. The avalanche of death will fall; but O ye saints, when it comes this is all it will do for you—your earthly house will be dissolved! Will you fret over so small a loss?

No evil will come nigh to you: the poor hut of the body will be buried beneath the earth, but as for yourself, what will you have to do but to sing an everlasting Te Deum unto him who delivered you from death and danger, and raised you to his own right hand?

It would not long affect a man if his tent should be overthrown; he would shake himself clear of it and come forth; it would not otherwise disturb him. So death shall not affect us for the worst, but for the better; the dissolution of this hampering frame shall give us liberty. To-day we are like birds in the egg; so long as the shell is whole we are not free: death breaks the shell. Does the fledgling lament the dissolution of the shell? I never heard of a bird in its nest pining over its broken shell; no, its thought runs otherwise: to wings, and flight, and sunny skies. So let it be with us. This body will be dissolved: let it be so; it is meet it should be. We have been glad of it while we have needed it, and we thank God for the wondrous skill displayed in it; but when we no longer require it we shall escape from it as from imprisonment, and never wish to return to its narrow bounds. Death, as it pulls away our sackcloth canopy, will reveal to our wondering eyes the palace of the King wherein we shall dwell for ever, and, therefore, what cause have we to be alarmed at it? I have set out the whole catastrophe before you, and surely no believer trembles in view of it.

II. So now we pass on to the second head, THE PROVISION OF WHICH THE APOSTLE PAUL MOST SURELY KNEW. He knew that if his tent-dwelling was overthrown he would not be without a home; he knew that he would not have to open his eyes in a naked condition, and cry, "Woe's me, whither am I to fly? I have no dwelling place." No, he knew that if this tent-house were gone he had "a building of God." Paul was not afraid of going to purgatory: though of late some even among Protestants have in a modified form revived that grim fiction, and have told us that even believers will have much to bear before they will be fit for eternal happiness. The apostle held no such opinion; but, on the contrary, he wrote: "We know that if our earthly house of this tabernacle were dissolved, we have a building of God." He did not expect to be roasted alive for the next thousand years, and then to leap from purgatory to Paradise, but he did expect to go, as soon as ever his earthly house was dissolved, into his eternal house which is in the heavens. He had not even the thought of lying in a state of unconsciousness till the resurrection. He says, "We know that if the earthly house of this tabernacle were dissolved we have [we have already] a building of God." He says not "we shall have it," but "we have it"; "we know that we have it." The picture seems to me to be as though one of you should dwell in his garden in a tent for a while. Somebody inquires what would happen if a gale of wind should blow your tent away in the night. "Oh," say you, "I have a house over yonder; I should go within doors and live there." What a comfort to know that, whatever occurs to our temporary gear, we have a fixed and settled abode to which we can at once repair. This makes us feel independent of all dangers, and helps us joyfully to welcome the inevitable, come when it may.

What did the apostle mean, however? for this text is said to be a very difficult one. He meant, first—the moment his soul left its body it would at once enter into that house of which Jesus said, "In my Father's house are many mansions: if it were not so, I would have told you." Do you want to know about that house? Read the Book of the Revelation, and learn of its gates of pearl, its streets of gold, its walls of rarest gems, of the river which windeth through it, and of the trees which bear their fruit every month. If after that you desire to know more concerning this house, I can but give you the advice which was given by John Bunyan in a similar case. One asked of honest John a question which he could not answer, for the matter was not opened in God's word; and therefore honest John bade his friend live a godly life, and go to heaven, *and see for himself*. Believe no dreams, but bide thy time, believing in the Lord Jesus, and thou shalt shortly know all about the house not made with hands, eternal in the heavens.

Paul, however, did mean that in the fulness of time he would again be clothed upon with a body. He regarded the waiting time as so short that he almost overlooked it, as men forget a moment's pause in a grand march. Ultimately, I say he expected to be housed in a body: the tent-house which was blown down and dissolved would be developed into a building, so rich and rare as to be fitly called " a building of God, a house not made with hands." This also is our prospect. At this present in this mortal body we groan being burdened, for our spirit is liberated from bondage, but our body is not yet emancipated, although it has been bought with a price. We are " waiting for the adoption, to wit, the redemption of our body," and so " the body is dead because of sin: but the Spirit is life because of righteousness." Our soul has been regenerated, but the body waits for the process which in its case is analogous to regeneration, namely, the resurrection from the dead. Disembodied saints may have to wait a few thousand years, more or less, dwelling in the Father's house above; but there shall come eventually the sounding of the trumpet and the raising of the dead, and then the perfected spirit shall dwell in a body adapted to its glory. The certainty of the resurrection raises us above the dread which would otherwise surround the dissolution of our body. A child sees a man throwing precious metal into a melting pot, and he is sad because fair silver is being destroyed; but he that knows the business of the refiner understands that no loss will come of the process: only the dross of that silver will be taken away, and the pure molten mass poured out into a comely mould will yet adorn a royal table. Well, my brethren, are we assured that to lose this vile body is clear gain since it will be fashioned according to the glorious body of the Lord Jesus?

Let us pass on to consider how Paul could say he knew this. This wonderfully enlightened nineteenth century has produced an order of wise men who glory in their ignorance. They call themselves "Agnostics," or know-nothings. When I was a boy it would have seemed odd to me to have met with a man who gloried in being an ignoramus, and yet that is the Latin for that Greek word "Agnostic." Is it not singular to hear a man boastfully say, "I am an ignoramus"? How different is our apostle! He says "we know." Whence came this confidence? How did he know?

First, Paul knew that he had a Father in heaven, for he felt the spirit of sonship: he knew also that his Father had a house, and he was certain that if ever he lost the tent in which he lived he should be sure to be welcomed into his own Father's house above. How do our children know that if ever they are in need of a house they can come home to us? Did they learn that from their tutors at school? No, their childhood's instinct teaches them that our house is their home, just as chickens run under the mother-hen without needing to be trained. Because they are our children they feel that as long as we have a house they have a house too; Paul, therefore, unhesitatingly said, "We know"; and, brethren, we know the same through like confidence in our Father's love. In the house of the many mansions we feel quite sure of a hearty welcome in due time. Shut out from our Father's home we cannot be! Houseless wanderers while our royal Father dwells in his palace we cannot be! We are not merely hopeful on this matter, but certain; and therefore we say, "We know."

Paul knew, again, that he had an elder brother, and that this brother had gone before to see to the lodging of the younger brethren. Paul remembered that Jesus had said, "I go to prepare a place for you, and if I go and prepare a place for you, I will come again, and receive you unto myself, that where I am ye may be also." So Paul had no question whatever; if the Lord had gone to prepare a place there would be a place for him; for he never knew his divine Lord set about anything and fail therein. Can we not all trust our Forerunner? Have we any doubts of him who has entered within the veil as our representative? No; as we are sure that Jesus has passed into the heavens on our behalf, so are we sure that when this tent-house body is dissolved, there remains a rest and home for our souls.

Doubtless, Paul also thought of the Holy Ghost, that blessed One who deigns to live with us in this frail house of clay, which is in many ways an uncomfortable and unsuitable abode for him by reason of the sin which has defiled it. He condescends to dwell in these mortal bodies, and, therefore, when we leave our earthly house he will leave it too; and we are persuaded that a place will be found where we may still abide in fellowship. As our bodies have been honored to entertain the Holy Ghost we may be sure that in our hour of need he will find an abode for us. He has been our guest, and in his turn he will be our host; this we know, for we know the love of the Spirit. He who has made our body his temple will find a rest for our souls. Thus, from the Father, the Son, and the Holy Ghost, we gather assurance that we shall not wander to and fro unhoused, even though this mortal frame should be dissolved.

Besides, let me tell you something. Paul knew that when he died there was a Paradise prepared, for he had been there already. You remember how he locked up that story till he could keep it no longer, and, then, fifteen years after its occurrence, he let out the blessed secret. Let me read his words, "I knew a man in Christ above fourteen years ago, (whether in the body, I cannot tell; or whether out of the body, I cannot tell: God knoweth;) such an one caught up to the third heaven. And I knew such a man, (whether in the body, or out of the body, I cannot tell: God knoweth;) how that he was caught up into paradise, and heard unspeakable words, which is not lawful for a man to utter." He says he was taken up to the third heaven; it was, therefore, idle to tell Paul that there was no home for him hereafter, for he had seen the place. "Well," say you, "*I* have not seen it." No; but you fully believe the witness of Paul, do you not? For my own part I am sure that Paul would not say that which is false, and inasmuch as he went into the third heaven or paradise, and saw it, I believe that there is such a place. Remember that this is the place to which the Lord Jesus admitted the dying thief, "To-day shalt thou be with me in paradise." This is the place where Jesus is, and where we shall be with him for ever, when the earthly house of this tabernacle shall be dissolved.

Yet, again, dear brothers and sisters, you and I know

that when this earthly tabernacle is dissolved there will be a new body for us, because our Lord Jesus Christ has risen from the dead. In my mind the ultimate answer to my deepest unbelief is the fact of the rising of Jesus from the dead. No matter of history is anything like so well attested as the fact that our Lord was crucified, dead and buried, and that he did upon the third day rise again from the dead. This I unhesitatingly accept as a fact, and this becomes my anchorage. Inasmuch as Jesus is the representative of all who are in him, it is as certain that the believer will rise as that Jesus has risen. The apostle says, "We know," and remembering these grand truths I am sure that his words are not a bit too strong. Nay, if I knew any word in the English language which would express more assurance than the word to know, I would use it this morning for myself. Much more, then, might the apostle use it for himself.

This we are also sure of, namely, that if our Lord Jesus be alive and in a place of rest he will never leave his chosen and redeemed ones without house or home. Where he has found a throne his people shall find a dwelling. Delightful is our old-fashioned ditty—

> "And when I shall die, Receive me, I'll cry,
> For Jesus has loved me, I cannot tell why;
> But this I do find, we two are so joined,
> He won't be in glory and leave me behind."

There is such an attachment between Christ and the believer; yea, more, such a vital, essential, indissoluble, tender marriage union that separation is impossible. As no man among us would ever be content to see his wife in prison if he could set her free, or to leave her outside in the cold when he could bring her to his fireside in comfort, so Christ, to whom our soul is espoused in eternal wedlock, will never rest until he has brought every one of his own beloved to be with him where he is, that they may behold his glory, the glory which the Father hath given him. No believer in Jesus has any doubts about that. I am sure you can all say, as Paul did, "We know that if our earthly house of this tabernacle were dissolved, we have a building of God, an house not made with hands."

"Ah," says one, "but how is a man to know that *he* has an interest in all this? Suppose I do know that the children of God are thus favored, how am I to know that I am one of them?" I invite you to self-examination on this point. Dost thou believe in the Lord Jesus Christ with all thine heart? Then it is written, "He that believeth in me though he were dead yet shall he live. He that liveth and believeth in me shall never die." Having believed in Christ, the Apostle knew that he was safe; for the promises are to believers, and if any man be a believer every promise of the covenant belongs to him. We obtain further assurance of this by our possessing the new life. Dear friend, have you entered into a new world? Do you feel within you a new heart and a right spirit? Have old things passed away, and have all things become new? Are you a new creature in Christ Jesus? Then it is all right with you: that new life cannot die, your new-born nature must inherit everlasting bliss. "Fear not, little flock; it is your Father's good pleasure to give you the kingdom." In addition to this, do you commune with God? do you speak with Christ? None perish who commune with the Father and the Son. Jesus cannot say at the last "I never knew you; depart from me;" for he does know you, and you know him. "Oh," say you, "he knows enough of me, for I am always begging." Just so, go on with that trade; be always a spiritual mendicant. The Lord of love will never cast away a pleading suppliant: he who frequents the throne of grace shall infallibly reach the throne of glory. Beside, does not "the Spirit itself also bear witness with our spirit that we are the children of God?" And if children and heirs, are we afraid of being left naked in the world to come? I hope that many of us have now reached the full assurance of faith, so that we believe and are sure. Can you not say each one for himself,—" I know whom I have believed, and I am persuaded that he is able to keep that which I have committed to him until that day"? These are the ways in which believers know that they are believers, and then by the word of God they know that all things are theirs, so that if their earthly house should fail they would be received into everlasting habitations.

III. Lastly, as to THE VALUE OF THIS KNOWLEDGE TO US. To be sure that when this body dies all is well, is not that worth knowing? Secularists twit us with taking men's minds away from the practical present that they may dream over a fancied future. We answer that the best help to live for the present is to live in prospect of the eternal future. Paul's confident belief that if his body should be dissolved he would be no loser, kept him from fainting. He knew what the worst would be, and he was prepared for it. Great storms were out, but the apostle knew the limit of his possible loss, and so was ready. All we can lose is the frail tent of this poor body. By no possibility can we lose more. When a man knows the limit of his risk it greatly tends to calm his mind. The undiscoverable and the unmeasured are the worst ingredients of dread and terror: when you can gauge your fears, you have removed them. Our apostle felt that he had been sent into the world with the great design of glorifying God, winning souls, and building up saints, and he was fully resolved to keep to the ministry which he had received. He argues with himself that his most dangerous course would be to faint in his life-service, for perseverance in his calling could bring with it no greater risk than death, and that he summed up as losing a tent and gaining a mansion. The Roman emperor might strike off his head, or a mob might stone him to death, or he might be crucified like his Master; but he made light of such a fate! It was to him only the coming down of the old tent; it did not affect his undying spirit; he smiled and sang, "For our light affliction, which is but for a moment, worketh for us a far more exceeding and eternal weight of glory."

The prospect of his heavenly house made his present trials seem very light; for he felt like a man who sojourns for a night at a poor inn, but puts up with it gladly because he hopes to be home on the morrow. If we were trying tent life for a season we should probably cry out, "A fearful draught comes in at that corner! How damp it is under foot! How cramped up one feels!" Yet we should smile over it all, and say, "It will not be for long. We shall soon be in our house at home." Ah, brethren, an hour with our God will make up for all the trials of the way. Wherefore, be of good courage, and press on.

This changed for Paul the very idea of death; death was transformed from a demon into an angel: it was but the removal of a tottering tent that he might enter into a permanent palace. Some of God's own children are much troubled through fear of death, because they do not know what it is. If they were better taught they would soon discover in their present source of sorrow a subject for song. I would like here to say that I have known some of my Master's doubting and fearing servants die splendidly. Do you remember how Mr. Feeblemind, when he crossed the river, went over dry shod. Poor soul, he thought he should surely be drowned, and yet he scarcely wet the soles of his feet. I have known men of God go like Jacob all day long weary and faint, feeling banished from their father's house; and yet when they have laid their head down for their final sleep they have had visions of angels and of God. The end of their journey has made amends for the rough places of the way. It shall be so with you, brother believer. There is usually a dark place in every Christian's experience: I have seen some travel in sunlight almost the whole of the way, and then depart in gloom, and I have thought none the worse of them for it; and I have seen others struggle forward through a fog for the first part of their pilgrimage, and then come out into cloudless day. At one period or another beneath these lowering skies the shadow falls across our way, but surely "light is sown for the righteous, and gladness for the upright in heart."

As I have thought of some of my dear brothers and sisters that I have seen die very sweetly, and I have remembered that they were, in life, lowly and self-distrustful, I have compared them to persons who, when they drink their tea, forget to stir the sugar at the bottom of the cup. How doubly sweet the drink becomes as they near the bottom: they have more sweetness than they can well bear. Would it not be wise to stir the tea at once and enjoy the sweetness from the brim to the bottom? This is the benefit of faith as to the future, for it flavors the present with delight. But what if saints should miss immediate comfort for awhile, how richly will they be compensated! What will it be to open your eyes in heaven! What a joy to fall asleep on the bed of languishing and to wake up amid the celestial Hallelujahs! "What am I? Where am I? Ah, my God! my Christ! my heaven! my all! I am at home." Sorrow and sighing shall flee away. Does not this view of things give a transfiguration to death? O you poor unbelievers, how I pity you, since you have no such glorious hopes. O that you would believe in the Lord Jesus and enter into life eternal.

Faith had such an effect upon Paul that it made him always calm, and brave. Why should he be afraid of a man that could not do him harm? Even if his persecutor killed him he would do him a service. What had he to fear? This made Paul wise and prudent. He could use his judgment, for he was not fluttered. He was not like some of you that are only a little ill, and straightway you are filled with fright, and so you make yourselves worse than you otherwise would be, so that the doctor has to contend with an affrighted mind as well as a diseased body. He who is calm, restful, happy is already on the road to a cure. He is quiet because he is in his Father's hands, and whether he lives or dies all is well; and this conviction helps the physician to remove his bodily malady. I say again, there is no way to live like learning to die, and he who can afford to be careless whether he lives or dies is the man who will so live as to die triumphantly. Oh, that all of you felt the quiet which comes of trusting in the Lord Jesus. How sad to know that you may die at any moment, and to be unprepared for the change! I do not wonder that you are unhappy: you have good reason for being so. Oh that you were wise, and would make the future sure by faith in the risen Lord.

In Martin Luther's time, and before his era, men who had lived evil lives were often in great fear when they came to die, and in their terror they would send to a monastery and procure a monk's dress in which to be buried. What a foolish fancy! Yet so it was that they hoped to fare better in the day of judgment for being wrapped in brown serge, and covered with a cowl! Be ours a better garment. Here is a wish of holy Rutherford—" His believed love shall be my winding-sheet, and all my grave-clothes; I shall roll up my soul, and sew it up in the web of his sweet and free love." Is not that your idea? It is surely mine! If we are laid to sleep in such a cerecloth, there will be no fear of our waking. It will happen to us as to the man who was laid in Elisha's grave, and at once arose as soon as he touched the prophet's bones. No man can lie dead if wrapped up in the love of Christ, for his love is life. He that has touched the love of Christ has touched the heart of the life of God, and he must live. So let us give ourselves up to that divine love, and trusting in our Lord, let us go onward to eternal bliss till the day break and the shadows flee away: let us triumph and rejoice that there is prepared for us a " building of God, a house not made with hands, eternal in the heavens."

IX.

GLORY!

May 20, 1883.

"Who hath called us unto his eternal glory."—1 Peter v. 10.

A fortnight ago, when I was only able to creep to the front of this platform, I spoke to you concerning the future of our mortal bodies:* "We know that if our earthly house of this tabernacle were dissolved, we have a building of God, a house not made with hands, eternal in the heavens." On the next Sabbath day we went a step further, and we did not preach so much about the resurrection of the body as upon the hope of glory for our entire nature,† our text being, "Christ in you, the hope of glory." Thus we have passed through the outer court, and have trodden the hallowed floor of the Holy Place, and now we are the more prepared to enter within the veil, and to gaze awhile upon the glory which awaits us. We shall say a little—and oh, how little it will be —upon that glory of which we have so sure a prospect, that glory which is prepared for us in Christ Jesus, and of which he is the hope! I pray that our eyes may be strengthened that we may see the heavenly light, and that our ears may be opened to hear sweet voices from the better land. As for me, I cannot say that I will speak of the glory, but I will try to stammer about it;

* "The Tent Dissolved and the Mansion Entered."
† "Christ in You."

for the best language to which a man can reach concerning glory must be a mere stammering. Paul did but see a little of it for a short time, and he confessed that he heard things that it was not lawful for a man to utter; and I doubt not that he felt utterly nonplussed as to describing what he had seen. Though a great master of language, yet for once he was overpowered; the grandeur of his theme made him silent. As for us, what can we do, where even Paul breaks down? Pray, dear friends, that the spirit of glory may rest upon you, that he may open your eyes to see as much as can at present be seen of the heritage of the saints. We are told that "eye hath not seen, neither hath ear heard, neither have entered into the heart of man, the things which God hath prepared for them that love him." Yet the eye has seen wonderful things. There are sunrises and sunsets, Alpine glories and ocean marvels which, once seen, cling to our memories throughout life; yet even when nature is at her best she cannot give us an idea of the supernatural glory which God has prepared for his people. The ear has heard sweet harmonies. Have we not enjoyed music which has thrilled us? Have we not listened to speech which has seemed to make our hearts dance within us? And yet no melody of harp nor charm of oratory can ever raise us to a conception of the glory which God hath laid up for them that love him. As for the heart of man, what strange things have entered it! Men have exhibited fair fictions, woven in the loom of fancy, which have made the eyes to sparkle with their beauty and brightness; imagination has revelled and rioted in its own fantastic creations, roaming among islands of silver and mountains of gold, or swimming in seas of wine and rivers of milk; but imagination has never been able to open the gate of pearl which shuts in the city of our God. No, it hath not yet entered the heart of man. Yet the text goes on to say, "but he hath revealed it unto us by his Spirit." So that heaven is not an utterly unknown region, not altogether an inner brightness shut in with walls of impenetrable darkness. God hath revealed joys which he has prepared for his beloved; but mark you, even though they be revealed of the Spirit, yet it is no common unveiling, and the reason that it is made known at all is ascribed to the fact that "the Spirit searcheth all things, yea, the deep things of God." So we see that the glory which awaits the saints is ranked among the deep things of God, and he that would speak thereof after the manner of the oracles of God must have much heavenly teaching. It is easy to chatter according to human fancy, but if we would follow the sure teaching of the word of God we shall have need to be taught of the Holy Spirit, without whose anointing the deep things of God must be hidden from us. Pray that we may be under that teaching while we dwell upon this theme.

There are three questions which we will answer this morning. The first is, *what is the destiny of the saints?* — "Eternal glory," says the text. Secondly, *wherein doth this glory consist?* I said we would answer the questions, but this is not to be answered this side the pearl-gate. Thirdly, *what should be the influence of this prospect upon our hearts?* What manner of people ought we to be whose destiny is eternal glory? How should we live who are to live for ever in the glory of the Most High?

I. First, WHAT, THEN, IS THE DESTINY OF THE SAINTS? Our text tells us that God has "called us unto *his eternal glory.*" "Glory!" does not the very word astound you? "Glory!" surely that belongs to God alone! Yet the

Scripture says "glory," and glory it must mean, for it never exaggerates. Think of glory for us who have deserved eternal shame! Glory for us poor creatures who are often ashamed of ourselves! Yes, I look at my book again, and it actually says "glory"—nothing less than glory. Therefore so must it be.

Now, since this seems so amazing and astonishing a thing, I would so speak with you that not a relic of incredulity may remain in your hearts concerning it. I would ask you to follow me while we look through the Bible, not quoting every passage which speaks of glory, but mentioning a few of the leading ones.

This glory has been promised. What said David? In the seventy-third Psalm and twenty-fourth verse we meet with these remarkable words: "Thou shalt guide me with thy counsel, and afterward receive me to glory." In the original Hebrew there is a trace of David's recollection of Enoch's being translated; and, though the royal Psalmist did not expect to be caught away without dying, yet he did expect that after he had followed the guidance of the Lord here below the great Father would stoop and raise up his child to be with himself for ever. He expected to be received into glory. Even in those dim days, when as yet the light of the gospel was but in its dawn, this prophet and king was able to say, "Thou shalt afterward receive me to glory." Did he not mean the same thing when in the eighty-fourth Psalm, verse eleven, he said, "The Lord will give grace and glory: no good thing will he withhold from them that walk uprightly"? Not only no good thing under the name of grace will God withhold from the upright, but no good thing under the head of glory. No good of heaven shall be kept from the saints; no reserve is even set upon the throne of the great King, for our Lord Jesus has graciously promised,

"To him that overcometh will I grant to sit with me in my throne, even as I also overcame, and am set down with my Father in his throne." "No good thing," not even amongst the infinitely good things of heaven, will God "withhold from them that walk uprightly." If David had this persuasion, much more may we who walk in the light of the gospel. Since our Lord Jesus hath suffered and entered into his glory, and we know that we shall be with him where he is, we are confident that our rest shall be glorious.

Brethren, it is *to this glory that we have been called.* The people of God having been predestinated, have been called with an effectual calling—called so that they have obeyed the call, and have run after him who has drawn them. Now, our text says that he has "called us unto his eternal glory by Christ Jesus." We are called to repentance, we are called to faith, we are called to holiness, we are called to perseverance, and all this that we may afterwards attain unto glory. We have another Scripture of like import in 1 Thessalonians ii. 12:—"Who hath called you unto his kingdom and glory." We are called unto his kingdom according to our Lord's word, "Fear not, little flock; for it is your Father's good pleasure to give you the kingdom." We are called to be kings, called to wear a crown of life that fadeth not away, called to reign with Christ in his glory. If the Lord had not meant us to have the glory he would not have called us unto it, for his calling is no mockery. He would not by his Spirit have fetched us out from the world and separated us unto himself if he had not intended to keep us from falling and preserve us eternally. Believer, you are called to glory; do not question the certainty of that to which God has called you.

And we are not only called to it, brethren, but *glory*

is especially joined with justification. Let me quote Romans viii. 30:—" Moreover whom he did predestinate, them he also called: and whom he called, them he also justified: and whom he justified, them he also glorified." These various mercies are threaded together like pearls upon a string: there is no breaking the thread, no separating the precious things. They are put in their order by God himself, and they are kept there by his eternal and irreversible decree. If you are justified by the righteousness of Christ, you shall be glorified through Christ Jesus, for thus hath God purposed, and so must it be. Do you not remember how salvation itself is linked with glory? Paul, in 2 Timothy ii. 10, speaks of " the salvation which is in Christ Jesus with eternal glory." The two things are riveted together, and cannot be separated.

The saved ones must partake of the glory of God, for *for this are they being prepared every day.* Paul, in the ninth of Romans, where he speaks about the predestinating will of God, says in the twenty-third verse: " The vessels of mercy, which he had afore prepared unto glory." This is the process which commenced in regeneration, and is going on in us every day in the work of sanctification. We cannot be glorified so long as sin remains in us; we must first be pardoned, renewed, and sanctified, and then we are fitted to be glorified. By communion with our Lord Jesus we are made like to him, as saith the apostle in 2 Corinthians iii. 18:—" But we all, with open face beholding as in a glass the glory of the Lord, are changed into the same image from glory to glory, even as by the Spirit of the Lord." It is very wonderful how by the wisdom of God everything is made to work this way. Look at the blessed text in 2 Corinthians iv. 17, where Paul says, " For our light affliction, which is but for a moment, worketh for us a far more exceeding and eternal weight of glory;" where he represents that all that we can suffer, whether of body or of mind, is producing for us such a mass of glory that he is quite unable to describe it, and he uses hyperbolical language in saying, "a far more exceeding and eternal weight of glory." Oh, blessed men, whose very losses are their gains, whose sorrows produce their joys, whose griefs are big with heaven! Well may we be content to suffer if so it be that all things are working together for our good, and are helping to pile up the excess of our future glory.

Thus, then, it seems we are called to glory, and we are being prepared for it; is it not also a sweet thought that *our present fellowship with Christ is the guarantee of it?* In Romans viii. 17 it is said, "If so be that we suffer with him, that we may be also glorified together." Going to prison with Christ will bring us into the palace with Christ; smarting with Christ will bring us into reigning with Christ; being ridiculed, and slandered, and despised for Christ's sake will bring us to be sharers of his honor, and glory, and immortality. Who would not be with Christ in his humiliation if this be the guarantee that we shall be with him in his glory? Remember those dear words of the Lord Jesus, "Ye are they which have continued with me in my temptations. And I appoint unto you a kingdom, as my Father hath appointed unto me." Let us shoulder the cross, for it leads to the crown. "No cross, no crown:" but he that has shared the battle shall partake in the victory.

I have not yet done, for there is a text, in Hebrews ii. 10, which is well worthy of our consideration, *we are to be brought to glory.* It is said of our Lord that it "became him, for whom are all things, in bringing many sons unto glory, to make the captain of their salvation perfect through sufferings." See, beloved, we are called to glory, we are being prepared for it, and we shall be brought to it. We might despair of ever getting into the glory land if we had not One to bring us there, for the pilgrim's road is rough and beset with many foes; but there is a "Captain of our salvation," a greater than Bunyan's Greatheart, who is conducting the pilgrim band through all the treacherous way, and he will bring the "many sons"—where?—"*unto glory*," nowhere short of that shall be their *ultimatum*. Glory, glory shall surely follow upon grace; for Christ the Lord, who has come into his glory, has entered into covenant engagements that he will bring all the "many sons" to be with him.

Mark this, and then I will quote no more Scriptures: *this glory will be for our entire manhood*, for our body as well as for our soul. You know that text in the famous resurrection chapter; in 1 Cor. xv. 43 Paul speaks of the body as being "sown in dishonor," but he adds, "it is raised in glory;" and then, in Philippians iii. 21, he says of our divine Lord at his coming, "Who shall change our vile body, that it may be fashioned like unto his glorious body, according to the working whereby he is able even to subdue all things unto himself." What a wonderful change that will be for this frail, feeble, suffering body! In some respects it is not vile, for it is a wonderful product of divine skill, and power, and goodness; but inasmuch as it hampers our spiritual nature by its appetites and infirmities, it may be called a "vile body." It is an unhandy body for a spirit: it fits a soul well enough, but a spirit wants something more ethereal, less earth-bound, more full of life than this poor flesh and blood and bone can ever be. Well, the body is to be changed. What alteration will it undergo? It will be rendered perfect. The body of a child will be fully developed, and the dwarf will attain to full stature. The blind shall not be sightless in heaven, neither shall the lame be halt, nor shall the palsied tremble. The deaf shall hear, and the dumb shall sing God's praises. We shall carry none of our deficiencies or infirmities to heaven. As good Mr. Ready-to-Halt did not carry his crutches there, neither shall any of us need a staff to lean upon. There we shall not know an aching brow, or a weak knee, or a failing eye. "The inhabitant shall no more say, I am sick."

And it shall be an impassive body, a body that will be incapable of any kind of suffering: no palpitating heart, no sinking spirit, no aching limbs, no lethargic soul shall worry us there. No, we shall be perfectly delivered from every evil of that kind. Moreover, it shall be an immortal body. Our risen bodies shall not be capable of decay, much less of death. There are no graves in glory. Blessed are the dead that die in the Lord, for their bodies shall rise never to know death and corruption a second time. No smell or taint of corruption shall remain upon those whom Jesus shall call from the tomb. The risen body shall be greatly increased in power: it is "sown in weakness," says the Scripture, but it is "raised in power." I suppose there will be a wonderful agility about our renovated frame: probably it will be able to move as swiftly as the lightning flash, for so do angels pass from place to place, and we shall in this, as in many things else, be as the angels of God. Anyhow, it will be a "glorious body," and it will be "raised in glory," so that the whole of our manhood shall participate of that wonderful depth of bliss which is summed up in the word—"glory." Thus I think I have set before you much of what the word of God saith upon this matter.

II. Secondly, may the Holy Spirit help me while I try very hesitatingly and stammeringly to answer the enquiry, WHEREIN DOTH THIS DESTINY CONSIST?

Do you know how much I expect to do? It will be but little. You remember what the Lord did for Moses when the man of God prayed—"I beseech thee show me thy glory!" All that the Lord himself did for Moses was to say, "Thou shalt see my back parts; but my face shall not be seen." How little, then, can we hope to speak of this glory! Its back parts are too bright for us: as for the face of that glory, it shall not be seen by any of us here below, though by-and-by we shall behold it. I suppose if one who had been in glory could come straight down from heaven, and occupy this platform, he would find that his discoveries could not be communicated because of the insufficiency of language to express such a weight of meaning.

The saints' destiny is *glory*. What is glory, brethren? What is it, I mean, among the sons of men? It is generally understood to be fame, a great repute, the sound of trumpets, the noise of applause, the sweets of approbation among the crowd and in high places. The Queen of Sheba came from afar to see the glory of Solomon. What was that glory, brethren? It was the glory of a rare wisdom excelling all others: it was the glory of immense riches expended upon all manner of magnificence and splendor. As for this last glory the Lord says of it that a lily of the field had more of it than Solomon; at least, "Solomon in all his glory was not arrayed like one of these." Yet that is what men mean by glory—rank, position, power, conquest—things that make the ears of men to tingle when they hear of them—things extraordinary and rare. All this is but a dim shadow of what God means by glory; yet out of the shadow we may obtain a little inkling of what the substance must be. God's' people shall be wise, and even famous, for they shall "shine as the stars for ever and ever." God's people shall be rich; the very streets of their abode are paved with gold exceeding rich and rare. God's people shall be singularly honored; there shall be a glory about them unrivalled, for they shall be known as a peculiar people, a royal priesthood, a race of beings lifted up to reveal their Maker's character beyond all the rest of his works.

I reckon that glory to a saint means, first of all, *purified character*. The brightest glory that really can come to any one is the glory of character. Thus God's glory among men is his goodness, his mercy, his justice, his truth. But shall such poor creatures as we are ever have perfect characters? Yes, we shall one day be perfectly holy. God's Holy Spirit, when he has finished his work, will leave in us no trace of sin: no temptation shall be able to touch us, there will be in us no relics of our past and fallen state. Oh, will not that be blessed? I was going to say it is all the glory I want—the glory of being perfect in character, never sinning, never judging unjustly, never thinking a vain thought, never wandering away from the perfect law of God, never vexed again with sin which has so long been my worst enemy. One day we shall be glorious because the devil himself will not be able to detect a fault in us, and those eyes of God, which burn like fire and read the inmost secrets of the soul, will not be able to detect anything blame-worthy in us. Such shall be the character of the saints that they shall be meet to consort with Christ himself, fit company for that thrice Holy Being before whom angels veil their faces. This is glory!

Next, I understand by "glory" *our perfected manhood*. When God made Adam he was a far superior being to any of us. Man's place in creation was very remarkable. The Psalmist says, "For thou has made him a little lower than the angels, and hast crowned him with glory and honor. Thou madest him to have dominion over the works of thy hands; thou has put all things under his feet: all sheep and oxen, yea, and the beasts of the field; the fowl of the air, and the fish of the sea, and whatsoever passeth through the paths of the seas." No king among men in these days could rival Adam in the garden of Eden: he was indeed monarch of all that he surveyed, and from the lordly lion down to the tiniest insect of all, living creatures paid him willing homage. Can we ever rise to this last honor? Brethren, listen, "It doth not yet appear what we shall be, but we know that when Christ shall appear we shall be like him, for we shall see him as he is." Is there any limit to the growth of the mind of a man? Can we tell what he may reach? We read of Solomon that God gave him largeness of heart as the sand of the sea: God will give to his people glory that will include in it more largeness of heart than Solomon ever knew. Then shall we know even as we are known by God. Now we see, but it is "through a glass darkly," but then we shall see "face to face." You have met with men of great intellect and you have looked up to them: but assuredly the smallest babe in Christ when he shall reach heaven shall have a greater intellect than the most profound philosopher who has ever astounded mankind by his discoveries. We shall not always be as we are to-day, contracted and hampered because of our little knowledge, and our slender faculties, and our dull perceptions. Our ignorance and prejudice shall vanish. What a man will become we can scarcely tell when he is remade in the image of God, and made like unto our divine Lord who is "the firstborn among many brethren." Here we are but in embryo: our minds are but the seeds, or the bulbs, out of which shall come the flower and glory of a nobler manhood. Your body is to be developed into something infinitely brighter and better than the bodies of men here below: and as for the soul, we cannot guess to what an elevation it shall be raised in Christ Jesus. There is room for the largest expectation here, as we conjecture what will be the full accomplishment of the vast intent of eternal love, an intent which has involved the sacrifice of the only-begotten Son of God. That can be no mean design which has been carried on at the expense of the best that heaven itself possessed.

Further, by "glory" and coming to glory I think we must understand *complete victory.* Dwelling in the age of the Romans, men said to themselves, as they read the Scriptures, "What does the apostle mean by 'glory'?" and they could scarcely help connecting it with conquest, and the return of the warrior in triumph. Men called it glory in those days when valiant warriors returned from fields of blood with captives and spoil. Then did the heroes ride through the streets of Rome, enjoying a triumph voted them by the senate. Then for the while the men of war were covered with glory, and all the city was glorious because of them. As Christians, we hate the word "glory" when it is linked with wholesale murder, and girt in garments rolled in blood; but yet there is a kind of fighting to which you and I are called, for we are soldiers of the cross; and if we fight valiantly under our great Captain, and rout every sin, and are found faithful even unto death, then we shall enter glory, and receive the honor which belongs to men who have fought a good fight, and have kept the faith. It will be no small glory to obtain the crown of life which fadeth not away. Is not this a full glory if we only place these three things together, a purified character, a perfected nature, and a complete victory?

An invaluable ingredient in true glory is *the divine approval*. "Glory" among men means approbation: it is a man's glory when he is honored of his Queen, and she hangs a medal on his breast, or when his name is mentioned in the high court of Parliament, and he is ennobled for what he has done. If men speak of our actions with approval, it is called fame and glory. Oh, but one drop of the approbation of God has more glory in it than a sea full of human praise; and the Lord will reward his own with this holy favor. He will say, "Well done, good and faithful servant," and Christ before the universe will say, "Come, ye blessed of my Father." Oh, what glory that will be! They were despised and rejected of men, they "wandered about in sheepskins and goatskins; destitute, afflicted, tormented;" but now God approves them, and they take seats among the peers of heaven, made noble by the approbation of the Judge of all. This is glory with an emphasis, substantial glory. One approving glance from the eye of Jesus, one accepting word from the mouth of the Father, will be glory enough for any one of us, and this we shall have if we follow the Lamb whithersoever he goeth.

But this is not all: children of God will have *the glory of reflecting the glory of God*. When any of God's unfallen creatures shall wish to see the greatness of God's goodness, and mercy, and love, they that dwell in heaven will point out a glorified saint. Whenever any spirit from far-off regions desires to know what is meant by faithfulness and grace, some angel will reply, "Go and talk with those who have been redeemed from among men." I believe that you and I will spend much of eternity in making known to principalities and powers the unsearchable riches of the grace of God. We shall be mirrors reflecting God; and in us shall his glory be revealed. There may be myriads of races of pure and holy beings of whom we have never heard as yet, and these may come to the New Jerusalem as to the great metropolis of Jehovah's universe, and when they come there they will gaze upon the saints as the highest instances of divine grace, wisdom, power, and love. It will be their highest pleasure to hear how eternal mercy dealt with us unworthy ones. How we shall delight to rehearse to them the fact of the Father's eternal purpose, the story of the incarnate God—the God that loved and died, and the love of the blessed Spirit who sought us in the days of our sin, and brought us to the cross foot, renewing us in the spirit of our minds, and making us to be sons of God. Oh, brothers and sisters, this shall be our glory, that God shall shine through us to the astonishment of all.

Yet I think glory includes somewhat more than this. In certain cases a man's *glory lies in his relationships*. If any of the royal family should come to your houses you would receive them with respect; yes, and even as they went along the street they would be spied out, and passers-by would say, "That is the prince!" and they would honor the son of our good Queen. But royal descent is a poor business compared with being allied to the King of kings. Many angels are exceeding bright, but they are only servants to wait upon the sons. I believe that there will be a kind of awe upon the angels at the sight of men; when they see us in our glory they will rejoice to know our near relation to their Lord, and to fulfil their own destiny as ministering spirits appointed to minister to the heirs of salvation. No pride will be possible to the perfected, but we shall then realize the exalted position to which by our new birth and the divine adoption we have been raised. "Behold what manner of love the Father hath bestowed upon us that we should be called the sons of God." Sons of God! Sons of the Lord God Almighty! Oh what glory this will be!

Then there will be connected with this the fact that *we shall be connected with Jesus in everything*. For do not you see, brethren, it was because of our fall that Christ came here to save men; when he wrought out a perfect righteousness, it was all for us; when he died, it was all for us; and when he rose again, it was all for us? And what is more, we lived in Christ, we died in him, we were buried in him and rose in him, and we shall ascend into heaven to reign with him. All our glory is by Christ Jesus and in all the glory of Christ Jesus we have a share. We are members of his body; we are one with him. I say, the creatures that God has made, when they shall come to worship in the New Jerusalem will stand and gaze at glorified men, and with bated breath will say one to another "These are the beings whose nature the Son of God assumed! These are the chosen creatures whom the Prince of heaven bought with his own blood." They will stand astonished at the divine glory which will be manifested in beings emancipated from sin and hell and made heirs of God, joint heirs with Jesus Christ. Will not even angels be surprised and awed as they look on the church and say to one another, "This is the bride, the Lamb's wife!" They will marvel how the Lord of glory should come to this poor earth to seek a spouse and that he should enter into eternal union with such a people. Glory, glory dwelleth in Immanuel's land! Now we are getting near to the centre of it. I feel inclined, like Moses, to put off my shoes from off my feet, for the place whereon we stand is holy ground, now that we are getting to see poor bushes like ourselves aglow with the indwelling God, and changed from glory unto glory.

And yet this is not all, for there in heaven *we shall dwell in the immediate presence of God*. We shall dwell with him in nearest and dearest fellowship! All the felicity of the Most High will be our felicity. The blessedness of the triune Jehovah shall be our blessedness for ever and ever. Did you notice that our text says, "He hath called us unto *his* glory"? This outshines everything: the glory which the saints will have is the same glory which God possesses, and such as he alone can bestow. Listen to this text:—" Whom he justified, them *he* also glorified." He glorifies them, then! I know what it is to glorify God, and so do you, but when we poor creatures glorify God it is in a poor way, for we cannot add anything to him. But what must it be for God himself to glorify a man! The glory which you are to have for ever, my dear believing brother, is a glory which God himself will put upon you. Peter, as a Hebrew, perhaps uses a Hebraism when he says "*his* glory:" it may be that he means the best of glory that can be, even as the Jews were wont to say— "The trees of God," when they meant the greatest trees, or "the mountains of God," when they intended the highest mountains; so by the glory of God Peter may mean the richest, fullest glory that can be. In the original the word "glory" has about it the idea of "weight," at which the apostle Paul hints when he speaks of a "weight of glory." This is the only glory that has weight in it, all else is light as a feather. Take all the glories of this world and they are outweighed by the small dust of the balance. Place them here in the hollow of my hand, all of them: a child may blow them away as thistledown. God's glory has weight; it is solid, true, real, and he that gets it possesses no mere name, or dream, or tinsel, but he has that which will abide the rust of ages and the fire of judgment.

The glory of God! How shall I describe it! I must set before you a strange Scriptural picture. Mordecai must be made glorious for his fidelity to his king, and singular is the honor which his monarch ordains for him. This was the royal order. "Let the royal apparel be brought which the king useth to wear, and the horse that the king rideth upon, and the crown royal which is set upon his head: and let this apparel and horse be delivered to the hand of one of the king's most noble princes, that they may array the man withal whom the king delighteth to honor, and bring him on horseback through the street of the city, and proclaim before him, Thus shall it be done to the man whom the king delighteth to honor." Can you not imagine the surprise of the Jew when robe and ring were put upon him, and when he found himself placed upon the king's horse. This may serve as a figure of that which will happen to us: we shall be glorified with the glory of God. The best robe, the best of heaven's array, shall be appointed unto us, and we shall dwell in the house of the Lord for ever.

Highest of all our glory will be *the enjoyment of God himself*. He will be our exceeding joy: this bliss will swallow up every other, the blessedness of God. "The Lord is my portion," saith my soul. "Whom have I in heaven but thee? and there is none upon earth that I desire beside thee." Our God shall be our glory.

Yet bear with me, I have left out a word again: the text has it, "Unto his *eternal* glory." Ay, but that is the gem of the ring. The glory which God has in reserve for his chosen will never come to an end: it will stay with us, and we shall stay with it, for ever. It will always be glory, too; its brightness will never become dim; we shall never be tired of it, or sated with it. After ten thousand thousand millions of years in heaven our happiness shall be as fresh as when it first began. Those are no fading laurels which surround immortal brows. Eternal glory knows no diminution. Can you imagine a man being born at the same time that Adam was created and living all these thousands of years as a king like Solomon, having all he could desire? His would seem to be a glorious life. But if at the end of seven thousand years that man must needs die, what has it profited him? His glory is all over now, its fires have died out in ashes. But you and I, when we once enter glory, shall receive what we can neither lose nor leave. Eternity! Eternity! This is the sweetness of all our future bliss. Rejoice, ye saintly ones! Take your harps down from the willows, any of you who are mourning, and if you never sang before, yet sing this morning—"God has called us unto his eternal glory," and this is to be our portion world without end.

III. I can only find time for a few words upon the concluding head, which is—WHAT INFLUENCE SHOULD ALL THIS HAVE UPON OUR HEARTS?

I think, first, it ought to excite *desire* in many here present that they might attain unto glory by Christ Jesus. Satan, when he took our blessed Lord to the top of an exceeding high mountain, tempted him to worship him by offering him the kingdoms of the world and all the glories thereof. Satan is very clever, and I will at this time take a leaf out of his book. Will you not fall down and worship the Lord Jesus when he can give you the kingdom of God and all the glory thereof, and all this, not in pretence, but in reality? If there was any force in the temptation to worship Satan for the sake of the glory of this world, how much more reason is there for urging you to worship the Son of God that you may obtain his salvation with eternal glory! I pray the Holy Ghost to drop a hot desire into many a poor sinner's breast this morning that he may cry, "If this glory is to be had, I will have it, and I will have it in God's way, for I will believe in Jesus, I will repent, I will come to God, and so obtain his promise."

Secondly, this ought to move us to the feeling of *fear*. If there be such a glory as this let us tremble lest by any means we should come short of it. Oh, my dear hearers, especially you that are my fellow members, brother church officers, and workers associated with me, what a dreadful thing it will be if any one of us should come short of this glory! Oh, if there were no hell, it would be hell enough to miss of heaven! What if there were no pit that is bottomless, nor worm undying, nor fire unquenchable, it would be boundless misery to have a shadow of a fear of not reaching to God's eternal glory? Let us therefore pass the time of our sojourning here in fear, and let us watch unto prayer and strive to enter in at the strait gate. God grant we may be found of him at last to praise and honor!

If we are right, how this ought to move us to *gratitude*. Think of this, we are to enjoy "his eternal glory"! What a contrast to our deserts! Shame and everlasting contempt are our righteous due apart from Christ. If we were to receive according to our merits, we should be driven from his presence and from the glory of his power. Verily, he hath not dealt with us after our sins, nor rewarded us according to our iniquities; for, after all our transgressions, he has still reserved us for glory, and reserved glory for us. What love and zeal should burn in our bosoms because of this!

Last of all, it should move us to a dauntless *courage*. If this glory is to be had, do we not feel like the heroes in Bunyan's picture? Before the dreamer there stood a fair palace, and he saw persons walking upon the top of it, clad in light, and singing. Around the door stood armed men to keep back those who would enter. Then a brave man came up to one who had a writer's ink-horn by his side, and said, "Set down my name;" and straightway the warrior drew his sword, and fought with all his might, until he had cut his way to the door, and then he entered, and they within were heard to sing—

"Come in, come in,
Eternal glory thou shalt win."

Will you not draw your swords this morning, and fight against sin, till you have overcome it? Do you not desire to win Christ, and to be found in him? Oh, let us now begin to feel a passion for eternal glory, and then in the strength of the Spirit, and in the name of Jesus, let us press forward till we reach it. Even on earth we may taste enough of this glory to fill us with delight. The glory which I have described to you dawns on earth though it only comes to its noontide in heaven: the glory of sanctified character, the glory of victory over sin, the glory of relationship to God, the glory of union with Christ,—these are all to be tasted in a measure here below. These glories send their beams down even to these valleys and lowlands. Oh, to enjoy them to-day and thus to have earnests and foretastes of glory. If we have them let us go singing on until we reach the place where God's eternal glory shall surround us. Amen.

X.

"KNOCK!"

May 27, 1883.

"Knock, and it shall be opened unto you."—MATTHEW vii. 12.

I HAVE no doubt that, taken very strictly, the three exhortations of this verse—which, indeed, are but one—were first of all intended for God's believing people. It was to his disciples that the Lord said, "Cast not your pearls before swine;" and perhaps certain of them who were poor in spirit might turn around and say, "Lord, we have few pearls; we are too poor to have the treasures of thy grace so plentifully. Thou hast bidden us not to give that which is holy unto dogs; but holiness is rather a thing we seek after than possess." "Well," saith the Lord, "you have only to ask and have; ye have not because ye ask not; you have only to seek and you will be sure to find, for holy things, like rare pearls, are to be discovered if you look for them; you have only to knock and spiritual secrets shall open to you, even the innermost truth of God." In each exhortation our Lord bids us pray. Beloved, let us abound in supplication. Depend upon it that failure in prayer will undermine the foundation of our peace and sap the strength of our confidence; but if we abound in pleading with God we shall grow strong in the Lord, and we shall be happy in his love, we shall become a blessing to those around us. Need I commend the mercy-seat to you who wait before it?

Surely prayer must have become such a joy to you, such a necessity of your being, such an element of your life, that I hardly need press it upon you as a duty, or invite you to it as a privilege. Yet still I do so, because the Master does it by a triple exhortation. A threefold cord is not easily broken—let not my text be neglected by you. Let me urge you to repeated, varied, ever intensifying prayer: ask! seek! knock! Cease not to ask till you receive; cease not to seek till you find; cease not to knock till the door is opened unto you.

In these three exhortations there would appear to be a gradation: it is the same thought put into another shape, and made more forcible. *Ask*—that is, in the quiet of your spirit, speak with God concerning your need, and humbly beg him to grant your desires: this is a good and acceptable form of prayer. If, however, asking should not appear to succeed, the Lord would arouse you to a more concentrated and active longing; therefore let your desires call in the aid of knowledge, thought, consideration, meditation, and practical action, and learn to *seek* for the blessings you desire as men seek for hid treasures. These good things are laid up in store, and they are accessible to fervent minds. See how you can reach them. Add to asking the study of the promises of God, a diligent hearing of his word, a devout meditation upon the way of salvation, and all such means of grace as may bring you the blessing. Advance from asking into seeking. And if after all it should still seem that you have not obtained your desire, then *knock*, and so come to closer and more agonizing work: use not alone the voice, but the whole soul; exercise yourself unto godliness to obtain the boon; use every effort to win that which you seek after; for remember that doing is praying; living to God is a high form of seeking, and the bent of the entire mind is knocking. God often giveth to his people when they keep his commandments that which he denies to them if they walk carelessly. Remember the words of the Lord Jesus, how he said, "If ye abide in me, and my words abide in you, ye shall ask what ye will, and it shall be done unto you." Holiness is essential to power in prayer: the life must knock while the lips ask and the heart seeks.

I will change my line of exposition and say: ask as a *beggar* petitions for alms. They say that begging is a poor trade, but when you ply it well with God no other trade is so profitable. Men get more by asking than by working without prayer. Though I do not discommend working, yet I most highly commend praying. Nothing under heaven pays like prevailing prayer. He that has power in prayer has all things at his call. Ask as a poor mendicant who is hungry and pleads for bread. Then seek as a *merchant* who hunts for goodly pearls, looking up and down, anxious to give all that he has that he may win a matchless treasure. Seek as a servant carefully looking after his master's interests and laboring to promote them. Seek with all diligence, adding to the earnestness of the beggar the careful watchfulness of the jeweller who is seeking for a gem. Conclude all by knocking at mercy's door as *a lost traveller* caught out on a cold night in a blinding sleet knocks for shelter that he may not perish in the storm. When you have reached the gate of salvation ask to be admitted by the great love of God, then look well to see the way of entering, seeking to enter in; and if still the door seem shut against you, knock right heavily, and continue knocking till you are safely lodged within the home of love.

Once again, ask for what you want, seek for what you have lost, knock for that from which you are excluded. Perhaps this last arrangement best indicates the shades of meaning, and brings out the distinctions. Ask for everything you need, whatever it may be: if it be a right and good thing, it is promised to the sincere asker. Seek for what you have lost; for what Adam lost you by the Fall, for what you have lost yourself by your neglect, by your backsliding, by your want of prayer: seek till you find the grace you need. Then knock. If you seem shut out from comfort, from knowledge, from hope, from God, from heaven, then knock, for the Lord will open unto you. Here you need the Lord's own interference: you can ask and receive, you can seek and find; but you cannot knock and open,—the Lord must himself open the door, or you are shut out for ever. God is ready to open the door. Remember, there is no cherub with fiery sword to guard this gate, but, on the contrary, the Lord Jesus himself openeth, and no man shutteth. But now I must drop this line of things, for my desire is to use the text in reference to those who are not yet saved.

Last Lord's-day, when we preached upon glory, we had before us the end of the pilgrim way. It was a very, very happy time; for in meditation we reached the suburbs of the Celestial City, and we tasted of eternal glory. This morning I thought we would begin at the beginning, and enter in at the wicket gate which stands at the head of the way to heaven. Mr. Bunyan, in his "Pilgrim's Progress," says, "Now over the gate there was written, 'Knock, and it shall be opened unto you.'" His ingenious allegory is always as truthfully instructive as it is delightfully attractive. I concluded that this should be my text. If it be thought worthy to be written over the gate at the entering in of the way of life it must have a great claim upon the attention of those who have not yet started for glory, but are anxious to do so. May God the Holy Ghost instruct and quicken them while we hear the Lord from within his palace say, "Knock, and it shall be opened unto you."

I. First, then, dear friend, whoever you are, if you are desirous of entering into eternal life, I would expound to you the inscription over the gate, by saying, first, THE DOOR OF MERCY MAY APPEAR TO YOU TO BE CLOSED AGAINST YOU. That is implied in the text: "Knock, and it shall be opened unto you." If to your consciousness the door stood wide open, there would be no need of knocking; but since in your apprehension it is closed against you, it is for you to seek admission in the proper way by knocking.

To a large extent this apprehension is the result of your own fears. You think the gate is closed because you feel it ought to be so; you feel that if God dealt with you as you would deal with your fellow-men, he would be so offended with you as to shut the door of his favor once for all. You remember how guilty you have been, how often you have refused the divine call, and how you have gone on from evil to evil, and therefore you fear that the Master of the house has already risen up and shut to the door. You fear lest like the obstinate ones in Noah's day you will find the door of the ark closed, and yourself shut out to perish in the general destruction. Sin lieth at the door, and blocks it. Your desponding feelings fasten up the gate of grace in your judgment. Yet, it is not so. The gate is not barred and bolted as you think it to be; though it may be spoken of as closed in a certain sense, yet in another sense it is never shut. In any case it opens very freely;

its hinges are not rusted, no bolts secure it. The Lord is glad to open the gate to every knocking soul. It is closed far more in your apprehension than as a matter of fact; for the sin which shuts it is removed so far as the believing sinner is concerned. Had you but faith enough, you would enter in at this present moment; and if you did once enter in, you would never be put out again, for it is written, "Him that cometh to me I will in no wise cast out." If you could with holy courage take leave and license to come in, you would never be blamed for it. Fear and shame stand in the sinner's road, and push him back; and blessed is he whose desperate need forces him to be bold.

One thing we should remember when we fear that the door is closed against us, namely, that *it is not so fast closed as the door of our hearts has been.* You know the famous picture of "The Light of the World." It seems to me to be one of the finest sermons the eye has ever looked upon. There stands the Ever-Blessed, knocking at the door of the soul, but the hinges are rusted, the door itself is fast bolted, and wild briars and all kinds of creeping plants running up the door prove that it is long since it was moved. You know what it all means; how continuance in sin makes it harder to yield to the knock of Christ, and how evil habits creeping up one after another hold the soul so fast that it cannot open to the sacred knocking. Jesus has been knocking at some of your hearts ever since you were children; and still he knocks. I hear his blessed hand upon the door at this moment: do you not hear it? Will you not open? He has knocked long, and yet he knocks again. I am sure that you have not knocked at mercy's door so long as incarnate mercy has waited at your door. You know you have not. How, therefore, can you complain if there should be an apparent delay in answering your prayers? It is but to make you feel a holy shame for having treated your Lord so ill. Now you begin to know what it is to be kept waiting, what it is to be a weary knocker, what it is to cry "my head is wet with dew and my locks with the drops of the night." This will excite you to repentance for your unkind behavior, and also move you to love the more intensely that gentle Lover of your soul who has shown such patience towards you. It will be no loss to you that the door was shut for awhile, if you do but gain a penitent heart and a tender spirit.

Let me, however, warn you that *the door can be closed and kept shut by unbelief*. He that believeth entereth into Christ when he believeth: he that cometh in by the door shall be saved, and shall go in and out and find pasture; so our Lord says in the tenth of John. "He that believeth in him hath everlasting life," there is no question about that; but we read on the other hand, "So then they could not enter in because of unbelief." Forty years the tribes were in the wilderness, going towards Canaan, yet they never reached the promised land because of unbelief. And what if some of you should be forty years attending this means of grace? Coming and going, coming and going, hearing sermons, witnessing ordinances, and joining with God's people in worship: what if after all the forty years you should never enter in because of unbelief? Souls, I tell you if you lived each one of you as long as Methuselah, you could not enter in unless you believed in Jesus Christ. The moment you have trusted him with your whole heart and soul you are within the blessed portals of the Father's house, but however many years you may be asking, seeking, and knocking, you will never enter in till faith comes, for unbelief keeps up the chain of the door, and there is no entering in while it rules your spirit.

Do you, however, complain that you should have to knock? *It is the rule of the Most High.* Am I addressing any who have been earnestly praying for several months? I can sympathize with you, for that was my case, not only for months, but even for years: through the darkness of my mind and my cruel misapprehensions of the Lord, I did not find peace when first I began to ask for it, although I also sought with much earnestness, going to the house of God every time I could, and reading the Bible daily with a burning desire to know the right way. I did not enter into peace till I had knocked long and heavily. Hearken, therefore, to one who knows your trouble, and hear from me the voice of reason. Ought we to expect to enter into the glorious house of mercy without knocking at its door? Is it so with our own houses? Can every straggler carelessly saunter in? Is it not God's way in the world to give great blessings, but always to make men knock for them? We want bread out of the earth, but the farmer must knock at the door of the earth with his plough and with all his instruments of agriculture ere his God will hand him out a harvest. Is anything gained in this world without labor? Is it not an old proverb, "No sweat, no sweet: no pains, no gains: no mill, no meal"? And may we not expect in heavenly things that at least these great mercies should be prayed for with fervency before they can be bestowed? It is the usual rule with God to make us pray before he gives the blessing. And how could it be otherwise? How could a man be saved without prayer? A prayerless soul must be a Christless soul. The feeling of prayer, the habit of prayer, the spirit of prayer are parts of salvation. Unless it can be said of a man, "Behold, he prayeth!" how can there be any sort of hope that he knows his God, and has found reconciliation? The prodigal did not come home dumb, neither did he enter his father's house in sullen silence. No, but as soon as he saw his father, he cried, "Father, I have sinned against heaven." There must be speech with God, for God gives not a silent salvation.

Besides, *to make us knock at mercy's gate is a great blessing to ourselves* upon the spot. It is a going to school for us when we are set to plead with God for awhile without realized success. It makes a man grow more earnest, for his hunger increases while he tarries. If he obtained the blessing when first he asked for it, it might seem dog cheap; but when he has to plead long he arrives at a better sense of the value of the mercy sought. He sees also more of his own unworthiness as he stands outside mercy's gate, ready to swoon away with fear; and so he grows more passionately earnest in pleading; and, whereas he did but ask at first, he now begins to seek, and he adds cries and tears and a broken heart to all the other ways of his pleading. Thus the man, by being humbled and aroused, is getting good by means of his sorrow while he is kept for a while outside the gate. Beside that, he is increasing his capacity for the future. I believe I never could have been able to comfort seekers in their anguish if I had not been kept waiting in the cold myself. I have always felt grateful for my early distress because of its after results. Many men, whose experiences are recorded in books which are invaluable in the Christian library, never could have written those books if they had not themselves been kept waiting, hungry and thirsty, and full of soul-travail, ere the Lord appeared to them. That blessed man, David, who always seems to be—

"Not one, but all mankind's epitome"

—the history of all men wrapped up in one—how he pictures himself as sinking in the miry clay! Lower and lower did he go till he cried out of the depths, and then at last he was taken up out of the horrible pit, and his feet were set on a rock that he might tell to others what the Lord had done for him. Your heart wants enlarging, dear sir. The Lord means to prepare you to become a more eminent Christian by expanding your mind. The spade of agony is digging trenches to hold the water of life. Depend upon it, if the ships of prayer do not come home speedily it is because they are more heavily freighted with blessing. When prayer is long in the answering it will be all the sweeter in the receiving, like fruit which is well ripened by hanging longer on tree. If you knock with a heavy heart you shall yet sing with joy of spirit; therefore, be not discouraged because for a while you stand before a closed door.

II. Secondly, A DOOR IMPLIES AN OPENING. What is a door meant for if it is always to be kept shut? The wall might as well have remained without a break. I have seen certain houses and public buildings with the form and appearance of doors where there were none: the sham doorway being made for architectural purposes; but nothing is a sham in the house of the Lord. His doors are meant to open: they were made on purpose for entrance; and so the blessed gospel of God is made on purpose for you to enter into life and peace. It would be of no use to knock at a wall, but you may wisely knock at a door, for it is arranged for opening. You will enter in eventually if you knock on, for *the gos-*

pel is good *news for men*, and how could it be good news if it should so happen that they might sincerely come to Christ and ask mercy, and be denied it? I fear that the gospel preached by certain divines sounds rather like bad news than good news to awakened souls, for it requires so much feeling and preparation on the sinner's part that they are not cheered nor led to hope thereby. But be you sure that the Lord is willing to save all those who are willing to be saved in his own appointed way. A dear brother beautifully said in prayer on Monday night—"Thou, O Lord, art perfectly satisfied with the Lord Jesus, and if we are satisfied with *him*, thou art satisfied with us." That is the gospel put into a few words. God is satisfied with Christ, and if you are satisfied with Christ, God is satisfied with you. This is glad tidings to every soul that is willing to accept the atonement made, and the righteousness prepared by the Lord Jesus.

Dear friend, *this gospel must be meant to be received by sinners*, or else it would not have been sent. "But," saith one, "I am such a sinner." Just so. You are the sort of person for whom the news of mercy is intended. A gospel is not needed by perfect men; sinless men need no pardon. No sacrifice is wanted if there is no guilt: no atonement is wanted where there is no transgression. They that are whole need not a physician, but they that are sick. This door of hope which God has prepared was meant to be an entrance into life, and it was meant to open to sinners, for if it does not open to sinners it will never open at all; for we have all sinned, and so we must all be shut out unless it be of free grace for those who are guilty.

I am sure this door *must open to those who have nothing to bring with them*. If you have no good works, no merits, no good feelings, nothing to recommend you, be not discouraged, for it is to such that Jesus Christ is most precious, and therefore most accessible, for he loves to give himself to those who will prize him most. A man will never have Christ while he has enough of his own; but he that is consciously naked, and poor, and miserable is the man for Christ's money, he it is that has been redeemed by price. You may know the redeemed man, for he feels his bondage, and owns that he must remain therein unless the redemption of Christ be applied for his deliverance.

Dear friends, that door of hope will be opened to you though you may be ignorant, and weak, and quite unable to fulfil any high conditions. When the text says, "*Knock*, and it shall be opened unto you," it teaches us that *the way of winning admission to the blessing is simple*, and suitable to common people. If I have to enter in by a door which is well secured, I shall need tools and science. I confess I do not understand the art; you must send for a gentleman who understands picklocks, "jemmies," and all sorts of burglarious instruments: but if I am only told to knock, fool as I am at opening doors, I know how to knock. Any uneducated man can knock if that is all which is required of him. Is there a person here who cannot put words together in prayer? Never mind, friend; knocking can be done by one who is no orator. Perhaps another cries, "I am no scholar." Never mind, a man can knock though he may be no philosopher. A dumb man can knock. A blind man can knock. With a palsied hand a man may knock. He who knows nothing of his book can still lift a hammer and let it fall. The way to open heaven's gate is wonderfully simplified to those who are lowly enough to follow the Holy Spirit's guidance, and ask, seek, and knock believingly. God has not provided a salvation which can only be understood by learned men; he has not prepared a gospel which requires half-a-dozen folio volumes to describe it: it is intended for the ignorant, the short-witted, and the dying, as well as for others, and hence it must be as plain as knocking at a door. This is it,—Believe and live. Seek unto God with all your heart and soul, and strength, through Jesus Christ, and the door of his mercy will certainly open to you. The gate of grace is meant to yield admission to unscientific people since it shall be opened to those who knock.

I am sure this door will open to you, because *it has been opened to so many before you.* It has been opened to hundreds of us now present. Could not you, dear brothers and sisters, stand up and tell how the Lord opened the gate of his salvation to you? That door has opened to many in this house during the last few weeks. We have seen persons coming forward to tell how the Lord has been pleased to give them an entrance into his mercy, though at one time they were afraid that the door was shut, and they were ready to despair. Well, if the door has been so often opened for others, why should it not turn on its hinges for you? Only knock, with faith in God's mercy, and before long it shall yield to your importunity.

It is for God's glory to open his door of grace, and that is one reason why we are sure he will do so. We cannot expect him to do that which would be derogatory to his own honor, but we do expect him to do that which will glorify his sacred attributes. It will greatly honor the mercy, the patience, the love, the grace, the goodness, the favor of God if he will open the door to such an undeserving one as you are; wherefore knock. Knock since God delights to give; knock at a door which every time it turns on its hinges unveils his greatness; knock with holy confidence at this present moment, for "it shall be opened unto you." It is a door which seems closed, but because it is a door, it must be capable of being opened.

III. Thirdly, knock, for A KNOCKER IS PROVIDED. When persons can be admitted by knocking, a knocker is usually placed on the door; and if not, we often see the words, NO ADMITTANCE. Before bells became so common, the habit of knocking at the door was well-nigh universal, and people were accustomed to make the door resound with their blows. There was a nail-head for the knocker to drop upon, and people used to smite it so heavily that it became remarked that such blows on the head were killing, and hence arose the mirthful proverb, "as dead as a door-nail." It betokens a hearty kind of knocking, which I would have you imitate in prayer. Knock at heaven's gate as earnestly as people knocked at doors in the olden times. Have you not had knocks at your own doors which could be heard all through the house? Some of our friends are vigorous, and knock as if they meant coming in. It may be that gentle folks give such tender taps that they are not heard by the servants, and so they have to wait; but these I am speaking of never fall into that error, for they so startle everybody that people are glad to let them in, for fear they should thunder a second time. In this style let us pray: let us plead in downright fashion, and never cease till we gain admission.

I have said that the Lord has provided a knocker. What is this knocker? First of all, it may be found in *the promises of God*. We are sure to speed well when we can plead a promise. It is well to say unto the Lord, "Do as thou hast said." What force abides in an appeal to the word, the oath, and the covenant of God. If a man presents to another a promissory note upon the day on which it is due he expects to receive the amount stated therein. God's promises are bills of exchange, and he will duly honor them. He was never known to dishonor a bill yet, and he never will do so. If you can only quote a promise applicable to your condition, and spread it before the Lord in faith, and say, "Remember this word unto thy servant upon which thou hast caused me to hope," you must obtain the blessing. Pleading the promise gives such a knock at the gate of heaven that it must be opened.

The great knocker, however, is *the name of the Lord Jesus Christ.* If a person were to call upon you in the name of some dearly-beloved son who is far away, if he brought you due credentials, and a letter, saying, "Father, treat the bearer well for my sake," you would be sure to show him kindness; and if the aforesaid person was authorized to receive a promised amount in the name of your son, would you not hand out the money? Now, when we go to God and plead the name of Christ, it means that we plead the authority of Christ, that we ask of God as though we were in Christ's stead, and expect him to give it to us as if he were giving it to Jesus. That is something more than pleading for Christ's sake. I suppose the apostles at first did plead with God for Christ's sake, but Jesus says to them, "Hitherto ye have asked nothing *in my name.*" It is a higher grade of prayer, and when we get to pleading Christ's name with the Father, then do we gloriously prevail. At a Primitive Methodist meeting a person was trying to pray, but did not get on at it, and presently a voice was heard from the corner of the room, " Plead the blood, brother! plead the blood!" I am not very fond of such interruptions, yet this was to be commended, for it gave the right note, and set the pleader in his right place. Plead the precious blood of Jesus Christ, and you have knocked so that you must be heard.

"Alas!" says one, "I see the knocker, for I know something of the promises and of the person of our Lord, but how am I to knock?" With the hand of faith. Believe that God will keep his promise; ask him to do so, and thus knock. Believe that Jesus is worthy, whose name you are pleading, and so knock in confidence that God will honor the name of his dear Son. "Alas! my hand is so weak," say you. Then remember that the Holy Spirit helpeth our infirmities. Ask him to put his hand upon your hand, and in that fashion you will be able to knock with prevailing vehemence. I beseech you knock with all the strength you have, and knock often. If you are not in Christ, my dear hearer, do not give sleep to your eyes nor slumber to your eyelids till you have found him. If you have prayed once, go and pray again; and if you have prayed ten thousand times, yet still continue in prayer. Knock with all your might, with all the vigor of your Spirit; plead as for life; knock at the door as a man would knock who saw a wolf ready to spring upon him. Knock as one would knock who found himself ready to die of cold outside the door. Throw your whole soul into the work. Say unto the Lord, "I beseech thee have mercy upon me, and have mercy upon me now. I faint, I die, unless thou manifest thy love to me and take me into thy house and heart, that I may be thine for ever." "Knock, and it shall be opened unto you." There is the knocker.

IV. Next, to you who are knocking at the gate A PROMISE IS GIVEN. That is more than having a door before you, or a knocker to knock with. The promise is above the gate in plain words. Read it. You are growing faint and weary; read the promise, and grow strong again. "Knock, and it shall be opened unto you." Observe how plain and positive it is with its glorious "shall" burning like a lamp in the centre of it In letters of love the inscription shines out amidst all the darkness that surrounds you, and these are its words, "It shall be opened unto you." If you knock at the door of the kindest of men you see no such promise set before you, and yet you knock, and knock confidently; how much more boldly should you come to the door of grace when it is expressly declared, "It shall be opened unto you"!

Remember that this promise was *freely given*. You never asked the Lord for such a word, it was uttered by spontaneous goodness. You did not come and plead with Jesus for a promise that you should be heard in prayer. Far from it—you did not even pray. Perhaps you have been living in the world forty years, and have never truly prayed at all; but the Lord out of his overflowing heart of generous love has made this promise to you, "Knock, and it shall be opened unto you." Wherefore do you doubt? Do you think he will not keep his word? A God who cannot lie, who was under no necessity to promise, freely out of the greatness of his divine nature, which is love, says to a poor sinner, "Knock, and it shall be opened unto you." Oh, be sure of this, that he means it; and till heaven and earth shall pass away his word shall stand, and neither you nor any other sinner that knocks at his door shall be refused admittance.

This inscription has encouraged many to knock: when they have been ready to faint and give up all further seeking, they have read again the cheering lines, "Knock, and it shall be opened unto you," and they have taken heart and made the gate resound again. Now, do you think God will tantalize us, that he will make fools of us, that he will excite hopes in poor sinners, for the mere sake of disappointing them? Will he induce you to knock by his promise, and then laugh at you? Did the God of mercy ever say, "I called and you came; I stretched out my hands and you drew near to me, and yet I will mock at your calamity, and laugh when your fear cometh"? Why, a bad man would scarcely speak so: such an act would be more like Satan than God. Do not tolerate the thought that the God of all grace could treat a seeker thus; if it ever crosses your mind, thrust it away and say, "He that taught me to pray has thereby bound himself to answer prayer. He will not invite me to knock in vain! Therefore, I will knock again, only this time more vigorously than ever, relying upon his word and his truth." Oh, that you may never stop your knocking till salvation's door is entered by you! The promise of the Lord was given freely, and on the strength of that promise we knock, therefore we are sure that the Lord will not deny his trusting servants.

The mercy is that *this promise is meant for all knockers*—" Knock, and it shall be opened unto *you*." The Lord has not denied to you, my hearer, the privilege of praying, or declared that he will not answer your requests. You may knock, and you may expect to see the door open. I know the blessed doctrine of election, and I rejoice in it; but that is a secret with God, while the rule of our preaching is,—" Preach the Gospel to every creature." I would, therefore, say to each one here, "Knock, and it shall be opened unto *you*." The Lord knows who will knock, for "the Lord knoweth them that are his." But knock, my friend, knock now, and it will soon be seen that you are one of God's chosen ones. Remember the story of Malachi, the Cornishman. When a Methodist friend had some money to give him he smilingly said, "Malachi, I do not think I shall give you this money, because I do not know whether you are predestinated to have it. Will you tell me whether you are predestinated to have it or not?" Malachi replied, "You put the money in my hand, and I will tell you." As soon as Malachi had the sum in hand he knew that he was predestinated to have it; but he could not know before he had it in possession. So the secret counsel of the Lord is revealed to our faith when it gets Christ in possession, and not before. Knock at once. If you are predestinated to enter, I know you will knock, and knock till you are admitted, for so it stands, and no exception is made to it—"Knock, and it shall be opened unto you." It is a rule with the Lord that to him that knocketh it shall be opened.

Blessed be God, this text of mine shines out as if printed in stars, and *it continues to shine from day-dawn of life to set of sun.* As long as a man lives, if he knocks at God's door, it shall be opened unto him. You may have been long a rebel, and you may have heaped up your sins till they seem to shut out all hope from you, but still knock at Christ, the door, for an opening time will come. Even if it were with thine expiring hand, if thou couldst knock at mercy's gate it would open to thee; but put not off thy day of knocking because of God's long-suffering mercy; rather to-day knock, knock now while sitting in the pew, and if you are not answered immediately, as I trust you will be, yet go home, and there in secret cry unto the Lord, "I will not let thee go except thou bless me. I am lost unless thou find me; I am lost unless I find my Saviour and Lord, I am not playing at prayer now, my very soul means it; I must have Christ or else I die just as I am; I cast myself upon him, and trust his atoning sacrifice. Oh, manifest thyself to me as a pardoning God!" I will be bound for God as a hostage that he will answer you. I sought the Lord, and he heard me; and since then I have never doubted of any living soul but that if he too will seek the Lord through Jesus Christ he will certainly be saved. Oh, that you would try it! The Lord move you thereto by his own blessed Spirit.

V. So I close with one more point. When the door opens IT WILL BE A GLORIOUS OPENING TO YOU. "Knock, and it shall be opened." What will come of it then? Immediately you who have knocked will *enter*. If you have knocked in sincerity, the moment you see Christ as a Saviour you will accept him as your Saviour. Enter into Christ by faith. Behold he sets before you an open door, and no man can shut it. Do not hesitate to enter in. Hitherto you have thought there were many difficulties and obstacles in your way, but indeed it is not so—Believe and live. When, in answer to your knocking, you see the door move, then arise, and tarry not.

Remember that the opening of that door will not only give you entrance, but it will ensure you *safety*. He who once enters into Christ is safe for ever. Only pass beneath that blood-besprinkled portal, only rest in the house of the Well-beloved, and you shall go no more out for ever. The life which he bestows is eternal, therefore you shall not die. The destroying angel, whenever he may take his flight, must pass you by. Only believe, and you are saved; only trust Christ with your whole heart, and soul, and strength, and salvation has come unto your house, and you have come unto the house of salvation.

But then there shall come to you more of blessing yet, for yours shall be *the adoption.* Once entered in you shall abide in the mansion of grace, no more a stranger or a guest, but like a child at home. You shall sit at the Father's table and eat and drink as a son, an heir, a joint heir with Christ. Yours shall be the liberty, the plenty, the joy of the great house of love. At God's right hand there are pleasures for evermore, and these shall be your heritage. Yes, and more than that; when you have once entered into the house of love you shall have access to its inner chambers. Even the vestibule of God's house is a place of safety, but afterwards the Master of the house shall take you into curious rooms, and show you his treasures, and open to you his storehouses, so that you shall go from grace to grace, from knowledge to knowledge, and glory to glory, by continued progress. All this can only be understood by experience, and that experience can only be obtained by knocking.

I want to say this, and I have done. Some people think if they have begun to pray, and are a little in earnest, that this is enough. Now, praying is not an end, it is only a means. Knocking is not the ultimatum: you must enter in. If any of you are seeking, I am glad of it; if you are knocking, I am glad of it; but if you say, "I am perfectly satisfied to stand outside the door and knock," then I am grieved for you. You are foolish to the last degree, because you are resting in the means as if they were the end. You must enter by the door or else knocking will be labor in vain. Would any of you be content to visit a friend, and merely to stand for an hour or two outside of his door knocking. Did you ever say, "I do not want anything more: I shall sit down comfortably on the doorstep, and then get up and have another knock or two?" Knocking would not give you a dinner, nor do your business for you. Knocking is only the way of entrance, but if you stop at knocking it is poor work. The most earnest praying is only a way of getting to Christ: the gospel itself is, "Believe in the Lord Jesus Christ, and thou shalt be saved." Come, then, to Christ. If you find the door shut, knock. But oh, remember, the door is not really shut; it is only so in your apprehension! Heaven's gate stands open night and day. At once believe and live. Trust in the merit of Jesus Christ, and you are clothed with it; trust in the blood of Christ, and you are washed in it. Faith saves in an instant. It touches Jesus, and the healing virtue pours forth from his garment's hem: faith steps over the threshold, and the soul is safe. The Lord grant that you may enter in at once, and then it shall be our joy, and the angels' joy, and the great Father's joy, for ever and ever, to see you rescued from destruction!

XI.

IMITATORS OF GOD.

June 10, 1883.

"Be ye therefore followers of God, as dear children."—EPHESIANS v. 1.

We shall read the text as it should more properly be translated: "Be ye therefore imitators of God, as beloved children." Upon the word *imitate* our discourse will hinge.

The division into chapters is often most unfortunate, and in this case it causes a break in a passage which in its sense is one and indivisible. The apostle had said, "Be ye kind one to another, tenderhearted, forgiving one another, even as God for Christ's sake hath forgiven you. Be ye *therefore* imitators of God, as dear children." He has forgiven you, therefore imitate him. It is a pity to have divided the argument from the conclusion.

Here, while your minds are fresh, let me remind you that this is Hospital Sunday, and let me add that my text is an argument, and a powerful one, for helping those houses of mercy. Your Lord would have you kind one to another and tenderhearted; but how can we be kind and tenderhearted if the sick poor are not cared for? When all the machinery and all the medical skill are waiting to relieve the suffering poor, it is a crying shame that beds in hospitals should be unused because of want of funds; yet this is sadly the case, and several of those grand institutions are running into debt.

We may ourselves have no surgical skill, or nursing art, but we can each give of our substance to aid those whose lives are consecrated to the Christ-like work of healing. We cannot be kind and tenderhearted unless we give according to our ability to such noble institutions as our hospitals. Preachers generally put the application at the end of a discourse, but on these warm days you are apt to grow tired, and therefore I put the application at the beginning, that you may not give faintly and scantily when the sermon is over. All sorts of religionists are contributing to the common fund, and we must not be lacking. When the box comes round, "be ye imitators of God, as dear children," in the largeness of your liberality and the freeness of your gifts.

The apostle urges us to give and forgive. If ye be imitators of God, give, for he is always giving. Give, for if he were not to give, our lives would end; give, for he giveth unto all men liberally and upbraideth not, and every good gift and every perfect gift is from above. Be ye imitators of God, the constant, generous Giver, who spared not his own Son. Thanks be to his name for that unspeakable gift! Then comes that which to most men is a harder task, but which to a Christian man is a delight—I mean to forgive. God for Christ's sake hath forgiven us; he has blotted out our transgressions like a cloud, and cast our sins into the depth of the sea, plunging them into oblivion; therefore let us forgive most freely all that have done us wrong, so that when we bow our knee we may say without hypocrisy, "Forgive us our trespasses as we forgive them that trespass against us." Let giving and forgiving be two prominent features of our lives as Christians—giving to the needy and forgiving the guilty; giving to such as ask of us, and forgiving such as offend us. By these two things let us show that we walk in love as Christ also hath loved us. He has given himself for us, and through his precious blood we are forgiven our iniquities; let us, therefore, blend giving and forgiving into one God-like life, imitating our God. This is our Father's commandment, let it be our delight.

I. With this as a preface, let us now come closely to the text, and let us CONSIDER THE PRECEPT here laid down—"Be ye imitators of God, as dear children."

I note upon this precept, first, that *it calls us to practical duty*. Many precepts of the word of God are thought by men of the world to be unpractical, but even in those instances they are in error, for the result and outcome of such precepts produces the practical holiness which all profess to desire. In this instance there can be no cavil at the too spiritual, sentimental, or speculative character of the text; there can be no question as to the eminently practical character of the exhortation—"Be ye imitators of God, as dear children," for it points to action, continued action of the best kind. "Be ye imitators"—that is, do not only meditate upon God and think that you have done enough, but go on to copy what you study. Meditation is a happy, holy, profitable engagement, and it will instruct you, strengthen you, comfort you, inspire your heart, and make your soul steadfast; but you may not stop at meditation, you must go on to imitation of the character of God. Let your spiritual life not only bud and blossom in devout thought, but let it bring forth fruit in holy act. Be not satisfied with feeding the soul by meditation, but rise up from the banquet and use the strength which you have gained. Sitting at the feet of Jesus must be succeeded by following in the footsteps of Jesus.

Neither does the text say to us, "Be ye admirers of

God." This we ought to be, and shall be if we are true Christians. The pure in heart who alone can truly see God are filled with a reverent admiration of him. With the angels, every gracious heart exclaims, "Holy, holy, holy, Lord God of hosts." "There is none holy as the Lord" (Sam. ii. 2). When the best of men are compared with the Lord their holiness is not to be mentioned. "Who is like unto thee, O God, glorious in holiness?" But we cannot rest satisfied with rendering such admiration: we must prove that we do really admire by closely copying. The world's proverb is that "imitation is the sincerest form of flattery"; I shall alter it, and adapt it to a higher use. Imitation of God is the sincerest form of admiring him; neither can we believe that you know God, and are at all charmed with his holiness, unless you endeavor, as he shall help you, to imitate him as dear children.

Neither does the text even stay at adoration, though that is a sublime height. Adoration springs out of meditation and admiration, and is a very high and noble exercise of the mind. Perhaps we rise to the highest possible service of God on earth when we are adoring him: this is the engagement of saints and angels before his throne, and never are we nearer heaven than when we follow the same occupation here below. Beloved, let your whole lives be adoration. Not only on Sabbaths, and at certain hours, and in your assemblies, but everywhere adore by good works—a manner of worship which is as real and acceptable as the most reverent public service. Remember that "to obey is better than sacrifice,"—holy living outshines all other solemnities. To love is to adore; to obey is to praise; to act is to worship. If ye are imitators of God as dear children your adoration will be proved to be sincere.

Worship unattended by imitation is feigned; true adoration dwelleth not in words only, but as it comes from the heart so it affects the entire nature and shows itself in the daily behavior. Let us spread our adoration over all the day, till from the moment when we open our eyes till we close them again at night, we shall be practically worshipping the Lord by reverencing his law, delighting in his commandments, and imitating his character. It is clear that the precept before us is eminently practical. You who boast in being such practical men give heed to this!

Next, *this precept treats us as children,* treats us as what we are; and if we are lowly in heart we shall be thankful that it is worded as it is. Some men are very high and mighty; measured by their own rod they are great men, and hence they must be original, and strike out a path for themselves. You are not commanded to do anything of the kind: the path is laid down for you— "Be ye imitators." This is a similar doctrine to that which we teach to boys at school. You, my boy, are not to invent a system of writing; yours is a much easier task, keep to your copy, imitate every letter, ay, every turn and twist of your master's hand. Scholars can only learn by imitation, and we are all scholars. It may be something to aspire to be the head of a school of painting; but the first thing for the young artist to do is to copy. He who cannot copy cannot originate; depend upon that. I have heard great outcries about young preachers imitating, but I would suggest that, in their early efforts, this is not blameworthy. What more natural than that Timothy should at first be much influenced by Paul's manner of speech? How could a man become an artist if he did not attach himself to some school of painting, and sit under a certain master?

He may be of the French school, or the Italian school or the Flemish school, but he must begin as a follower even if he grows up to be a leader. When he has been well trained, and has done much work, he may outgrow his master and become an original, but he must begin as a careful copyist. Here you are invited to become imitators; but the Master is such an one that you will never be able to learn all that he can teach, and so strike out a better path. Though you be immortal, yet throughout eternity you will never advance beyond your model; for it is written, "Be ye imitators of God." Listen to me, ye aspiring minds: if ye must needs be original, the most wonderful originality in this world would be for a man's character to be a precise copy of the character of God: in him there would be novelty indeed, for he would be like him whose name is called "Wonderful." When our Lord Jesus exhibited on earth the character of God, his life was so original that the world knew him not; they were puzzled and amazed at the sight of One who was so like unto the Father. His life struck men as being the most singular thing they had ever seen; and if we are close copyists of God our characters will also stand out in relief, and we shall each one be "a wonder unto many." You see it is a humbling exhortation which only men of childlike spirit are likely to regard. Wisely does the Scripture address it only to such—"Be ye therefore imitators of God, as dear children"; if you are not his children you cannot imitate him, and you will not even desire to do so.

Observe next, that while it thus humbles us, *this precept ennobles us;* for what a grand thing it is to be imitators of God! It is an honor to be the lowliest follower of such a leader. Time has been when men gloried in studying Homer, and their lives were trained to heroism by his martial verse. Alexander carried the Iliad about with him in a casket studded with jewels, and his military life greatly sprung out of his imitation of the warriors of Greece and Troy. Ours is a nobler ambition by far than that which delights in battles, we desire to imitate the God of peace, whose name is love. In after ages, when men began to be a less savage race, and contests of thought were carried on by the more educated class of minds, thousands of men gloried in being disciples of the mighty Stagirite, the renowned Aristotle. He reigned supreme over the thought of men for centuries, and students slavishly followed him till a greater arose, and set free the human mind by a more true philosophy. To this day, however, our cultured men remain copyists, and you can see a fashion in philosophy as well as in clothes. Some of these imitations are so childish as to be deplorable. It is no honor to imitate a poor example. But, oh, beloved, he who seeks to imitate his God has a noble enterprise before him: he shall rise as on eagle's wings. We are copying infinite goodness, we seek after moral perfection. We are to be "blameless and harmless, the sons of God without rebuke"; but as God is infinitely more than that, so are we to rise above mere innocence into actual holiness. To refrain from evil is not enough, we must be filled with all goodness by the Spirit of God. Is not this a mark worth aiming at? Judge ye what that grace must be which is to raise us to this height! O angels, what happier task could be laid before *you*? What higher ambition can *you* know? God's only-begotten Son, who is this day Lord of all, weareth his Father's image in his glory, even as on earth he was such a copy of God that he could truly say, "he that hath seen me hath seen the Father." "I do always," said he, "the things that please him." The perfect Son of God is as his Father in holiness. You see your calling, brethren; to a high place in the rank of intelligences you are bidden to ascend by God himself. In this respect take your seats in the highest room. Imitate, but note well that ye do not select an imperfect example: "Be ye imitators of God, as dear children."

While it ennobles us, *this precept tests us*—tests us in many points. "Be ye imitators of God;" this tests our knowledge. A man cannot imitate that which he has never seen. He who does not know God cannot possibly imitate him. Do you know God, my hearer? Have you turned unto him with repentance? Have you ever spoken with him in prayer? Have you had fellowship with him in Christ? Can you say, "I have set the Lord always before me"? You cannot possibly follow a copy except you fix your eye upon that copy, and have some intelligent knowledge of what it is. We must have a spiritual idea of God or we cannot imitate him; hence the need of the Holy Ghost. How can we know the Lord unless the Spirit reveal him in us?

What is more, this precept tests our love. If we love God, love will constrain us to imitate him; but we shall not do so from any other force. We readily grow somewhat like that which we love. In married life persons who have truly loved, though they may begin with great dissimilarity, will gradually be conformed to one another in the process of years. Likeness is the natural product of love; and so if we love God truly we shall by very force of that love through his blessed Spirit grow more and more like unto him. If we do not love the Lord we shall not follow him, but if we truly love him we shall cry with David, "My soul followeth hard after thee; thy right hand upholdeth me."

Our text does even more than this: it tests our sincerity. If a man is not really a Christian he will take no care about his life; but in the matter of close copying a man must be careful; a watchful care is implied in the idea of imitation. You cannot copy a document without being intent to read and mark each word. If I sit down to write an article out of my own mind, I have nothing to do but to make my own track, and there is my work, such as it is: but if I have to copy from a book, then I must needs look to each line, and I must read it over attentively, for otherwise I may misrepresent the writer whose language I transcribe. In copying from nature how careful the artist has to be at every touch, or he will fail in his picture. If a sculptor is producing a replica of an ancient statue, he must keep his eyes open and follow every line and mark. My friend, you cannot imitate God if you are one of that sort of Christians who are habitually in a condition between sleeping and waking, with one eye a little open and the other closed. Such men live a slovenly life, and attempt a sort of happy-go-lucky religion, which may be right or which may be wrong, but its character they cannot tell, for they run with their neighbors and never examine for themselves. Such people live at random, and never take a day's life at night and examine it to see its faults; thus sin grows upon them like weeds in a sluggard's garden. Such persons, playing at hit or miss with holiness, are sure to come short of it; but he that is in earnest will give his prayerful thought and anxious desire to it, that he may become in very deed a successful imitator of God. He will also call in the aid of the Holy Spirit, and thus be led into holiness.

Moreover, the precept tests us as to our spirit, whether

it be of the law or of the gospel. "Be ye imitators of God, as dear children": not as slaves might imitate their master—unwillingly, dreading the crack of his whip; but loving, willing imitators, such as children are. You do not urge your children to imitate you; they do this even in their games. See how the boy rides his wooden horse, and the girl imitates her nurse. You see the minister's little boy trying to preach like his father; and you all remember the picture of the tiny girl with a Bible in front of her and an ancient pair of spectacles upon her nose, saying, "Now I'm grandmamma." They copy us by force of nature: they cannot help it. Such will be the holiness of the genuine Christian. He is born from above, and hence he lives above. His imitation of God springs out of his relationship to God. Holiness must be spontaneous, or it is spurious. We cannot be driven to holiness like a bullock to his ploughing; we must delight in the law of God after the inward man. "Be ye imitators of God, as dear children," because you do not wish for anything better than to be like your Father, and have no ambition in the world that approaches your aspiration to be holy even as God is holy, according to that word, "Be ye perfect even as your Father which is in heaven is perfect." Have you that filial spirit? Have you a burning love to holiness? or is sin your delight, and God's service a weariness? Where your pleasure is there your heart is. If you love evil you are not the children of God at all, and cannot imitate him nor render to him any acceptable service whatever. The Lord make us to be imitators of him, even as children from a natural bent copy their parents.

While it tests us, *this precept greatly aids us.* It is a fine thing for a man to know what he has to do, for then he is led in a plain path because of his enemies.

What a help it is to have a clear chart, and a true compass! We have only to ask,—"What would our heavenly Father do in such a case?" and our course is clear. As far as we are capable of imitating the Lord out pathway is plain. We cannot imitate God in his power, or omnipresence, or omniscience; certain of his attributes are incommunicable, and of them we may say—they are high and we cannot attain to them: but these are not intended in the precept. Creatures cannot imitate their Creator in his divine attributes, but children may copy their Father in his moral attributes. By the aid of his divine Spirit we can copy our God in his justice, righteousness, holiness, purity, truth, and faithfulness. We can be tenderhearted, kind, forbearing, merciful, forgiving; in a word, we may walk in love as Christ also hath loved us. To know what to do is a great aid to a holy life. This puts us into the light, while the poor heathen gropes in darkness, for his false gods are monsters of vice which he may not dream of imitating.

Another blessing is that it backs us up in our position; for if we do a thing because we are imitating God, if any raise an objection it does not trouble us, much less are we confounded. We did not expect when we commenced a holy life that everybody would applaud us, but we reckoned that they would criticise us; and so, when their censure comes, we are supported by the consideration that those who blame the imitation find fault with the copy,—if, indeed, the imitation be well done. He who follows God minds not what the godless think of his way of life. A clear conscience is our portion when we have in all things endeavored to please God.

I will leave my first head when I have made one more observation: *this precept is greatly for our usefulness*

—"Be ye imitators of God, as dear children." I do not know of anything which would make us so useful to our fellowmen as this would do. What are we sent into the world for? Is it not that we may keep men in mind of God, whom they are most anxious to forget? If we are imitators of God, as dear children, they will be compelled to recollect that there is a God, for they will see his character reflected in ours. I have head of an atheist who said he could get over every argument except the example of his godly mother: he could never answer that. A genuinely holy Christian is a beam of God's glory and a testimony to the being and the goodness of God. Men cannot forget that there is a God so long as they see his servants among them, dressed in the livery of holiness. We ought not only to be reminders of the careless, but teachers of the ignorant by our walk and conversation. When they look us up and down, and see how we live, they ought to be learning somewhat of God. Holy men are the world's Bibles: they read not the Testament, but they read our testimony.

Brethren, a close imitation of God would make our religion honorable. The ungodly might still hate it, but they could not sneer at it; nay, the more candid among unbelievers, perceiving our holiness to be the result of our faith, would say nothing against it. The name of Christ would not be so evil spoken of if our lives were not so faulty. Holiness is true preaching, and preaching of the most successful kind. What a support it is to the preacher when he has a people around him who are daily witnessing for God at home and in business. If the pastor can turn to his church and say, "See, here, what the doctrines of grace can do! See in the lives of our church-members what the Spirit of God can produce;" then he will have an unanswerable argument wherewith to silence gainsayers. Doth not the Lord say, "Ye are my witnesses?" Are we not detained in this world on purpose that we may bear testimony to our Lord? How can we bear forcible witness for him unless our lives are pure? An unclean professor is a fountain of scepticism, and a hindrance to the gospel. To be useful we must be holy. If we would bless men as God blesses them, we must live as God lives. Therefore, "Be ye imitators of God, as dear children." Thus much upon the precept.

II. Secondly, I invite you, dear friends, as we are helped of God's Spirit to WEIGH THE ARGUMENT. The argument is this, "Be ye imitators of God, *as dear children.*'

First, *as children.* It is the natural tendency of children to imitate their parents: yet there are exceptions for some children are the opposite of their fathers, perhaps displaying the vices of a remoter ancestor. Absalom did not imitate David, nor was Rehoboam a repetition of Solomon. In the case of God's children it is a necessity that they should be like their Father; for it is a rule in spirituals that like begets its like. Those who live wickedly are the children of the Wicked One: no proof is wanted, you may take it for granted: life is the evidence of nature. Those who live godly and righteously in Christ Jesus, believing in him, are God's children: and though the godly sin, yet they do not love sin, nor remain without repenting of it. Holiness of life is the proof of regeneration, neither can we accept any other. "By their fruits ye shall know them," is a rule of universal application. God's children *must* be like him. With all their faults and failings there must be about their lives as a whole a likeness to God. The copy may be blurred, but it is a copy. I say to any man here who bears the name of Christian and professes to be a child of God, either be like your Father or give up your name. You remember the old classic story of a soldier in Alexander's army whose name was Alexander, but when the battle was raging he trembled. Then Alexander said to him, "How canst thou bear the name of Alexander? Drop thy cowardice, or drop thy name." So say I to those who are unholy, unclean, impure, unkind, ungracious: be like God, or cease to bear the name of a child of God. What need is there that thou shouldest aggravate thy sin by pretending to a character which thou dost not possess! Be like Christ, or be not called a Christian. Do not play the Judas unless thou hast a mind to be a second "son of perdition."

The argument, then, is that if we are children we should imitate our Father; but it is also said "as *dear* children." Read it as "*children beloved.*" Is not this a tender but mighty argument? How greatly has God loved us in that he permits us to be his children at all. "Behold, what manner of love the Father hath bestowed upon us, that we should be called the children of God." A "behold" is placed there, as if it were a thing of wonder. Do you not wonder at it in your own case that you should be called a child of God? Behold the love which chose you when you were dead in trespasses and sins, and quickened you into the life of God! Do you not remember the text—"As many as received him, to them gave he power to become the sons of God, even to them that believe on his name"? What love was that which revealed itself in your new birth and your adoption, giving you thus the nature and the status of a child of God! Furthermore, since you have been a child, was there ever such kindness received by a child from a father as you have received? Behold, he dealeth with you as with sons. You could not wish for God to improve upon his dealings with you, since he acts towards you as he uses to do unto those that love his name. Behold how he has borne with your ill manners! How he has put up with your mistakes and your forgettings! how he has cared for you in all your cares, helped you in all your difficulties, and pardoned you in all your sins! I do not know what *you* have to say, my brother, but this I can say, I am filled with admiration at the love of God to myself. I have been a child greatly beloved of his Father. His love to me is wonderful; I am a deep debtor to his grace. Are you not the same? Then imitate your Father, for the more the love of a child to his Father the more his admiration of his Father, and the stronger his desire to be like him in all things. Let it be so with you.

However, this word "*as dear children*" bears yet another meaning. Children differ. A father loves all his children, but he cannot be said in all respects to love them all alike, for some force him to love them beyond the rest. You have one dear son who lies nearest your heart. What a sweet child he is! You have got another boy; —he is your child, and you love him, and do your best with him, but he is an awkward bit of stuff. He gives you little pleasure, and you are not particularly anxious to have him about you all day long. The first child loves you with all his heart and strives to please you. How obedient he is! How content and happy! In all things he is a comfort in the house. Your heart binds its tendrils about your Joseph more closely than about the wayward boy: you do not make a favorite of him, and so excite the jealousy of the others; yet you must own to a nearer and dearer love than usual when you think of him. You cannot help your heart clinging to him; his behavior is such that he is the son of your right hand,

and he has a tender place in your soul,—in a word, he is one of those whom the text calls, "dear children." Just so the Lord has certain *dear* children. Master Trapp says, "God hath but a few such children." I am afraid that the quaint old commentator is correct, and that few imitate the Lord as they should. Yet some of the Lord's children give themselves up wholly to him, are watchful and tenderly obedient, and walk in such closeness with him that they deserve the title of "dear children." Brethren, aim at this. Here happiness lies; here heaven lies this side of heaven! To be not only children, but *dear* children, is to antedate eternal bliss. Our Lord Jesus had disciples, but of some he said, "Then are ye my disciples indeed." Be such. May the Holy Spirit make you such! Around us there are troops of third-rate Christians: oh, for more first-class believers! We have many who appear to come into the Father's house at mealtimes to get a bit of bread, and then they are off again into the world. I counsel you in one thing to be like the elder brother, to whom his father said, "Son, thou art ever with me, and all that I have is thine." "Blessed are they that dwell in thy house." Oh, to be of David's mind: "I will dwell in the house of the Lord for ever." Be ye imitators of God, then, in so high a sense that ye become dear children, whose one thought is how to please their father, whose sorrow it is to grieve him, whose beauty it is to be like him.

III. In the third place, I desire, dear friends, to sug-gest encouragements. Did I hear one cry, "Oh, sir, this imitation of God is beyond us. How are we to be copyists of God?" I will encourage you by giving hints, which you can work out for yourselves.

First, *God has already made you his children.* I speak to you that are believers: you are God's sons and daughters. The greater work is done. If you are to be imitators of God, as dear children, you must first be his children: that is already accomplished. You could not have made yourselves children of God, but he has done that for you. "Beloved, now are we the sons of God." It must be a much easier thing to imitate the Father than to become a child. You might adopt a child, and call it yours, but you could not make it really your offspring, do what you might; but the Lord has "begotten us again unto a lively hope." We are "born, not of blood, nor of the will of the flesh, nor of the will of man, but of God"; and by this new birth we are renewed in his image. Hence the greater part of the task, the insurmountable hill of difficulty, is over, and that which remains is but our reasonable service. Should not the child imitate his father? Will he not do so naturally?

Next remember that *God has given you his nature already.* Does not Peter speak of our being "partakers of the divine nature, having escaped the corruption which is in the world through lust"? It remains for you to let the new nature act after its own manner. A well of living water is within you, sing ye unto it, "Spring up, O well." Let the holy thing that has been born in you now occupy the throne, and subdue the body of this death. Pray God it may. It seems to me a small thing to let the new nature have scope and freedom compared with the giving of that nature. A clean heart and a right spirit have been bestowed, let these show themselves in clean lives and right feelings. The living and incorruptible seed will produce a harvest of good works, water it with your prayer and watchfulness. If anything doth hinder it, repent and do your first works.

Next, *the Lord has given you his blessed Spirit to help*

you. "Likewise also the Spirit helpeth our infirmity." Never forget that. Things impossible with men are possible enough to the Spirit of God. We have the Spirit abiding in us, vitalizing our whole nature. The most beautiful harp you ever saw has no music in itself, but must be struck by the fingers of a musician; but the Holy Spirit makes us into living harps, which from themselves pour forth a natural and spontaneous melody. Is not this marvellous? We have not to look abroad for power to be holy, for the Spirit of God abideth in us, and worketh in us, creating in us "the spirit of power and of love and of a sound mind." Oh, to be filled with the Spirit of God! Meanwhile, it is no small help in the imitation of God to have the anointing of the Holy One, and to be instructed by him. The Holy Spirit is the Spirit of God, and hence he can teach us to imitate God; he is also the Spirit of holiness, and none can the better promote our holiness. Be of good cheer! With such a Helper you cannot be defeated.

Again remember, dear friend, that *the Lord allows you to commune with himself.* If we had to imitate a man, and yet could not see him, we should find it hard work; but in this case we can draw nigh unto God; some of us can shut the closet door and be alone with God when we will, we can even walk with God all the day What better conditions could we be under for imitating our God? Nearness to God brings likeness to God. The more you see God, the more of God will be seen in you. You know the Persian story of the scented clay. One said to it, "Clay, whence hast thou thy delicious perfume?" It answered: "I was aforetime nothing but a piece of common clay, but I lay long in the sweet society of a rose till I drank in its fragrance and became perfumed myself." Oh, if you dwell much with God in seasons of retirement, and abide with him in all the affairs of life, you will be changed into his image. As surely as the type will make its impress upon the paper, and the seal will stamp itself upon the wax, so will the Lord impress himself upon you, and stamp his image upon you if you dwell in him.

This ought also to inspire you with ardor to remember that you *have* to imitate God or you cannot go to heaven, for this is one of the main delights of heaven, to be like Christ because we shall see him as he is. "They are without fault before the throne of God." His name shall be in their foreheads; that is to say, the character of God shall be most conspicuous in them. Surely that which is to be our destiny eternally should be our desire to-day. We should strive after holiness according to his working who worketh in us mightily. We must become close copyists of God that we may enjoy everlasting communion with him. May his Spirit work us to that end.

IV. Now by turning our subject a little round we shall CLOSE WITH CERTAIN INFERENCES. I have hitherto spoken only to saints, but here is an inference for seekers. "Be ye imitators of God, as dear children;" what do I infer from this? I infer that *God is ready to forgive those who have offended him.* O you that have never been pardoned, listen to this: the Lord must be ready to forgive. We are to make God our pattern, but if God were unwilling to forgive he could not be a pattern to us. We are to be ready to pass by the offences of others, therefore if God is set forth as our example he must certainly be more ready to forgive than any of us can be. O you that are covered with sin to-day, I would urge you to catch at this fact. Suppose I were to bid you imitate your earthly father in frankly and freely forgiving all who vexed him; then you might reply "Do you know my father?" If I answered "Yes," you would say, "Is he really a fair example of patience and forgiveness? for I offended him some time ago, and I have always been afraid to go to him, lest he should refuse to receive me." If I could answer, "Yes, your father is an example that you may safely follow in that respect," then you would reply, "I will go home to him and tell him that I desire his forgiveness, and am sorry to have caused him pain." O poor sinners, you do not know what a forgiving spirit the heavenly Father has. He gave his son Jesus that he might be able to pass by our sins and yet be the righteous Judge of men. There have been good men in the world who have delighted to pass by offences. Some here present have been taught of the Lord till it has become easy and pleasurable to overlook injuries and forget wrongs; but our heavenly Father is much more kind, and with far more delight blots out the sinner's iniquities. They said of Cranmer that he was more than ready to forgive, for he always returned good for evil. It was a common saying, "Do my lord of Canterbury an ill turn, and he will be your friend as long as you live." That was fine; but my lord of Canterbury was nothing in gentleness compared with the Father of our Lord and Saviour Jesus Christ. The holy Leighton, also, was of such a gentle spirit that one day when he went out for a walk and came back he could not get into his own house, for it was locked up, and his servant had gone away for a day's fishing without leave or notice. All the good man said was, "John, next time you go fishing, please to let me know, or at least leave me the key, so that I may open the door." That was all. If even men have come up to such a degree of patience, much more will you find longsuffering in God. Oh, trembler, do believe that our Father in heaven is willing to forgive you. You backsliders, you great sinners, have right thoughts of God, and come to him at once for reconciliation. There is forgiveness with him. "He delighteth in mercy." "The Lord is good, and ready to forgive."

Christian friends, is there one among you who thinks God will not keep his promise to him. Now, listen. God is an example to us, therefore *he will surely keep his word*. He must be faithful and true, for you are bidden to copy him. If God could be false to his word we could not be exhorted to imitate him, and therefore we are sure that he is faithful and true, because we are bidden to imitate him closely. You may be sure that every word of his will stand fast, for he would have us righteous and upright in all our ways. "God is not unrighteous to forget your work and labor of love which ye have showed towards his name."

Another inference—only a hint at it—is, if you are told to be "imitators of God, as dear children," then you may depend upon it *the Lord is a dear Father*. The dear children of God have a dear Father. We may rest assured that he will be kind and tender to us, since he would have us loving towards himself. I know you are heavy in spirit at this time: I know you are depressed and troubled; but your Father is kind and good. Believe it if you cannot see it. If reason says that he deals somewhat harshly with you, for he chastens you, remember that this is his way with his beloved. Has he not said, "As many as I love I rebuke and chasten"? These stripes are seals of love. Chastisement is a high proof of wise affection. Your heavenly Father is much better to you than you are to him. He is dearer, and kinder, and more loving as a Father than you have been as a child to him. Rejoice in your Father though you cannot rejoice in yourself.

Lastly, when the text says, " Be ye imitators of God," it bids us keep on imitating him as long as we live: therefore I conclude that God will always be to us what he is. He will continue in his love since he makes that love the example of ours. God will persevere in bringing us home to heaven, for he teaches us to persevere, and make this a part of our likeness to himself. The Lord will not turn away his heart from us; he will not fail nor be discouraged: having begun to make us meet for heaven he will never stay his hand till that work is done. Wherefore rest ye upon the immutable goodness of your Father, and pray for grace evermore to imitate him until ye come to see his face. May his presence be with you, and may he give you rest. Amen.

XII.

BUYING WITHOUT MONEY.

June 17, 1883.

'He that hath no money; come ye, buy, and eat." Isaiah lv. 1.

There is a semicolon in our translation, but we need not take notice of it. It should not be there, since the text is the second of two parallel sentences arranged according to the method of Hebrew poetry.

> "Ho, every one that thirsteth, come ye to the waters,
> And he that hath no money, come, buy, and eat."

We have before us the figure of a merchant selling his wares, and crying like a chapman in the market, "Ho!" To attract attention he calls aloud, "Come! Come! Come!" three several times; and he adds to this the cry of "Buy! Buy!" Shall the Great King thus liken himself to a trader in the market earnest to dispose of his goods? It is even so, and I therefore call upon you to admire the mercy of the Lord.

In the fifty-third and fifty-fourth chapters this Divine Merchantman has been spreading out his wares. What treasures they are! Look to the fifty-third chapter: what see you there? Behold that pearl of great price, *the Lord Jesus Christ.* Behold him wounded for our transgressions, and bruised for our iniquities. This is so costly a treasure that heaven and earth could not match it. Where else should we find a sacrifice for sin, a justifier of many? This anointed One of God, upon whom the chastisement of our peace was laid—who would not have him to be his Saviour? Surely with such a treasure to display we ought not to cry long for buyers, for every truly wise man will exclaim, "This is what I need: a Saviour, and a great one. An atonement for sin is the one thing needful to me." To this you are invited in these words, "He that hath no money, come, buy, and eat."

In the fifty-fourth chapter the Divine Merchantman sets forth the rare possession of *his everlasting love*. Read from verse seven, "For a small moment have I forsaken thee; but with great mercies will I gather thee. In a little wrath I hid my face from thee for a moment; but with everlasting kindness will I have mercy on thee, saith the Lord thy Redeemer. For the mountains shall depart, and the hills be removed; but my kindness shall not depart from thee, neither shall the covenant of my peace be removed, saith the Lord that hath mercy on thee." What more can be set forth to win men's hearts? First, a full atonement and now love everlasting, making a covenant confirmed by oath. Shall there be need often to cry, "Come and buy," when such celestial wares are displayed before us?

Added to this, we see a little further on the blessing of *heavenly edification*. Notice the eleventh verse:—" I will lay thy stones with fair colors, and lay thy foundations with sapphires. And I will make thy windows of agates, and thy gates of carbuncles, and all thy borders of pleasant stones." This is rare building, is it not? There should be a quick market for such an array of choice things: sapphires and agates—what would you have more? Here are all manner of precious stones, and all of these given freely! The only terms are "everything for nothing! Heaven for the asking!" All the treasures of God are freely bestowed upon the sons of men who are willing to accept them as gifts of grace.

As if this were not enough, the Lord brings out a fourth blessing, namely, *everlasting* safety by faith: "In righteousness shalt thou be established: thou shalt be far from oppression; for thou shalt not fear: and from terror; for it shall not come near thee. No weapon that is formed against thee shall prosper; and every tongue that shall rise against thee in judgment thou shalt condemn." Security is worth infinitely more than gold. To be protected by Divine wisdom from every possible harm is the portion of believers in Jesus. To be saved, and made safe for ever, is not this worth worlds? Never was there a market like the gospel market; and never were such wares spread out before the eyes of men as those which are here presented to you. I shall therefore with the more hopefulness speak to those who have not yet been buyers, and urge upon you the invitation of the text, "He that hath no money, come ye, buy, and eat."

In handling this text we shall notice, first, *the description* of the buyer, "He that hath no money"; secondly, *the selection* of this particular buyer—why is he invited beyond all others? Thirdly, *the invitation* to purchase, "Come, buy, and eat"; and fourthly, we shall add *the assurance* that this gospel market is no deception, for these things are really to be had.

I. First, then, here is A DESCRIPTION of the buyer. I believe he is here this morning. I hope he will recognize his own portrait, though it is by no means a flattering one. It is truth itself, a photograph taken by the sunlight of heaven. It is the portrait of a poor, penniless, broken-down creature reduced to the extremity of want: here it is—" He that hath no money."

Of course, by this is meant among other things the man who literally has no money. Among the Jews of our Lord's day there existed an idea that a man who had money was at a great advantage with regard to heavenly things, so that when the Lord said " How hardly shall they that have riches enter into the kingdom," they exclaimed with wonder, " Who then can be saved?" as if they thought that if the rich could not be easily saved then none could be. The word of God contains nothing to encourage such a notion. The rich man is never extolled in the Old Testament, but he is often spoken of most slightingly. It is the glory of the Messiah that "the poor have the gospel preached unto them," and it is the glory of the gospel that it is freely provided by the bounty of God for the beggar on the dunghill. Let no man's heart fail him this day because he saith " Silver and gold have I none." Having nothing, you may yet possess all things. You are at no disadvantage in God's market because your pocket is empty: you may come penniless and bankrupt and receive the exceeding riches of his grace. But we understand the reference of the text to be mainly spiritual, and so the portrait here is that of a man who has no spiritual money, no gold of goodness, no silver of sanctity,—he it is that is invited to come and buy the wine and milk of heaven.

His fancied stock of natural innocence is spent. At first he thought himself to be pure as the newly fallen snow, forgetting the question—How can he be clean that is born of a woman? They told him that he was made "a member of Christ, a child of God, and an inheritor of the kingdom of heaven" while he was yet a babe; and thus he was led to think that he had started life's business with a respectable stock-in-trade. He knows better now; he has seen this fancied goodness melt away like the mist of the morning. He has gone, like the prodigal, into the far country, and there he has wasted his substance till not a groat remains. If he searches himself through and through he cannot find a relic of innocence; the whole head is sick and the whole heart faint: from the sole of the foot even to the head he is all wounds, and bruises, and putrefying sores. There is no health in him. Innocence is utterly gone, if it was ever there.

He thought that he had accumulated some little savings of good works; but *his imaginary righteousness turns out to be counterfeit*. Had he not been honest? had he not been sober? had he not attended a place of worship, and repeated forms of prayer? Did not all this make up a little fortune of righteousness? He thought so, but then he was ignorant and deluded: he knows better now, for he has found out that all his righteousness is base metal: he could not pass a penny's worth of it in the shop of his own conscience, much less in the market of heaven; he knows that it would at once be detected, and nailed to the counter. He finds that his silver is white metal of the basest sort, and that his gold is a sham: he has not the face to offer it anywhere; yea, he is so afraid of being seized by justice as a coiner that, like a wise man, he has hidden his sham righteousness in the earth, and has run away from it. He is now more afraid of his righteousness than of his unrighteousness. He would think it just as possible for him to be saved by cursing and swearing as by the merit of his own works. His good works are in ill odor with his conscience, for he sees them to be defiled within and without with sin: a rottenness is in the bones of his righteousness, and thus he is without merit of any sort.

See his poverty: his original stock is gone, and all his savings have melted away!

He is in a still worse plight, for he is also too poor to get anything: *the procuring power is gone*, for he has "no money." Now that he has come into his sober senses he would repent, but he cannot find a tender heart; he would believe, but he cannot find faith. He has no money; that is to say, nothing wherewith he can procure those good things which are necessary unto salvation and eternal life. He sees them all before him, like many a poor man who walks the streets of London, and sees just what he wants behind the glass of the shop window; but he puts his hand into his pocket, and despairingly passes on, for he has no money. As without money nothing is to be bought in the world's mart, so is this poor man afraid that no blessing of grace can ever be his because he has no good thing to offer, no righteousness to give in exchange. If God would sell him even a pennyworth of righteousness he has not the penny to buy it with; and if the Lord would pardon all his sins for one sixpennyworth of holiness, he has not so much as that to offer—he has no money.

Moreover, *his stock with which to trade is gone*. Money makes money, and he that has a little to begin with may soon have more; but this man, having no stock to start with, cannot hope to be rich towards God in and by himself. He cannot open the smallest shop, or sell the most trifling wares, for he has no money to start with. Even the poorest will buy a few matches and hawk them about the streets, but this poor creature has "no money," and cannot even invest a twopence in goods. He has no power even to think aright, much less to act aright, so as to become pleasing to God: he is as much without strength as without merit. Not only is he without good, but he appears to himself to be without power to get good. He is a broken trader who cannot again try his fortune, for he has "no money." He is worse than a common beggar, for he does not even know how to beg —"We know not what we should pray for as we ought." He needs even to be taught how to beg. What a pass to come to!

There is your portrait, my poor friend! Do you recognize it? I hope you do. I hear you say, "Yes, that is myself. I am without money." Then to you the word of this salvation is sent—"He that hath no money, come, buy, and eat."

"No money!" Then *he cannot pay his old debts.* His sins rise up before him, but he cannot make amends for them. What a long file is needed to hold the record of his debts; it must be deep as the bottomless pit, and high as heaven. He owes ten thousand talents, and has "nothing to pay": he has not a stiver, he has no money whatever! He is reduced to bankruptcy, and cannot pay a farthing in the pound.

Moreover, *he cannot meet his present expenses.* Poor man! he must live; he must eat the bread of heaven, and he must drink of the water of life: but he has nothing with which to procure these good things. His soul hungereth, yea, even fainteth after the mercy of God, but he has no price with which to procure it. This day he would pluck his eyes out to be pleasing with God: but he has nothing to offer which the Lord could accept. He is reduced to such beggary that like the prodigal he cries, "I perish with hunger."

He cannot face the future. He hardly dares to think of it; and yet the thought of it will come in. He remembers the needs which will surround him on a dying bed, and the terrible demands of the resurrection morning when the ringing **trump** shall introduce him to the dread Assize, and he shall stand before his God to render his account. He knows that he cannot answer him for one sin of a thousand. He dreads the thought of the world to come! He has nothing with which to meet the demands of the eternal future. He has "no money," nothing that will pass current in the day of judgment. He is brought to the last stage of spiritual destitution; poverty has come upon him like an armed man. This is a terrible plight to be in; yet I wish that every sinner here might be reduced to it, for when he is so reduced and brought low, grace will come in, and the tide will turn.

The only hope for a man who has "no money" must be outside himself. It is idle for him to look into his own coffers: he must look away from himself; and his only chance in thus looking is to appeal to charity, and plead for mercy's sake. He cannot buy—it is only God's mercy that talks about his buying: he must beg, he must entreat for love's sake. This is an essential part of spiritual poverty; and I would that every unregenerate person knew that in him there dwelleth no good thing, and that he were convinced that he must look out and look up for salvation, and that upon the ground of mercy, since he cannot expect to obtain any blessing upon the footing of justice, or as a matter of debt.

This is the man who is called to buy heaven's wine and milk. Do you want a fuller portrait of him? Look at the twenty-first verse of the fourteenth of Luke's Gospel, where he that made the feast said, " Bring in hither the poor and the maimed and the halt and the blind." This man is so poor that he cannot buy bread, so maimed that he cannot run for it, so halt that he cannot stand up to receive it, and so blind that he cannot see it; yet such a person we are to bring into the royal banquet of mercy. If you would like another photograph turn to Revelation iii. 17, 18: "Thou knowest not that thou art wretched, and miserable, and poor, and blind, and naked." This portrait was taken by John, who had an eagle's eye, and saw deep into the inward misery of the heart. To the "wretched, and miserable, and poor, and blind, and naked," the Lord says, "I counsel thee to buy of me gold tried in the fire, that thou mayest be rich; and white raiment, that thou mayest be clothed, and that the shame of thy nakedness do not appear; and anoint thine eyes with eyesalve, that thou mayest see." Gospel riches are sent to remove our wretchedness, and mercy to remove our misery. It is to these wretches, these blind beggars, these naked vagrants, that the gospel is sent. This day I have to present the promise of God and the exhortation of mercy to those who have failed in life, who are down at the heel, broken and crushed. Oh, you utterly lost ones, to you is there opened a door of hope. The Lord has come into the market, and he bids you buy of him without money and without price.

II. Now a minute or two upon the second point: THE SELECTION of the buyer. It is a strange choice, and it leads to a singular invitation, "He that hath no money; come, buy, and eat." In the streets round about this Tabernacle, especially on a Saturday evening, you may note the salesmen standing before their shops, and crying out vociferously, "Buy! Buy! Buy!" No one can refuse to hear their noise; but if they knew that a person had no money, I think they would save their breath so far as he is concerned. They want ready-money customers, and plenty of them. What would be the use of crying, "Buy! Buy!" to a man whose purse is empty? Yet these are the very persons whom the Lord selects, and to them he cries, "Come, buy, and eat." What is the reason?

Well, first, *these need mercy most.* Oh, poor souls, when the Lord Jesus looks on you he does not look at what you have, but at what you have not. He does not look at your excellences, but at your necessities. He is not looking out for man's fulness but for man's emptiness. The Lord Jesus never gave himself for our righteousness; but he "gave himself for our sins." Salvation is by grace, and it is presented to those who are lost, for they are the people whom it will suit: how should those who are not lost value salvation? I say that God selects the most poverty-stricken first because this character most needs his pitying love. The greatness of your necessity is that which gives you a first call from the God of all grace. Not merit, but demerit; not desert of reward, but desert of wrath, is the qualification for mercy.

Again, this character is chosen because *he is such an one as will exhibit in his own person the power of divine grace.* If the Lord Jesus Christ takes one that is wretched, and miserable, and poor, and blind, and naked, and if he satisfies all his necessities by being riches for his wretchedness, comfort for his misery, wealth for his poverty, eyes for his blindness, and raiment for his nakedness, then all the world will see what a great Saviour he is, and how wonderfully his salvation meets the necessities of the case. If you and I were only little sinners I do not see how Christ could be anything but a little Saviour to us; and if he only met our smaller wants, a small supply would suffice. Ah, friends, it pleased the Father that in him should all fulness dwell, and he wills that this fulness should be seen. When he takes a man whose needs are as large as the sea, whose wants are as many as the sands on the shore, whose danger is deep as the bottomless pit, and whose sin is black as Tophet's midnight; and when he makes that man into a child of God and an heir of heaven, ah, then all intelligences are amazed, and cry out, " What a Saviour is this! What precious blood is this! What a fulness this must be which satisfies such immeasurable wants!" As it is one end of Christ's work to glorify divine grace, therefore he calls first upon those who have the most need, for in them his grace will be best displayed.

Next, *the Lord Jesus delights to make evident the freeness of his grace.* Now, if those were first called who have the money of merit, it might be imagined that they had paid their way: but if those are called who have no good thing in them, it is clear that grace is free. When a poor wretch cannot do a stroke of work, or contribute a button to you, then your lodging him must be of pure charity, and nothing else. The Lord Jesus is very jealous of the freeness of his grace: he will not let a sixpence of our merit cross his hand, lest we should glory in our flesh, and think that we have made Jesus rich.

If you ask me yet again why is he that hath no money so expressly called, I would answer, because *he is the kind of man that will listen.* The man who is needy is the man that will hearken to the tidings of a full and free supply. It is the guilty man who loves to hear of pardon, it is the bond-slave whose ear is charmed with the word "redemption." If you are no sinner you will not care about a Saviour. Only real sinners rejoice in a real atonement. The Lord sends the gospel to every creature under heaven; but he knows, as we do, that the most of men will not regard it, for they fancy that they need it not: but if there is one that has no merit or claim he will listen with eagerness to the tidings of mercy for him. He that hath no money is the man for Christ's money. He that is shivering in his nakedness will rejoice to be clothed. A wretched sinner jumps at mercy like a hungry fish leaping at the bait. When a soul is empty then it longs for the fulness of Christ, but not till then. Full souls quarrel over honeycombs, they are not sweet enough for them; but to the hungry man even every bitter thing is sweet. A man who is conscious of sin will not quibble about the way of grace, but if pardon is to be had he will have it at once: whoever may be silent, you will hear his voice crying aloud, "Thou Son of David, have mercy on me!"

Let me add that such an empty, penniless soul, when he does get mercy, *will prize it and praise it.* He that has been shut up in the dark for years values the light of the sun. He that has been a prisoner for months, how happy he is when the prison doors are opened, and he is at liberty again! Let a man once get Christ, who has bitterly known and felt his need of him, and he will prize him beyond all things, and find his sole delight in him. The impotent man at the beautiful gate of the temple, when his ankles received strength, walked, ay, and ran, ay, and leaped. He leaped, praising God, before all the people. He could not do enough to show his delight and his gratitude. Oh, for a few leaping Christians. The Lord Jesus loves us to prize the mercy which cost him so dear. Shall he die on the tree and give us blessings to treat with contempt? No, no. We will love him much because of his priceless gifts to us. Therefore the Well-beloved delights to invite those who manifestly have no merit, and no spiritual power. because he knows that when they taste of his love they will overflow with praise to his name for ever and ever. You have heard of the old woman who said that if ever she got to heaven the Lord Jesus Christ should never hear the last of it; many of us are of that mind: we shall never praise the Lord sufficiently throughout eternity. If I do but once cross the golden threshold, and stand within the pearly gate, my heart, my soul, my tongue shall extol my Redeemer world without end. This shall be the one and only contention among the birds of Paradise, who shall sing the most sweetly to the praise of infinite compassion. None of us will yield the palm in that contest; we will see which can sink lowest in sense of obligation, which can rise highest in adoring love. Singers are wanted for the celestial choirs and there are no voices so sweet as those which have known the force of spiritual hunger and thirst: these take the *alto* notes, and sing "Glory to God in the highest."

In any case, be the reason what it may, it is clear that there are special invitations issued for the royal feasts, and these are all directed to those whose need has reached the extremity of distress.

But I may not linger. How I wish that I knew how to preach. I long with my whole heart to use great plainness of speech. I would not utter a single sentence which would seem to have the wisdom of words in it. I aim not at fine language, but only to get at poor sinners' hearts. Oh that I could bring the sinner to his Saviour. Oratory has been the curse of the Christian church; it has hidden the cross under roses, and taken men's minds away from Christ. To strain after eloquence when preaching the gospel is a sin worthy of eternal destruction. To point the sinner to Christ must be our sole desire. Pray for me, brethren and sisters, as I go on, for I need aid from the Holy Ghost.

III. I have now in the third place to notice THE INVITATION. The man who has no money is to *come, buy, and eat*. It looks odd to tell a penniless man to come and buy, does it not? and yet what other word could be used? Come and *buy*, has a meaning of its own not to be otherwise expressed.

In buying there are three or four stages, and the first is *desiring to have* the thing which is exhibited. The man who buys has first the wish that the property in the article should be vested in himself. Will you not desire that Christ, that forgiveness, that eternal life, that salvation should become yours? Do you not long for the Lord to grant it to you? Men in the streets, as I have said before, cry "Buy! buy!" because buying means business. They are not unwilling that people should stop and look at their goods—they even ask them to walk in and see for themselves; but they aim at finding buyers and not gazers. If a man were to come into the shop and turn over all the goods, and never purchase anything, the tradesman would begin to cry, "Buy! buy!" with quite another accent; for he does not want a crowd to look at him, but he wants people to buy of him. Many of you who are here this morning have only come to hear what the preacher has to say, and to criticise his style and language; I pray you rise to something better than that. Come, and *buy!* Let us do business this morning for God, and for our own souls. Do not waste the precious market-day of the Sabbath. People come and go, and hear sermons, and read books, and all for a sort of amusement; they do not come to downright business with the Lord. See, how they select striking sentences and cull sparkling and delightful extracts, and take notes of telling anecdotes; but all this is comparatively wasting time. "Come, *buy!* Buy! Buy!" Do you mean business? Then, come and buy. Do not stand huckstering by the year together. Come to terms, and make an end of hesitation. If you have no desire you will not buy, and I shall effect no sales. Again I cry, "Come, buy, and eat." Oh that the Spirit may work in you that strong desire without which no man will ever buy! Alas! there are thousands who are always discussing knotty points, not because they have a wish to understand the gospel, but because they do not care to come to serious dealings. Perhaps you have read the story of a governor of one of the American States who called at a hotel where there was a colored waiter, who was well known to hold Calvinistic opinions, and was, therefore, made the butt for many a jest. So the Governor said to him, "Sam, you do not really believe that doctrine of election, do you?" "'Deed I do, sah," said he. "Well, then," replied the Governor, "tell me whether I am elect or not." "Sah," said the negro, "I did not know you were a candidate, and I know nothing about a man's being elected if he has not put up for it." Now, that is common sense. It is a business-like way of answering an absurd question. Certain people who are not even candidates for heaven will yet shelter themselves behind wrong ideas of predestination—playing with the blessings of grace instead of desiring them. Have you not seen a man with a pack stand at a door trying to sell a few trinkets to a servant. He does not mind half-an-hour's talk about his goods; but when at last he finds that the maid does not mean buying, see how he shuts up his boxes, folds up his packages, and indignantly takes himself off, saying by his gestures, "I wish I had not wasted so much time over you." It is just so with earnest preachers; they grow sick at heart when they see that men will not come to business. They cry, "Who hath believed our report?" and are anxious to carry their heavenly burden to another people. Oh, dear hearers, let us not have to shake off the dust of our feet for a testimony against you! Oh, that you would hunger and thirst after Christ and his salvation, and then we should soon do a trade with you.

"*Buy*":—This means next to *agree to terms*, for there cannot be any purchasing, however much the buyer desires to buy and the seller to sell, till they agree to terms. Now, our difficulty with God's goods is this: whereas ordinarily the buyer cannot be brought *up* to the seller's price, in our case we cannot get men *down* to God's price. They *will* persist in offering something as a price. They talk to us thus—"I cannot be saved, for I do not see any good thing in myself. Sir, if I had a deep sense of need, then I could be saved"; or, "Sir, if I could pray better"; or, "Sir, if I had more repentance, or more love, I could then believe in Jesus." Oh, yes, if you had a price in your hand, you would pay for heaven's blessings, would you not? But then, you see, they are not presented to you upon such terms. Price is out of the question. God's terms are that there shall be no terms of purchase at all: you are to be nothing, and Jesus is to be your all in all. When you will come down to that, then take the goods, the bargain is made; eternal life is yours.

The next thing in a purchase is that, when the terms are carried out, *the buyer appropriates the goods to himself*. If I buy a thing it is mine, and I take it into my possession. You do not see a man buy a thing and then leave it behind him for the seller to do as he likes with it. In the things of God you are to appropriate the blessing to yourself. Put out the hand of faith, and say, "Here is Christ for a sinner. I am a sinner, and I take Christ to be my Saviour. Here is washing for the filthy: I am filthy, and I wash. Here is a robe of righteousness for the naked: I am naked, I take the raiment to be mine." Make Christ your own, and he has made you his own. Take the Lord by an appropriating act of faith to be yours for ever, and the bargain is struck.

But the text says a little more than that—it says, "Buy, *and eat*," as much as to say, make it yours in the most complete sense. If a man buys a loaf of bread it is his: but if he eats it, then all the lawyers in the world cannot dispute him out of it—he has it by a possession which is not only nine points of the law, but all the law. When a poor soul hath confidence enough to take Christ and to live upon him as his own, saying, "This Christ is able to save me, I take him into me and I am saved," why, the devil himself cannot unsave you. What is to divide him from Christ? There is the bath, and I wash therein and am clean: what then? Who can obliterate the fact that I have washed? The righteousness of Christ is bestowed upon me, and put on by me, who can tear off that glorious dress? Christ fed upon is ours beyond all question. No method of possession is more sure and safe than that of eating what you have bought. Feed, then, on Christ, the bread of heaven, and though you be in yourself the poorest of the poor, yet he is yours for ever and ever.

See, then, the blessed invitation, the whole of God's mercy in Christ, infinite love and boundless compassion are to be had for no price at all; they are freely given to every man who has no money with which to procure them. The height of love meets the depths of poverty and fills them up. He that has nothing is invited to have all things, for he is the person for whom they were provided in the eternal purposes of God.

IV. I conclude now by saying a few things by way of ASSURANCE, to show that this is all real and true and no make-believe. Every needy, thirsty soul may have this day all the grace of God. Oh, may the Spirit of God make him willing, he shall have all the blessings of the covenant of grace to be his own for ever and ever! This is no sham; there is an honest offer made to every one who is conscious of soul-poverty!

For, first, *it is not God's way to mock men.* He hath himself declared, "I said not unto the seed of Jacob, seek ye my face in vain." God has not said one thing in one place and another in another to contradict himself. He has not in the Scriptures bidden men to come to him with the promise that he will not cast them out, all the while meaning of some of them that he will cast them out. No, there are no exceptions made in the promises of God to empty sinners who come to him. You must not dream of exceptions which do not exist. Jesus says, "Him that cometh to me I will in no wise cast out," and this includes all who come. I am speaking to some this morning who have come across the Atlantic and are not yet saved: you may have been careless and thoughtless all your lives, but if you come to Jesus Christ this morning he will not refuse you his salvation. Many have come in from the country to-day: oh, that this may become their spiritual birthday! Come to the Lord Jesus Christ, my friend, and he will welcome you. He never did reject one, and he never will. He will not find pleasure in tantalizing you. He is too good, too true, to become a deceiver even to one poor lonely seeker. His word of promise to you is true and real: every word is full of meaning, sweeter meaning than you dream of. Grace shall be had by you at once if you will but take it "without money and without price." Men mock men, but God never deludes. We may say of him "Thy word is truth."

Note that these mercies must be really meant to be given gratis to the poor, because *God is under no necessity to sell his benefits.* He is not impoverished: he is so rich that none can add anything to his wealth. All things are his, therefore he must give freely, since it would be beneath his all-sufficiency to be chaffering for compensation, or demanding a price at a creature's hand. He means the penniless to have everything for nothing, since nothing can be imagined to be a price to him. If a poor tradesman began to give away his goods you would say, "There is some trick about this"; but when the Most High God, the possessor of heaven and earth, who has everything, freely gives to us, then there can be no design for his own advantage: his motive must be pure compassion.

There is no adequate price that we could bring to God for his mercy. How could there be? Would it be mercy if it could be bought? Grace is without price because it is priceless. You can buy gold if you will: there is some medium of exchange for the purchase of every finite thing; but what medium of exchange could there be for the purchase of infinite blessings? Huge heaps of such things as the native Africans call money would be of no value to us, and what self-righteous men call merit is utterly despicable to God. Is there any comparison between a man's giving all his wealth and the possession of eternal glory? No comparison can be instituted between metals and spiritual joys. As you cannot bring any price, I do pray you believe that God is honest when he declares that he will give you pardon of sin and all the blessings of his grace of God without money and without price. You cannot have them otherwise; do believe that he means you to receive them by grace. Remember that Jesus must be meant for sinners, for *if sin-*

ners had not existed there never *would* have been a *Saviour*. When the Lord Jesus Christ set up in business to save he must have known there was no sphere for his operations except among sinners, and hence he entered on his office with the view of saving sinners. If a doctor comes into a town, and there is nobody ill, and it is certain that nobody ever will be ill, he had better drive off somewhere else: he will do most business where there is most sickness. When Christ Jesus became a soul-physician he had his eye on the spiritually sick, and on them alone. They are the patients who make up his practice, and they only. If, then, thou art sick even unto death, put thy case into the hands of Christ, for he will heal thee.

Remember, too, that it must be true that God will give these blessings to men who have no merits, and will bestow them as gifts, because *Jesus himself is a gift*. Did anybody ever dream of buying Christ? Stand at the foot of the cross and say to yourself, "Could I ever have procured this vast display of love by any merit of mine? Could I have done anything which could have merited that the Son of God should become man, and that being found in fashion as a man he should die such a death as this for me?" Salvation must be a gift, for Jesus is a gift. Away with your sacraments, your ceremonials, your prayers, your alms, your good works, if these are made the brass pence with which you hope to buy such inestimable things as pardon, sonship, heaven! Salvation is seen to be such when it is given to those who have no money of their own.

Beside that, *Christ is all*. Men have no notion what Christ is when they talk of getting ready for Christ, or, bringing something to him. What would you bring to Christ? Everything is in Christ, and therefore you cannot bring anything to him. "Oh, but," say you, "I must come with a broken heart." I tell you no, you must come *for* a broken heart. "Oh, but I must come with a sense of need." I tell you that a true sense of need is his work in you. True repentance and a sense of need spring from his grace, and you must get them from him without money and without price. "Ah, but I must *be* something." Say, rather, you must be nothing. We cannot drill this into men's brains: nay, if we were to use steam power to work upon the mind, we could not get this thought fixed in their proud hearts. They will cling to merit, they must *be* something, *feel* something, *say* something, *do* something. Out of the way with your somethings! Subside into nothingness. The Spirit of God brooded of old over chaos, so that order was clearly his work; and when the mind seems to be all chaos and darkness, then the Spirit of God is sure to work, and the Lord's voice is heard, saying, "Let there be light!" Go to the Lord Jesus just as you are, you will never be better —you may be worse; go now, just as you are, to Jesus, and buy and eat without money, means, or merit.

One thing more I would say, and that is the gospel of Jesus Christ is blessedly free from all clogging conditions because *all supposed conditions are supplied in Christ Jesus.* We have heard of men advertising to give things away, but when you read the advertisement carefully you find that you are to pay after all: the gospel is not so, its freedom is real. Many a good thing is to be had, but when you see how it is to be obtained, you say to yourself "the conditions shut me out:" but the conditions of eternal life shut no man out who needs to be saved and wills to be saved. Over the gate of heaven is written "Come, and welcome." But you remind me that it says "Buy," and you insist upon it that therefore you must pay. Not so; salvation is paid for already: all the paying has been done by him who opened his veins to find the only price that is current in heaven—the sin-atoning blood. If price may be spoken of—that price was all paid long before you were born. Nearly nineteen hundred years ago on Calvary's cross the purchasing work was done, and Jesus bowed his head and said, "It is finished." Will you add to that which is finished? Will you tag on your rags to the Lord's glistering cloth of gold, and add your base farthings to the infinite price which he poured forth so lavishly at the foot of the Eternal Throne? Oh, do not so. To yoke you with Christ can never be. You and Christ together! An archangel and an emmet would make a better pair than you yoked with Christ. Nay, my friend, sink, sink, sink; by a mighty descent sink to nothing, and let Jesus rise, rise, rise, till he fills the whole horizon of your thoughts and hopes, for then are you saved. Let us sing—

>"'Tis done! the great transaction's done;
>I am my Lord's, and he is mine:
>He drew me, and I follow'd on,
>Charm'd to confess the voice divine."

XIII.

THE VOICE FROM THE CLOUD AND THE VOICE OF THE BELOVED.

June 24, 1883.

"While he yet spake, behold, a bright cloud overshadowed them: and behold a voice out of the cloud, which said, This is my beloved Son, in whom I am well pleased; hear ye him. And when the disciples heard it, they fell on their face, and were sore afraid. And Jesus came and touched them, and said, Arise, and be not afraid."—MATTHEW xvii. 5, 6, 7.

IT is exceedingly important to have clear evidences of the truth of our holy religion. Sometimes, I dare say, you have wished that God would speak out of heaven in your hearing, or that he would work some extraordinary marvel before your eyes, that you might know beyond all question the truth of the gospel of Jesus. This desire for signs and wonders is no new thing. Ah, my dear friends, we know not what we ask, nor what we desire; for if such a voice were to come to us out of the excellent glory, we are made of the same flesh and blood as Peter, and James, and John, and it would therefore produce the same effect upon us as upon them: we should fall upon our faces, and be sore afraid. Spirituals must grow out of spirituals: saving faith can never be produced by carnal sight and hearing. The Holy Ghost can work faith in us apart from any form of miracle; and miracle alone can never create a spiritual faith. Do we wish to receive a sign in order to confirm our belief in God? Suppose that we had it, we should soon need to have it repeated, for unbelief dies hard. I cannot tell how often we should need to hear the voice out of the cloud; but certainly life would soon become a misery to us, for we should be so frequently lying on our faces, so often cast into a swoon of fear, that we should be shattered, and nervous, and incapable of the ordinary duties of life. Like Israel at Sinai, we should begin to entreat that the Lord would not speak to us any more. The fact is that the voice of God, as absolute God, is too awful, too majestic, for mortal ears, and the sight of overwhelming miracles would put such a strain upon the human mind that it is better for us to be without them. It is plain from the example of Israel in the wilderness that even the lowest form of grace does not grow out of frequent miracles, for the tribes fell into every form of evil, though they lived on miracles, and even ate and drank the result thereof. Not signs and wonders without, but a new heart within, is the grand cure for unbelief. Christ in you is the hope of glory and the death of doubt: anything else will fall short of your need.

According to our text, what is wanted is, not an audible voice of God to confirm the evidences of our religion, but the touch and the voice of Christ to make us conscious within ourselves of the power of him to whom God bears witness. Not external, but internal evidences are what we need. The best evidences in the world are what we call experimental, such as grow out of actual experience. It is a better thing for a man to live near to Christ, and to enjoy his presence, than it would be for him to be overshadowed with a bright cloud, and to hear the divine Father himself speaking out of it. The voice out of the cloud would but dismay and distract: the voice of Christ would cheer and comfort, and at the same time would be an equally powerful assurance to us of the divinity of the whole matter. Assurance is the thing which we so much desire, and we can better obtain it by personal test than by any external witness. Brethren, the most profitable thing for me at any rate is not so much to study evidences or to seek them, as to enjoy the gospel itself by personal contact with the Christ of God. You may be told that this is the bread of heaven, but you will not know it, however heavenly the voice, one half so vividly as if you eat thereof and live: then shall you know when Jesus touches you and bids you "be not afraid." A miraculous interposition would crush as well as convince; a spiritual visitation and a consoling word will convince as certainly, and it will comfort at the same time.

The verses which I have selected seem to me to teach us just this—that even the voice of God the Father would need to be supplemented by the voice and by the touch of our Lord Jesus Christ the incarnate Son, or else we should not be so assured as to become active witnesses for gospel truth. To preach Christ we must hear Christ; no other voice will suffice unless he speak to us.

This morning I propose to treat the subject thus: first, *let us hear the voice out of the cloud;* and then, secondly, *let us hear the voice of Jesus.* May the Holy Spirit sweetly enable us to hearken diligently in each case.

I. First: LET US HEARKEN TO THE VOICE THAT SPEAKETH OUT OF THE CLOUD.

Observe at the outset the words, "*Behold, a bright cloud overshadowed them.*" When God draws near to man it is absolutely necessary that his glory should be veiled. No man can see his face and live. Hence the cloud, in this instance, and in other cases; hence that thick veil which hung over the entrance to the most holy place; hence the need of the incense to fill that place with smoke when the high priest once in the year went within the veil; hence above all the need of the body and the manhood of Christ that the Godhead may be softened to our view. The God shines graciously through the man, and we behold the brightness of the Father's glory without being blinded thereby. There must be a cloud. Yet it was a *bright* cloud which in this case yielded the shadow, and not a thick darkness like that which became the canopy of Deity at the giving of the law. Then Mount Sinai was altogether on a smoke, and the Lord sat enthroned amid thick darkness. On other occasions we read, "He made darkness his secret place; his pavilion round about him were dark waters and thick clouds of the skies"; but now on Tabor, where God bears peaceful witness to his well beloved Son, he veils himself in a brightness significant of his good pleasure towards the sons of men.

There were but three who saw this glory of the Transfiguration, and heard the Father's voice; such signs are not for unholy eyes and ears. There were sufficient to bear complete witness, for "the testimony of two men is true," and "in the mouth of two or three witnesses the whole shall be established." It is not needful that you and I therefore should see the transfigured Saviour: the fact of the transfiguration is quite as sure as if we did see it, for three men saw it of whose truthfulness we have no question. It is not needful that these ears should hear the attesting words of the divine Father, for those three apostles heard him speak, and they bore witness thereof by their honest lives and martyr deaths. We know that their witness is true, and to us to-day there is an absolute certainty of belief that the Lord God Almighty did with an audible voice declare Jesus of Nazareth to be his Son, in whom he is well pleased. The testimony of honest men is all that we can have about most things, and we are accustomed to accept it and act thereon; in this case we may be as sure as if we had ourselves been there, and had ourselves seen and heard.

It is a very instructive fact that *the utterance of God out of the cloud was made up of words out of Scripture.* We are told, "If any man speak, let him speak as the oracles of God;" and what honor has the Father put upon holy Scripture here! He did but utter three brief sentences, and each of them might be called a quotation. The Lord God is the master of language, for he is the creator of tongues; he need not, therefore, confine himself to language used by prophets and seers in the volume of inspiration, and because he did so in this instance we conclude that he intended to put special honor upon the words of Scripture. The occasion was most august, yet no better words are needed by the Lord himself concerning his own Son than those recorded in former ages in the pages of Holy Writ. First the Father said, "This is my beloved Son." Turn to Psalm ii. 7, and there you read, "Thou art my Son." Then the Father said, "In whom I am well pleased." Look to Isaiah xlii. 1, and there you will read of our Lord that he is called "Mine elect, in whom my soul delighteth." This passage is quoted in Matthew xii. 18 in a rather different form—"In whom my soul is well pleased," thus showing how nearly the words agree in all respects. Then comes the last word, "Hear ye him," which is a repetition of Deuteronomy xviii. 15, where Moses saith, "The Lord thy God will raise up unto thee a Prophet from the midst of thee, of thy brethren, like unto me; unto him ye shall hearken;" or as Stephen puts it, "him shall ye hear." The words of Moses are as much imperative as prophetic, and contain the sense,—"hear him."

So that this voice of the Lord utters three Bible words, and surely if the Lord speaks in the language of Scripture, how much more should his servants? We preach best when we preach *the word of God*. We may be confident in what we say when we preach the truth in the words which the Holy Ghost teacheth, and endeavor to convey the mind of the Holy Ghost in his own words. I take it that the scripturalness of the divine witness is noteworthy, and full of instruction.

Coming to the words themselves, the Father said, "*This is my beloved Son.*" "*This.*" As if he called their attention away from Moses and Elias and said, "*This* is he of whom I speak to you. He is above the law and the prophets; he is my Son." There was a question among the Jews who the Messiah should be: they believed in the Messiah, but they did not know when he would come, nor where, nor how; and hence, when he did come, they made a mistake and missed him. Here the great Father points to Jesus of Nazareth, who is the Son of Mary as to his flesh, and he says, "*This* is my beloved Son." It is a word of demonstration and distinction, by which he marks him out from all others as his own nearest and dearest one. By this also he points him out as being present there and then; not as yet to come, but as actually with them, their Master and friend. "*This* is my beloved Son." It is not a finger pointing into history, but a hand laid upon the true Messiah, who in very flesh and blood stood before them, of whom they afterwards said, "We were eyewitnesses of his majesty. For he received from God the Father honor and glory, when there came such a voice to him from the excellent glory, This is my beloved Son, in whom I am well pleased. And this voice which came from heaven we heard, when we were with him in the holy mount." In this very place, upon this Tabor, Jesus stood among them, and the Father pointed him out, saying, "*This* is my beloved Son." They could make no mistake whatever about the person: the word of the Lord so distinctly pointed him out.

While it thus pointed him out personally as being present it separated him from all others, and set him apart by himself as the sole and only one. "*This* is my beloved Son," and no one else may claim that title. Truly, other sons are the Lord's by adoption and regeneration, but none are such in the sense in which the Lord said, "*This* is my beloved Son." Beyond all others and in a special sense he is "the only begotten Son." "Unto which of the angels said he at any time, Thou art my son, this day have I begotten thee?" We do not understand, we cannot understand, the doctrine of the eternal filiation of the Son of God. I suppose it to be well-nigh profane to endeavor to look into that sublime mystery: a holy delicacy forbids; and besides, the glory is too bright: we lack the eyes which could perceive anything in such a blaze of light. This, however, we may observe: namely, that Jesus is not the Son of God so that the idea exactly tallies with sonship among men; for he is co-equal and co-eternal with the Father; and he is himself called "the Mighty God, the everlasting Father." He is not of fewer years than the Father, for "in the beginning was the Word." Concerning this matter we may sing,—

> "Thy generation who can tell,
> Or count the number of thy years?"

Yet doubtless sonship is the nearest approach to the great mystery which could be found among human similitudes, and the word "Son" is the nearest description that could be given in human language. Hence the

Father, looking at Jesus and at none other beside him, says of him, and of him only, "This is my beloved Son." He says, "I proceeded forth and came from God." He is "the only begotten Son," which is in the bosom of the Father. Oh, dear friends, how we ought to fix our gaze upon Jesus! He is a most singular personality, the wonder of wonders, for he is Son of God as truly as he is Son of man. Verily, he is man, and we err not when we so think of him, for he both suffered and died: yet verily he is God, for he liveth for ever and ever, and upholdeth all things by the word of his power.

"This is *my Son*." Moses and Elias were his servants—Jesus alone was his *Son*. By his being thus called *Son* we are taught that Jesus is of the same nature as God—is indeed God. A man is the father of a man; a man is not the father of that which he makes with his own hands, such as a statue or a painting; but a man is the father of another who is of the same nature as himself, and the Lord Jesus Christ is of the same nature as God in all respects—a true Son. The Lord Jesus Christ is equal in nature to the Father, and therefore he counts it not robbery to be equal with God, and he receives the same honor and worship as the Father, as saith the Scripture, "that all men should honor the Son even as they honor the Father. He that honoreth not the Son honoreth not the Father which hath sent him."

A son bears the likeness of his father, and assuredly the Lord Jesus is described as "the brightness of his Father's glory and the express image of his person"; so that he said himself, "He that hath seen me hath seen the Father." "He is the image of the invisible God:" in him is the Godhead better seen than in all the works of creation.

Not only is there a likeness between them, but there

is a perpetual union: "I and my Father are one." "I am in the Father," said Christ, "and the Father in me." This leads to continual communion with each other, and a participation in plans and designs. "The Son can do nothing of himself, but what he seeth the Father do: for what things soever he doeth, these also doeth the Son likewise. For the Father loveth the Son, and showeth him all things that himself doeth." The Lord Jesus was for ever in the bosom of the Father, and he saith, "All things are delivered unto me of my Father: and no man knoweth the Son, but the Father: neither knoweth any man the Father, save the Son, and he to whomsoever the Son will reveal him." It was with the Son of God that the Father took counsel when he said, "Let us make man in our own image, after our likeness." Our Lord knows and reveals the inmost heart of the Father; yea, the being and essence of God, unknown to all besides, are with him, for he himself is "God over all, blessed for ever, Amen." Let us never, brethren, think of the Lord Jesus without the lowliest reverence of him as very God of very God, co-equal, co-eternal with the Father. While we call him Master and Lord let us take care that we render unto him the glory which is due unto his name. There must be no trifling with him, nor with the things which he speaks, for he is Lord of all, and to him every knee shall bow, and every tongue shall confess that he is Lord to the glory of God the Father.

For a minute let me dwell upon this declaration. "This is my Son."—Does it not teach us the great love of God to us guilty creatures? "He spared not his own Son." You perceive the love of Abraham to God when he is ready to offer up Isaac at the Lord's bidding. Remember the words, "Take now thy son, thine only son, Isaac, whom thou lovest, and offer him for a burnt-offering." This is just what the great Father did for us; and yet we were his enemies, living in alienation and in open rebellion against him. Hear, O heavens, and wonder, O earth! he spared not his own Son, but freely delivered him up for us all! "Herein is love, not that we loved God, but that God loved us, and sent his Son to be the propitiation for our sins." What gratitude this should create! What devotion it should bring! "This is my Son." When you see Jesus on Tabor or on Calvary, you see God giving himself to us, that we might not perish, but have everlasting life.

Does the Father say, "This is my Son"? What a Saviour this must be! How confidently may you and I trust him! If the Lord Jesus Christ be no common person, but nothing less than God himself, who shall doubt his power to save? If he be God's only begotten Son, how safely we may trust our souls' affairs in his almighty hands! He is indeed "a Saviour, and a great one!" "It pleased the Father that in him should all fulness dwell." What an intercessor have we! So dear to him with whom he pleads, for he is his beloved Son! What a sacrifice have we that may well cover all our sin, for "he gave himself for us, an offering and a sacrifice to God, for a sweet smelling savor." However black our sin, and however deep our despair, we may readily rise out of it and say, "Verily, there is salvation here!" If the Son of God has made his own person the price of our redemption, then are we indeed redeemed, and none can hold us in bondage.

One thing more is worthy to be noted here. If the Father says, "This is my Son," observe the graciousness of our adoption! With such a son the Lord had no need of children. He did not make us his children because he needed sons, but because we needed a father.

The infinite heart of the Father was well filled by the love of the Only-begotten. There was enough in Jesus to satisfy the love of the divine Father, and yet he would not rest till he had made him " the firstborn among many brethren." Herein we ought to admire exceedingly the grace of God. "Behold what manner of love the Father hath bestowed upon us that we should be called the sons of God." When a man is childless, and desires an heir, it may be that he adopts a child to fill the vacancy which exists in his house; but the heavenly Father had no such want, for he saith, "This is my beloved Son." Our adoption is, therefore, not for his gain, but for ours: it is a matter of divine charity, arising out of the spontaneous love of God. Thanks be unto the Father evermore!

Do you remind me that I have left out one word? The Father said, "This is my *beloved* Son." I have by no means forgotten it, for though I cannot speak as I would upon that word yet it is exceedingly sweet in my ears. "This is my *beloved* Son." We none of us know how much beloved our Lord is of the Father. We love our children, we love them as our own souls, we could not measure our affection for them; but still we are finite and so are our children, and the finite to the finite yields but a finite love; but here is an Infinite Father with an Infinite Son, and he loves him infinitely. Why should he not? He is most near to him: his own Son. Why should he not? He is in all things like unto him in nature, dignity, character, and glory. Why should he not? For he in all things doth his will. Jesus said, "And he that sent me is with me: the Father hath not left me alone; for I do always those things that please him." If we had such a son as God has in Jesus then we should love him indeed, for there has been nothing in the Son throughout eternity which is in the least opposed to the Father's mind. These are wonderful words of the man Christ Jesus—"Therefore doth my Father love me, because I lay down my life, that I might take it again." When Solomon speaks of wisdom, which is but another name for our Lord Jesus, he represents him as saying, "The Lord possessed me in the beginning of his way, before his works of old. I was set up from everlasting, from the beginning, or ever the earth was. When he gave to the sea his decree, that the waters should not pass his commandment: when he appointed the foundations of the earth: then I was by him, as one brought up with him: and I was daily his delight, rejoicing always before him." He has been in the bosom of the Father from of old; and when he left the bosom of the Father it was to do his Father's will and to be obedient to him even unto death. His will and his Father's will are perfectly joined together in one spirit, and therefore we cannot fathom the depths of love which are indicated in these words which came from the Father who himself is love; he, looking at his own Son, saith plainly, "This is my beloved Son." Oh, that we might have grace to trust without wavering in this glorious Son of God!

Permit me now to introduce to you the second of the sentences: "*In whom I am well pleased.*" I have heard it quoted, "With whom I am well pleased." The alteration cannot be tolerated: it robs the language of half its sense. True, God is pleased with Christ, but that is not all that he says here: he is pleased *in* him, which means not only that God is eternally, infinitely pleased with Jesus Christ himself, but that God himself is reconciled and pleased as we view him in his Son. I thought this over last night till my heart seemed ready to dance for joy, for I thought—"then, however much I have displeased the Father, my Lord Jesus, who stands for me, has pleased him more than I have displeased him. Mine is finite sin, but his is infinite righteousness. If my sins have vexed the Lord God, yet Christ's righteousness has pleased him more. I cannot be more than finitely displeasing to God, but Jesus is infinitely pleasing to him; and if he stands in my room, and place, and stead, then the pleasure which the Father derives from his Son is greater than the displeasure which he has ever felt towards me." My brethren, how displeased the great God has been with men. He said that it repented him that he had made men upon the earth. That was a striking expression which is used in Genesis vi. 6: "It grieved him at his heart." He seemed to grow so weary of man's wanton wickedness that he was sorry that he ever made beings capable of so much evil. Yet he is so well content with his beloved Son, who has assumed our nature that we read of him, "The Lord is well pleased for his righteousness' sake: he will magnify the law, and make it honorable." (Is. xlii. 21). The Lord looks down upon those who are in Christ with an intense affection, and loves them even as he loves the Son, for that is the meaning of this word, "In whom I am well pleased." All who are in Christ Jesus are pleasing to God; yea, God in Christ looks with divine satisfaction upon all those who trust his Son: he is not only pleased, but *well* pleased. If you are pleased with Jesus, God is pleased with you: if you are in the Son, then you are in the Father's good pleasure. Out of Christ there is nothing but divine displeasure for you. Concerning you who are out of Christ it is written, "The Lord will take vengeance on his adversaries." Who can stand before his indignation? Who can abide the fierceness of his anger? He cannot look on sin without hatred. He says of sinners, "My soul loathed them, and their soul also abhorred me." There is no peace between a Christless soul and God, neither can there be. But when a poor sinner by faith enters into Christ, then such is the Father's delight in Christ's person, that he delights in all that are in him. Jesus said, "The Father himself loveth you." God is pleased with every hair of Christ's head: the meanest member of Christ's body is delightful to the Father. If I am pleased with a man, I am not angry with his foot or with any part of him. So, then, if I am a member of Christ, if I am joined unto him by a living, loving, lasting union, then I am well-pleasing unto God, because Jesus is well-pleasing to him. Indeed, the Scripture speaketh of all saints as one with Christ; they are so perfectly joined unto him that they are one body with him, and God has not hatred to some part of the body and love to another part of it. Is Christ divided? It cannot be. The Father is well pleased with the entire mystical body for the sake of Jesus Christ its head. I wish I could speak at length upon this; but I might weary you upon this close and sultry day, when your spirit truly is willing but your flesh is weak. Oh, the charm of this voice of God! Each word has divine emphasis upon it. It is not the voice of a man, but of the Eternal himself. "This is my beloved Son, in whom I am well pleased."

Consider, next, the third word, which is, "*Hear ye him*." Listen to what he says; remember it carefully; endeavor to understand it; heartily accept and believe it; confidently trust in it, and cheerfully obey it. All these precepts are wrapt up in the expression " Hear ye him"; as we could prove if there were time available. " Hear ye him": it is as if the Father said, "You need not hear Moses any longer; hear ye *him*. You need not listen to Elias any more; hear ye my Son." There are thousands of priests in the world who say, "Hear us"; but the Father says, "Hear *him*." Many voices clamor for our attention: new philosophies, modern theologies, and old heresies revived, all call to us and entreat us to hearken, but the Father says, "Hear *him*." As if he said, "Hear him and none besides." Does any man claim to be a successor of Christ? The Father speaks of no succession, but bids us, "Hear *him*." If Jesus were dead and his prophetic office extinct we might hear others; but since he liveth, we hear the celestial voice rolling along the ages and distinctly crying, "Hear ye *him*." Brethren beloved, do not hear *m* as though I spake of myself, for I have no more claim upon your attention than any other man. I speak faultily, for I know but in part, and prophesy in part. So far as I speak my own mind, I speak in vanity; but if I speak the words of Christ, and the truth which the Spirit of God has revealed, then it is no longer I that speak, but Christ himself that speaks, and then you are bound by the word from the Father, which saith, "Hear ye *him*." Oh, to be content with hearing Christ, and letting other voices go away into the eternal silence. Is he God's Son? Then "hear him." Is he God's beloved Son? Then "hear him." Is the Father well pleased with him? Then "hear him." Is the Father well pleased in him, and with you in him? Then "hear him." What less can you do? Ought you not to do this always, and with all your might? Peter, you need not build the tabernacles: the Father bids you hear Jesus, your Lord. It is better to hear Christ, that is, to believe his teaching and obey it, than it would be to build cathedrals for him, much more such frail tents as Peter intended. Peter, you need not cumber yourself with much serving, and play the Martha; you will do better if you sit at his feet with Mary and *hear* him. The highest honor we can render to Christ as a prophet is to hear him, trusting him in his promises and obeying him in his precepts. Jesus came on purpose to teach, and we are in our best position for adoration when we lend him our ears and hearts, and are determined to believe what he says, and to do what he commands.

"This is my beloved Son: hear ye him." It does seem to me as if the great Father said, "*I* have spoken to you once, with my own voice, and I see you fall upon your faces with fear; evidently you cannot bear my immediate presence. I see your faces blanched with fright; you lie prone upon the ground, stiff with dismay: I will speak no more directly from myself; I have made my beloved Son your Mediator; hear *him*." The Psalmist David said, "The voice of the Lord is powerful; the voice of the Lord is full of majesty. The voice of the Lord shaketh the wilderness; the Lord shaketh the wilderness of Kadesh." Is it not gracious on his part that he should no more speak with us himself, but reveal himself by his Son, whose name is "*the Word of God*"? Remember what Israel said at Sinai to Moses, the typical mediator: "Speak thou with us and we will hear; but let not God speak with us, lest we die." To this the Lord replied to Moses, "They have well said all that they have spoken." The Lord recognized at once the need of a mediator, and he finds us one in the person of the Well-beloved as he says, "Hear ye *him*." It is like Pharaoh saying to those who came for corn, "Go unto Joseph." This day God saith to men, "Come not to me at the first: go to my Son. No man cometh to the Father but by Jesus Christ his Son. I will not speak with you, for you are but dust and ashes, and you would be overwhelmed by the thunder of my voice. Hear ye HIM."

Blessed ordinance of that gracious One who knoweth our frame and remembereth that we are dust! He hath spoken to us by his Son: let us incline our ear and come unto him, let us hear that our soul may live.

This links on the first part of my discourse to the second, upon which I will speak as briefly as I can, though the subject might well demand a full sermon.

II. Secondly, LET US HEAR THE VOICE OF JESUS. The Father himself has sent us to Jesus, and unto Jesus let us go.

"When the disciples heard it, they fell on their face, and were sore afraid. And Jesus came and touched them, and said, Arise, and be not afraid." Dear friends, I think you will be cured of desiring miracles, and of wishing to hear voices from God, if you well consider the effect of the Divine voice upon these favored apostles. You could not bear the voice divine any better than they could; if, indeed, so well. I hope that you will now be content with what the Father recommends to you, namely, that you hear his beloved Son Jesus Christ our Lord. The apostles, one would have thought, needed not to have been afraid, for they were holy men; engaged in the best possible business, and in the company of their Lord who was their protector and friend; and yet such is the amazing power of the glory of God upon the human mind that they fell on their faces. So was it with Job, and Daniel, and Isaiah, and Habakkuk, and all such holy men: the presence of the Lord filled them with fear and trembling and self-abhorrence.

See how Jesus acts to his three disciples. We might have thought that they would have hastened to their Lord. Why did they not? Why did they not cry out to him, "Master, we perish?" Why did not Peter say, as he did on another occasion, "If it be thou, bid me to come unto thee?" No; they are overpowered, bewildered, confounded: the glory of the Lord has laid them on their faces as dead, and a sore fright is upon them. Then the incarnate God, their Lord and yet their brother, interposes his sacred ministry. First, *he comes to them.* Wycliffe's version puts it, "He came nigh." He approached to them; for any distance is painful when a heart is afraid. Jesus came near to the affrighted three. This is the beauty of our Lord Jesus Christ, that he comes so near to us, poor troubled ones, when we are overwhelmed with the glory of God and our own sense of sin. "The man is near of kin unto us: one of our next kinsmen." God, the glorious, must ever seem to be far off as to our weakness, however near he comes to us in condescending grace. He is in heaven, and we upon earth; he is the Creator, and we are the creatures of an hour. The Lord Jesus comes so very near to us because he bears our nature, and is bone of our bone and flesh of our flesh. We may be familiar with him, and yet incur no censure. Little children climbed his knee, and he said, "Suffer the little children to come unto me." We feel that we may come where children are welcomed; yea, we rejoice that when we cannot come to him, our Lord Jesus comes to us, and when our weakness makes us fall upon the ground, he stoops over us to help us up. His sympathy makes him quick to draw near, and calm our troubled breasts. When a child falls, how fast the mother runs to set it on its feet again. Yet she is not more in haste than Jesus, who leaves not his own to remain long in their distress. He draws very near to his poor, fainting, swooning disciples. He will not leave them comfortless, he will come unto them. He is the same Christ at this hour as in the days of his flesh: he is still in the habit of visiting his people and manifesting himself to them as he doth not to the world. Brothers, do not ask evidence any more; do not begin searching books to find out arguments and reasons. Ask Jesus to come to you: his presence will stand in stead of all reasoning, and be better far. Communion with Christ supplies the soul with irresistible arguments as to his being, his love, his power, his Godhead. Actual nearness to him clothes the mind with a coat of mail which wards off every arrow of unbelief. Let Christ come to us, and questions and doubts are heard no more. Quibblings are nailed to his cross; insinuations fall dead at his feet. This assurance works in an infinitely better manner than if out of yon black cloud God himself were to speak to us in thunder-tones.

When Jesus came, the next thing he did was, *he touched them*. This is to me most precious: as they lie there all fainting he touches Peter, and touches James, and touches John, just as in after days we read, "He laid his right hand upon me, saying unto me, Fear not." That was his way of healing those diseased with leprosy. The blind man he touched and gave him sight, and the dead maiden was thus revived. Oh, the power of his touch! Our touch of Jesus saves us; what will not his touch of us do? We are so much made up of feeling, after all, that we want to know that the Lord really feels for us, and will enter so tenderly into our case as to touch us. That touch reassures our fainting hearts, and we know our Lord to be Emmanuel, God with us. Sympathy! This is the meaning of that human touch of a hand which is nevertheless divine. Oh, how sweetly Christ has touched us by being a partaker in all that is human! He touched us everywhere: in poverty, for he had not where to lay his head: in thirst, for he sat by the well and said, "Give me to drink:" in anguish, for he was betrayed by his friend.

He has touched us in depression of spirit, for he cried, "My soul is exceeding sorrowful even unto death." He is touched with a feeling of our infirmities, "for he was tempted in all points like as we are." An absolute God does not seem to touch us with a fellow-feeling: he pities us as a father pitieth his children, yet in this he is above us, and our fears prevent our reaching up to him: for tenderest sympathy in adversity a brother must be born, and Jesus is that brother. We are frail and sinful; and Jesus touches us in both respects, for he has taken our flesh and carried away our sins. He was "numbered with the transgressors," thus he touched transgressors; and he became frail even as we are, until at last he said, "I am a worm, and no man"; thus he touched our infirmities. Dear friends, nothing so cheers the heart as the divine touch of Christ, for if you have felt it you will bear witness that contact with his wondrous person is like life from the dead. Virtue comes out of Christ to us when his garment's hem and our finger meet. The contact of grace on his part and faith on our part brings into us strength, light, joy, and all else that is laid up in Jesus to meet our wants. The hand of Jesus is laid upon us, and in the strength which it gives a man might dash through hell and climb to heaven. Ezra said, "I was strengthened as the hand of the Lord my God was upon me." Touched with the almighty Sufferer's sacred sympathy, we glory in tribulation, and triumph in death. Is not this more effective evidence of the truth of the gospel and of the commission of Christ than if the Lord God should again speak out of a cloud? To feel the wondrous power of Christ strengthening our hearts, surely this is the most certain witness.

Next time you read of the Red Sea, and of God's dividing it for his people, and drowning Pharaoh in the deep waters, do not say to yourself, "I wish I had been there!" but pray God to make a way for you through your troubles, and to dry up the Red Sea of your sins, and lead you into Canaan. Pardoned sin will make you rejoice in him. It must have been a fine demonstration of God's glorious majesty when he sent a thick darkness over all the land, even darkness that might be felt. For my part I count it a more-to-be-desired demonstration of the power of God when he took away my thick darkness and brought me into his marvellous light. When he turned all the waters of Egypt into blood, so that they loathed to drink of the river, it was a sure proof that God was there; but to my soul it was a more assuring proof when he turned my water into wine, and made my ordinary life to become like the life of those in heaven by his sovereign grace. He has raised us up together from the depths of our natural ruin, and made us sit together in the heavenly places,—is not this as great a proof of his power and Godhead as when he raised up Israel from the brick-kilns, and set his people free? It was a sure proof of God's being in Egypt when he called for the frogs, and they came, even into the king's chambers; but what a proof of his being with us is given to our mind when the Lord sweeps out of our soul all the frogs of fear that used to croak within us, even in the king's chambers of devotion and communion. We could not worship God for their croaking, but everywhere we were defiled and disturbed with doubts and fears, and when Jesus comes and clears them all away it is a kindlier proof and more effectual to the heart than a thousand plagues could be. So there were two actions of Christly sympathy—Jesus came near, and touched them.

But always the great thing with Jesus is his word—*he spake to them.* He is the Word, and as the Word he proves his Godhead. "Where the word of a king is, there is power." Jesus, after he had touched them, said, "Arise, be not afraid." Precious word! "Arise, be not afraid." When the word of Jesus Christ comes with power to our discouraged souls, and we are made strong in confidence, then we are persuaded of the truth of the gospel. When we are disabled from the divine service through fear, and Jesus renews our strength by saying, "Arise," so that we are able to work again, then do we believe and are sure, "The joy of the Lord is our strength." Whenever the blessed Comforter reveals Christ to us so that we are cheered and made glad in the midst of our tribulations, then we need not ask for signs and wonders, nor for voices speaking out of the cloud: it is enough, the truth is sealed in our consciences. The voice of Christ is better far than all other manifestations, for it does not leave us swooning with fear, but sends us out to fight the battles of the Lord.

This is the sum of what I have spoken unto you. Ask not signs and wonders which God will not give; but, "Hear ye him." Listen to Jesus by faith, and your personal experience of his presence shall be to you all that you need by way of assurance. Live on Christ, live in Christ, live with Christ, and this shall be better to you than visions or bright clouds, or celestial voices, or all supposable evidences. This shall make your spirit leap and your heart rejoice, till the day break and the shadows flee away, and you see God, even the Father, face to face in glory. May the grace of our Lord Jesus Christ be with you evermore. Amen.

XIV.

ACCEPTED OF THE GREAT FATHER.

July 15, 1883.

"He hath made us accepted in the beloved."—EPHESIANS i. 6.

A FEW Sabbath mornings ago I spoke to you upon those memorable words of the great Father, "This is my beloved Son, in whom I am well pleased." We now go a step farther, and see how the love of God to his beloved Son overflows, and runs like a river of life to all those who are in Christ Jesus. To him he saith, "This is my beloved Son," and then he turns to all who are in union with him and says, "These also are my beloved for his sake." As believers we are assured by the text that we are "accepted *in the Beloved*," to the praise of the glory of God's grace. Why is that peculiar title here used? It might have been said, we are accepted in Christ, or accepted in the Mediator; there must be some motive for giving him this special name in this place. The motive is declared to be that we may praise the glory of divine grace. God did not want for a beloved when he made us his beloved: his heart was not pining for an object; his affections were not lone and desolate. His only-begotten Son was his delight, and there was room enough in him for all the Father's love; it was *we* that needed to be loved, and so the Beloved is mentioned that we may remember the unselfishness of divine grace. He makes us his beloved, but he had a Beloved before.

We are also reminded that we are "accepted in the Beloved" to let us know that God has not shifted his love—his first beloved is his Beloved still. We have not supplanted his dear Son, nor even diverted a beam of love from him. The Lord has called us beloved who were not so, and made us a people who were not a people; but he has not withdrawn a grain of love from Jesus, whom he still calls "mine elect, in whom my soul delighteth." All the infinite love of God still flows to Jesus, and then to us in him. It pleased the Father that to him a fulness of love should be given, that out of it we might each one receive. God's love to us is his love to his Son flowing in a hundred channels. For his sake he makes the wedding-feast, and we are the happy guests who sit at the table. Not for our sakes is this done, but for Jesus' sake, that so it might be all of grace. His perpetual acceptance with God is our acceptance, that nothing legal, nothing whereof we might boast, might be mingled with the work of sovereign grace.

We are "accepted in the Beloved." Do you not love that sweet title? Is it not the highest quality of the acceptance, that it comes through such an One? He is beloved in the highest conceivable degree by the Father, and in this you imitate the great God, for to you also the Lord Jesus is altogether lovely. He is your Beloved as well as God's Beloved, and this is one proof that you are accepted; for all who truly love the Son are approved by the Father. Thus saith the Scripture: "Because he hath set his love upon me, therefore will I deliver him: I will set him on high because he hath known my name." Is Christ your Beloved? Then, as he is the Father's Beloved, you and the Father have evidently come to a sweet agreement; you have come to look at things from the same standpoint as the glorious Jehovah; the Lord and you evidently have a mutual interest in one common person—the incarnate God. Your recognition of Christ as your Beloved is thus a sure proof that you are accepted in the Beloved. See you not this? It is because he is the Father's Beloved that the Father loves you in him, and because he is your Beloved therefore you have an evidence within yourself that you have come to an agreement with the Father, and so to an acceptance by him. I delight in being *accepted* all the more because therein I am still further linked with him who joins God and man in one grand affection.

God's love of his dear Son covers all believers, as a canopy covers all who come beneath it. As a hen covereth her chickens with her wings, so God's love to Christ covers all the children of promise. As the sun shining forth from the gates of the morning gilds all the earth with golden splendor, so this great love of God to the Well-beloved, streaming forth to him, enlightens all who are in him. God is so boundlessly pleased with Jesus that in him he is altogether well pleased with us. Oh, the joy of this blending of our interests with those of the Well-beloved! I scarcely know whither I am borne even by a single word of my precious text.

Let this stand for our preface, and now let us come close to our subject, upon which I do not desire so much to descant myself as to lead you individually to meditate, and personally to feed. I would much rather put the text into your mouths as a sweet fruit from the garden of the Lord, most mellow and ripe, than be judged myself to handle it well. I seek not to exhibit my own skill in words, but I long that you may be refreshed with the marrow and fatness of the choice word. I desire that you may this morning experimentally enjoy the precious drop of honey from the rock Christ Jesus which

is contained in the four words—"Accepted in the
Beloved." Oh that the Holy Spirit may make you enter
into the treasures which they contain!

I. I will begin by treating the text by way of CON-
TRAST. Brethren and sisters, the grace of God hath made
us to be this day "accepted in the Beloved"; but it was
not always so. As many of us as have, through grace,
believed in Christ are now, to a certainty, at this very
moment "accepted in the Beloved"; but in times past
it was very different. It is not a matter of question, nor
of imagination, nor of sentiment; but a matter of fact,
declared by the Holy Ghost himself, that the Lord hath
"made us accepted in the Beloved"; but it was far
otherwise a little while ago. What a contrast is our
present condition of acceptance to our position under
the law through Adam's fall. By actual sin we made
ourselves to be the very reverse of accepted, for we were
utterly refused. It might have been said of us, "Reprobate silver shall men call them, because God hath rejected them." Our way was contrary to God's way, our
thoughts were not his thoughts, our hearts were not
according to his heart. Oh, if he had dealt with us then
after our sins what must have become of us? At that
time we were condemned, "condemned already," because we had not believed on the Son of God. We had
no acceptableness before God; he could take no complacency in us; his pure and holy eyes could not look upon
us, we were so full of everything that provoked him to
jealousy; but now we are—(oh, let me pronounce it like
music!)—"accepted in the Beloved." The criminal is
now a child, the enemy is now a friend, the condemned
one is now justified. Mark, it is not said that we are
"acceptable," though that were a very great thing, but
we are actually accepted; it has become not a thing pos-

sible that God might accept us, but he has accepted us in Christ. Lay this to your soul, and may it fill you with delight. The Lord has chosen you; he has received you to himself, and set his love upon you, and his delight is in you now. What a contrast from what you were a season ago in your own consciousness, in your own judgment. Refresh your memories a little. If you passed through the same state of mind as I did, you loathed your very selves in the sight of God; you felt that God must abhor you, for you abhorred yourselves; you saw sin to be exceeding sinful, and that sinful thing was permeating your entire being, saturating your thoughts, putrefying your aims, making you to be corrupt and offensive in the sight of the Most High. I know I felt that if the Lord swept me away with the besom of destruction, and cast me into the lowest hell, I well deserved it. But now that condemnation is no more to be dreaded; we receive not the spirit of bondage, but the spirit of adoption. Lift up your eyes out of the thick darkness, and behold the light. You, who in your own judgment were cast away for ever; you, who thought that the Lord would never be favorable to you, nor blot out your sins, are this day accepted, "accepted in the Beloved." No contrast could be more sharp and clear, and no reflections could be more joyful than this contrast suggests to the heart.

Think, again, of the contrast between what you are now and what you would have been had not grace stepped in. Left out of Christ as we then were, we might at this time have been going from sin to sin, revelling and rioting in it, as so many do: we might at this moment have been sinning with a high hand, finding even in the Sabbath-day a special opportunity for double transgression. In our daring rebellion we might have been crying, "The better the day the better the deed," and so might have shown how completely we had thrown off the yoke of allegiance to the great King. Ay, by this time we might have been dead, as the result of our own sins. The measure of our iniquity might have been full, and we might have been in hell. Be startled, my soul, at this thought, that nothing but infinite longsuffering has kept thee out of the pit that is bottomless, "where their worm dieth not, and their fire is not quenched." But, brothers, we are not in hell, and, what is more, we never shall be, for those iron gates can never close upon a soul that is "accepted in the Beloved," and that is our condition now. We have fled for refuge to the hope set before us, and now no more need we be in terror of the great white throne and the righteous Judge, and the stern sentence, "Depart, ye cursed." Clinging to the cross, and beholding ourselves covered with the righteousness of Christ, we know that we are saved, and, what is far more, we are *accepted*. This blessed fact is true of those who might have been among the damned. Our laments might have been going up to-day amidst the wailings of the wretched who are eternally cast away from hope; and now, instead thereof, we lift the joyful song of praise unto our God, and bless and magnify his name in whom we are accepted this day. Oh, my soul, sing thou thine own song to thy Beloved—

> "Just as thou art—how wondrous fair,
>   Lord Jesus, all thy members are!
>   A life divine to them is given—
>   A long inheritance in heaven.
>
> "Just as I was I came to thee,
>   An heir of wrath and misery;
>   Just as thou art before the throne,
>   I stand in righteousness thine own.

> "Just as thou art—nor doubt, nor fear,
> Can with thy spotlessness appear;
> Oh timeless love! as thee, I'm seen,
> The 'righteousness of God in him.'"

One more point I cannot quite pass over, and that is, the contrast between what we now are and all we ever could have been in the most favorable circumstances apart from the Beloved. If it had been possible for us out of Christ to have had desires after righteousness, yet those desires would all have run in a wrong direction; we should have had a zeal of God, but not according to knowledge, and so, going about to establish our own righteousness, we should not have submitted ourselves to the righteousness of God. We should have been weaving a righteousness of our own with heavy labor, which would have proved no better when completed than a cobweb that could never conceal our nakedness. At this moment the prayers we offered would never have been received at the throne; the praises we presented would have been an ill savor unto God; all that we could have aimed to accomplish in the matter of good words, had we striven to our utmost, would have been done in wilfulness and pride, and so must necessarily have fallen short of acceptance. We should have heard the voice of the Eternal saying, "Bring no more vain oblations; incense is an abomination unto me"; for out of Christ our righteousness is as unacceptable as our unrighteousness, and all our attempts to merit acceptance increase our unworthiness. Oh, strive as ye will, ye self-righteous; labor as ye may after a righteousness of your own, what can come of it but confusion? Whence is it that the people labor as in the very fire? This shall they have at the Lord's hands— they shall lie down in sorrow. The bed is shorter than that a man may stretch himself on it, and the covering is narrower than that a man may wrap himself in it. Woe is unto the man who is out of Christ, wherever he may be. In any case the wrath of God abideth on him. But we are not out of Christ, we are not striving in vain, we are not spending our strength for naught, for here is the blessed contrast, we are "accepted in the Beloved."

A touch of the black pencil brings out the bright lights, and therefore I have laid on these shades. Such were some of you, but now ye are washed, now ye are sanctified, now ye are justified, now ye are "accepted in the Beloved." All glory be unto the grace by which we have received this heavenly benefit.

II. Secondly, we will say a little by way of EXPLANATION, that the text may sink yet deeper into your hearts, and afford you richer enjoyment. Recollect, brethren, that once we were pitied of God as poor, lost, self-destroyed creatures: that was in a degree hopeful. We were chosen of God while in that pitiable condition, and although forlorn, wretched, and ruined, yet were we marked by his electing love—this was still more encouraging. Then came a time of dealing with us, and we were pardoned, our transgressions were put away, we were renewed in the spirit of our minds by the Holy Ghost, and the righteousness of Christ was imputed to us, and at length burst forth the light of this word, " He hath made us accepted in the Beloved." Much went before this, but, oh, what a morning without clouds rose upon us when we knew our acceptance and were assured thereof. Acceptance was the watchword, and had troops of angels met us we should have rejoiced that we were as blest as they.

Understand that this acceptance comes to us entirely as a work of God—" He hath made us accepted in the

Beloved." We never made ourselves acceptable, nor could we have done so, but he that made us first in creation, hath now new made us by his grace, and so hath made us accepted in the Beloved.

That this was an act of pure grace there can be no doubt, for the verse runs thus, "*Wherein* he hath made us accepted in the Beloved"—that is, in his grace. There was no reason in ourselves why we should have been put into Christ, and so accepted; the reason lay in the heart of the Eternal Father himself. He will have mercy on whom he will have mercy, and by this will we were saved. To the great First Cause we must ever trace the motive for our acceptance. Grace reigns supreme. It is a gracious acceptance of those who but for grace had been rejected. Do notice this, and dwell upon the truth, glorifying God therein. Again, our acceptance is "*in the Beloved.*" It is only as we are in Christ that we are accepted. Let no man steal out of Christ, and then say, "God has accepted me." Nothing of the kind. If the Lord views you apart from Christ, whoever you may be, you are a thing to be consumed, and not to be accepted. "In the Beloved," that is, as it were, within the gates of the city of refuge. You must abide within that wall of fire of which the cross is the centre, or else you are not accepted. You must remain within the arms of the Well-beloved, living in the very heart of Christ, and then you shall know yourself to be "accepted in the Beloved." For Christ's sake, and because you are a part of him, you shall be approved of the Father. He has taken you into covenant union, so that you can say with the favored apostle, "Truly our fellowship is with the Father and with his Son Jesus Christ." Therefore the Father accepts you, because he cannot dissociate you from his Son, nor his Son from you, nor think of Christ without you, nor of you without Christ; hence it is you are "accepted in the Beloved." That explains the words.

The following remarks may make the sense somewhat more transparent. No man, my brethren, can be accepted of God while he is guilty of sin, so that our acceptance in the Beloved involves the fact that our sin at this moment is for ever put away. Covered is our unrighteousness, and therefore from condemnation we are free, and we are accepted. Realize this truth. It does not require any oratory to set it forth; it needs only that your faith should fully apprehend it. Realize that you are forgiven to-day. With your eye upon the wounds of Christ, say unto your soul by the Spirit, " I am without spot or wrinkle in the sight of God; for Christ hath washed me whiter than the driven snow." He has said of his people, " Ye are clean every whit." Rejoice in this. You could not be accepted if he had not made you clean, for the filthy are not accepted of the Lord.

Neither could God accept a man devoid of righteousness. A mere colorless person, whose sin was forgiven, but who had no righteousness, could not be acceptable with him. I cannot suppose the existence of such a being; but if there were such, he would be like one who was neither cold nor hot, and must be spewed out of God's mouth. He that is accepted with God must be positively righteous. Very well, then, if he has made believers "accepted in the Beloved," they that believe in Christ are righteous in the sight of God. Mark you, they are not righteous with a sham righteousness, an imaginary, fictitious righteousness; no, the righteousness which is of faith is the most real righteousness under heaven. The righteousness of works may be questioned, but the righteousness of faith cannot be, for it is the righteousness of God himself. Now drink that in. Do not let me hold it up, and show you what a draught it is; but drink it up for yourselves. You are righteous in Christ, or else you could not be accepted. Sin is gone, and righteousness is positively yours.

Now to come back again. If we be indeed "accepted *in the Beloved*," does it not show how close, how real our union with the Beloved must be? Do we even share in Christ's acceptance with God? Then we are one with him in everything. Here is a father who has no particular interest in such and such a woman, but his son takes to himself that woman to be his wife, and now the loving father says, "That woman is my daughter," and so she is received into his love for his son's sake. He says to her; "You are my dear son's wife; therefore you are my daughter, and dear to me, and welcome to my house at any time." Thus it is with the great God. He says to us, whom Christ has espoused unto himself, that we may be his bride in blessed conjugal union for ever and ever, "Come to my heart, my children, for he is my Son, and I love you for his sake; I accept you in him." Is not that a wonderful union, closer than the marriage bond, which causes us to share in Christ's righteousness, so that the holy God can say to us who are sinful by nature, "You are acceptable to me because of your connection with my Son"? If a woman of base character were married to the best of men it would not make her acceptable. A father would scarcely know what to do with such a daughter-in-law: we should try and carry out our relationship as far as we could with all kindness, but we could hardly say that such a person brought into our family by marriage would be acceptable to us; but, oh, the Lord sees his people so wrapped up in Christ that he must accept them in him. If I accept a man, I cannot quarrel with his little finger; if I accept a man, I accept his whole body: and so, since the Father accepts Christ, he accepts every member of his mystical body. If I am one with Christ, though I be but as it were only the sole of his foot, and exposed oftentimes to the mire of the streets, yet, because the glorious Head is accepted, the meanest member joined in living union to that Head is accepted too. Is not this glorious? Can you get a firm hold of it? Unless you intelligently grasp its full significance you will not heartily enjoy this unspeakable privilege. But if your faith receives and welcomes it, you will not need any further explanation. You are "accepted in the Beloved," and it is clear that there is a blessed union between you and Christ. The acceptance which the Father gives to Christ he gives to you. Now, see if you can measure it. How acceptable is Christ to God? Must it not be an infinite acceptance?-for it is an infinite Being infinitely accepting an infinitely holy and well-pleasing One, and then accepting us who are in him with the self-same acceptance. Oh, how acceptable is every believer to the eternal Father in Christ Jesus!

III. Can we get a step farther? Will the Holy Spirit help us while I say a few words by way of ENLARGEMENT? If we are "accepted in the Beloved," then, first, our persons are accepted: we ourselves are well-pleasing to him. God looks upon us now with pleasure. Once he said of men that it repented him that he had made them, but now when he looks at his people he never repents that he made us; he is glad he made us, he takes delight in us. Look at your own children; sometimes they grieve you, but still you are pleased with them; it is a pleasure to have them near you; and if they are long out of your sight you grow anxious about them. They are coming home for their holidays soon: they are glad to return home, and I am sure their mothers are glad at the thought of seeing them again. Our Father is as truly pleased with us: our very persons are accepted of God. He delights in us individually; he thinks of us with joy, and when we are near to him it gives pleasure to his great heart.

Being ourselves accepted, the right of access to Him is given us. When a person is accepted with God he may come to God when he chooses; he is one of those sheep who may go in and out and find pasture; he is one of those courtiers who may come even to the royal throne and meet with no rebuff. No chamber of our great Father's house is closed against us; no blessing of the covenant is withheld from us; no sweet smile of the Father's face is refused us. He that accepted us gives us access into all blessings. "See, I have accepted thee concerning this thing also." You remember the story of King Ahasuerus and his poor trembling spouse Esther, how she ventured in at the peril of her life, for if her royal lord and master did not stretch out the golden sceptre then the guards that stood about the throne would cut her down, the queen royal though she was, for daring to come unbidden into the despot's presence; but to-day, when you and I come to God, we have no fear of that kind, because we are accepted first; he hath already stretched out to us the golden sceptre, and he bids us come boldly. All is well between us and him. We have access with boldness into this grace wherein we stand.

And, being accepted ourselves, our prayers are also accepted. Children of God, can you sincerely believe this? Do you not sometimes pray as if you were beggars in the street, pleading with unwilling persons to give you a gratuity of coppers? I believe many children of God do so; but when we know we are "accepted in the Beloved" we speak to God with a sweet confidence, expecting him to answer us. To us it is no surprise that our heavenly Father should hear our prayers. He does it so often and so generously that we expect him to do so always. It is a way of his to hear the prayers of the Well-beloved. When unaccepted men pray they pray unaccepted prayers, and when accepted men plead with God he says, "In an acceptable time have I heard thee, and in a day of salvation have I succored thee." When God delights in men he gives them the desires of their hearts. Oh, the splendor of that man's position who is "accepted in the Beloved!" To him the Lord seems to say, "Ask what thou wilt, and it shall be given to thee, not even to the half of my kingdom, but my kingdom itself shall be thine: thou shalt sit with me upon my throne." Oh, the blessedness of being "accepted in the Beloved," because the acceptance makes our prayers to be as sweet incense before the Lord!

It follows, then, as a pleasant sequence, that our gifts are accepted, for those who are accepted with God find a great delight in giving of their substance to the glory of his name. I know that when money is wanted for the church of God, and one of the brethren goes round to collect the offerings, the subjects of the kingdom are wont to say, "Here comes the tax-gatherer again." Yes, that is what the subjects say. Oh, but when the children are about, they cry, "Here is another opportunity of presenting an offering to our Father, a welcome occasion of proving that our love to him is pure, without greed or grudging." They clap their hands to think that they may come before the Lord with their sacrifices. Their only question is, "Will he accept it? Oh, what would I not give if I did but know that he would accept it!" Many a poor woman will take her two mites, and not more stealthily than joyfully cast them into the treasury, as she says, "Will he really accept them when dropped into the offering-box; will he even know about them?" And some of God's children get schemes into their heads of doing great things for God, but they say, "May I not after all be working for myself? May it not be that pride and vain-glory so leaven my labors that 'the odor of a sweet smell,' like to that 'sacrifice acceptable' which the Philippians presented, will be all a-wanting." Nay, my friends, my helpers in every good work, you need not ask that question if he has accepted you, for the accepted man brings an accepted offering. It is wonderful how God sees good things in his people where we cannot see them. He saw in Abijah some good thing towards the Lord God of Israel when perhaps no one else saw it. Mistress Sarah once made a rather naughty speech; yet there was one good word in it. I doubt very much if any one of us would have been quick enough to discern it. Yet the Holy Spirit picked out that one word, and put it into the New Testament to her praise. She spoke unbelievingly as to her bearing a child at her advanced age, though the promise was pronounced that she should bring forth a son. She said, "Shall it be, I being old, my lord being old also?" This was a bad speech, but we are somewhat startled to read in the New Testament, "As Sarah also obeyed her husband calling him lord." If God can find a speck of good in us he will. Then let us try what we can do for him. Here is a great lump of quartz, but if the Lord can see a grain of gold he will save the quartz for the sake of it. He says, "Destroy it not, for a blessing is in it." I do not mean that the Lord deals thus with all men. It is only for accepted men that he has this kind way of accepting their gifts. Had you seen me when a young man, and an usher, walking through the streets with rolls of drawings from a boys' school, you would have guessed that I considered them of no value and fit only to be consigned to the fire; but I always took a great interest in the drawings of my own boy, and I still think them rather remarkable. You smile, I dare say, but I do so think, and my judgment is as good as yours. I value them because they are his, and I think I see budding genius in every touch, but you do not see it because you are so blind. I see it since love has opened my eyes. God can see in his people's gifts to him and their works for him a beauty which no eyes but his can perceive. Oh, if he so treats our poor service, what ought we not to do for him? What zeal, what alacrity should stimulate us! If we are ourselves accepted our sacrifices shall be acceptable. The Almighty will permit us to be called his servants, and we shall find his blessing resting on all that we do. If the tree be good the fruit is good. As is the man, so is his strength; and as is his prestige, so is his power. "Accepted in the Beloved" has for its accompaniment "God hath accepted thy works."

IV. We have thus pursued our train of thought in a contrast, an explanation, and an enlargement; let us now indulge in a few REFLECTIONS.

"Accepted in the Beloved." May not each believer talk thus with himself—I have my sorrows and griefs, I have my aches and pains, and weaknesses, but I must not repine, for God accepts me. Ah me! How one can laugh at griefs when this sweet word comes in, "accepted in the Beloved." I may be blind, but I am "accepted in the Beloved:" I may be lame, I may be poor, I may be despised, I may be persecuted, I may have much to put up with in many ways, but really these troubles of the flesh count for little or nothing to me since I am "accepted in the Beloved."

I have to mourn over a multitude of infirmities and imperfections, and there is never a day but what when night comes on I have repenting work to do, and feel compelled to fly to the precious blood again for a renewed sense of pardon. Yes, but I am "accepted in the Beloved." Ah me, I have been struggling with this evil and that, and I hope I have got the victory, though I have had many a wound in the battle; yes, but I am "accepted in the Beloved." I have just now been blaming myself for my shortcomings, and mourning over my many slips and failures; yes, but I am "accepted in the Beloved." I am speaking for you, or at least I am trying to interpret your meditations; I want you to let this blessed fact go down sweetly with you, that whatever may be the trials of life, whatever the burdens that oppress you, whatever the difficulties of the way, whatever the infirmities of the body, whatever the frailties of the mind, yet still, as being "in the Beloved" you are accepted. Oh, will you not be accepted when you stand where golden harps ring out perpetual hallelujahs, where every robe is spotless, and every heart is sinless? Yes, but you will not be a jot more accepted *then* than you are now, in all this noise, and strife, and turmoil of every-day life, for you are "accepted in the Beloved" *now*. Is not this present grace in the highest perfection? What more can you have till you behold the unveiled face of infinite love. Drink down that truth, I pray you.

Let a further reflection be added also to the sweetness of your enjoyment. Think of who it is that doth accept you. It is no common person who admits us to his favor; it is the God whose name is Jehovah, the jealous God. "Holy, holy, holy," cry the seraphim unceasingly, and nothing that is defiled can ever enter his palace-gates, nor can his heart endure the thought of iniquity, and yet it is he that hath accepted you. Did your brethren cast you out? Did your friend condemn you? Did your own heart accuse you? Did the devil roar upon you? What matters it, for he hath accepted you. "Who shall lay anything to the charge of God's elect? It is God that justifieth. Who is he that condemneth?" He hath made us "accepted in the Beloved," and if that be so, we need not fear what men can do unto us.

Now, just think again, he has made you "accepted in the Beloved." He, that is, God, has accepted you in Christ. Would you have liked any other way of acceptance one half as well? For my part, I had infinitely rather receive everything through Christ than reach it for myself. Mercy seems so much the sweeter and the better from the fact that it all comes from that dear, pierced hand. If I were this day accepted in myself, I should fear that I might lose my acceptance, for I am a poor, changeable being, but if I am "accepted in the Beloved," then the Beloved will never change, and I always must and shall be accepted, come what may. Is not this a word to die with? We will meet death and face his open jaws with this word, "Accepted in the Beloved." Will not this be a word to rise with amidst the blaze of the great judgment-day? You wake up from your tomb, lift up your eyes, and ere you gaze upon the terrors of that tremendous hour, you say, "I am accepted in the Beloved," what can then fill you with alarm? For ever and ever, as the cycles of eternity revolve, will not this be the core and centre of heaven's supremest bliss, that still we are "accepted in the Beloved?" I hear strange theories nowadays of what may happen to the saints: they tell us the sinners will die out, or be restored, or something else; for they are not content with the Scripture teaching of eternity, but must needs invent strange notions about the punishment of the ungodly. Then they begin to picture new destiny for saints too, and the heaven of our fathers has sad doubts cast on it. I care not for their dreams, for I am "accepted in the Beloved." It matters nothing what all the eternities can reveal: he that is accepted in Christ, and eternally one with him, has nothing before him at which he need tremble.

My time is gone: I heard the warning bell just now, and so I must forbear to amplify on the many reflections that spontaneously flow out of our text; all fitted to stifle anxious care, to sweeten mortal life, and to set our souls a-longing for the home which is above where so hearty a welcome awaits us.

V. And now I wish to finish with this one PRACTICAL USE. If it be so that we are "accepted in the Beloved," then let us go forth and tell poor sinners how they can be accepted too. Are you, to-day, though unconverted, anxious to be found right at last? Listen, friend. If you want to be accepted, you must accept. "And what," do you ask, "must I accept?" You must accept Christ as the free gift of God; you must accept Christ as God's way of accepting you, for if you get into Christ you are accepted. The guiltiest of the guilty *may be* accepted in Christ: no matter how great and grievous their transgressions may have been, the atoning sacrifice can take all their guilt away, and the perfect righteousness can justify the most heinous sinner before God. You may be accepted. Listen. If you come to Christ now and trust him you *will be* accepted. Never did one come to Christ to be rejected. You shall not be the first. Try it; and though you came into this house condemned you shall go out accepted, if you come now and hide in those dear wounds of his as doves do hide them in the clefts of the rocks. Listen again. It is not only that *you may be* accepted; it is rather that *you will be* accepted, *you cannot but be* accepted in Christ: there is no sort of fear nor possibility that you shall come to Christ and be cast out. Christ must change, truth must change, God must change towards his Well-beloved, he must cease to love him ere he could refrain from loving a soul that is in him. Guilty as you are, come to Christ this morning. Come, despise not the exhortation, for you must be accepted; it cannot but be that you should be accepted if you come. And you shall be accepted *at once*. If at this moment you are as vile as vile can be, if while I speak you know that you are black as hell's dark night, yet the moment that you come to Christ you are "accepted in the Beloved." Trust him: trust him. Have you done so? Your sin is gone; righteousness is imputed; you are saved.

And, then, to close, if you get into Christ you shall be accepted as long as you are in Christ, and as the grace of God will never let you go out of Christ you shall be accepted for ever, "accepted in the Beloved" world without end. If that be the verdict of this day it shall be the verdict of every day till days shall be no more; the hope for you dying, the song for your rising again, the verdict which shall be given out when the great assize shall sit, and you shall be tried for your life for the last time. They that sit in judgment shall say, "Let that man go; he is accepted in the Beloved." If thou believest in Jesus it shall be; it is so; it shall be so for ever and ever. God bless you all by his good Spirit, for Christ's sake. Amen.

XV.

ON HUMBLING OURSELVES BEFORE GOD.

July 22, 1883.

"Humble yourselves therefore under the mighty hand of God, that he may exalt you in due time."—1 PETER v. 6.

PRIDE is so natural to fallen man that it springs up in his heart like weeds in a watered garden, or rushes by a flowing brook. It is an all-pervading sin, and smothers all things like dust in the roads, or flour in the mill. Its every touch is evil as the breath of the cholera-fiend, or the blast of the simoom. Pride is as hard to get rid of as charlock from the furrows, or the American blight from the apple-trees. If killed it revives, if buried it bursts the tomb. You may hunt down this fox, and think you have destroyed it, and lo! your very exultation is pride. None have more pride than those who dream that they have none. You may labor against vainglory till you conceive that you are humble, and the fond conceit of your humility will prove to be pride in full bloom. It apes humility full well, and is then most truly pride. Pride is a sin with a thousand lives; it seems impossible to kill it, it flourishes on that which should be its poison, glorying in its shame. It is a sin with a thousand shapes; by perpetual change it escapes capture. It seems impossible to hold it; the vapory imp slips from you, only to appear in another form and mock your fruitless pursuit. To die to pride and self one would need to die himself.

Pride was man's first sin, and it will be his last. In

the first sin that man ever committed there was certainly a large admixture of pride, for he imagined that he knew better than his Maker, and even dreamed that his Maker feared that man might grow too great. It has been questioned whether pride was not the sin by which the angels fell when they lost their first estate: I will not go into any controversy upon that subject; but there was certainly pride in the sin of Satan and pride in the sin of Adam. This is the torch which kindled hell and set the world on fire.

Pride is a ringleader and captain among iniquities: it attaineth unto the first three of Satan's champions. It is a daring and God-defying sin, arraigning divine justice, as Cain did; challenging Jehovah to combat, as Pharaoh did; or making self into God, as Nebuchadnezzar did. It would murder God if it could, that it might fill his throne. While it is first to come, and first in horrible supremacy, it is also last to go. As Paul said, "The last enemy that shall be destroyed is death." I think I might say that the least enemy but one is pride, for even at our death-bed pride will be found in attendance. In his last moments John Knox had a sharp conflict with self-righteousness though he had preached against it with all his might, and knew, with a clearness seldom given to men, that salvation is of the Lord alone. Even within an hour of glory he had to make a stand against the vile thing, the pride of the human heart. Many others of the Lord's valiant ones have been sorely assailed by the same crafty foe, which shoots with feathered flatteries shafts of destruction. In the most quiet minds the deadly calm of self-conceit may be found. Our hearts are deceitful above all things, and in nothing less to be trusted than in this matter of pride. Even while we breathe out our souls unto God it will attempt to puff us up;—yes, it will puff up poor dying worms! Brothers and sisters, for certain, you and I are in danger of pride; possibly we are even now victims of it: let us be on our guard, for it may be ruining us without our knowledge even as the moth in secret eats up the garment, or as unseen rust cankers the hidden treasure.

Let pride lodge where it may, it does its entertainer great mischief, for it bars out the favor of God, "God resisteth the proud." It must be sent adrift ere God can visit us with favor, for no grace comes to the proud, "but he giveth grace unto the humble." Humility is the grace that attracts more grace. As money makes money, so humility increases humility, and with it every other spiritual gift. If you would have much grace have much humility. God hath assistance for the humble but resistance for the proud. You know how he fought Pharaoh. What blows he struck at the haughty monarch! He would have him down from the pinnacle of defiance one way or another, and make him learn in bitterness the answer to his own insolent question, "Who is the Lord?" Remember how Nebuchadnezzar had to eat grass like an ox because he spake with haughty tongue. Wherever God sees pride lifting itself on high, he resolves to level it with the dust. He draws his bow, he fits his arrow to the string, and pride is the target that he shoots at. The more pride enters into the Christian's heart the less grace will enter there, and the more opposition from God will come there; for pride is never so hateful to God as when he sees it in his own people. If you see disease in a stranger you are very sorry, but if you discover its symptoms in your own child your grief is much more deep. A viper is loathsome anywhere; but how it would make you start if you saw the head of one of those creatures peeping out from the bosom of a beloved friend! So pride is detestable anywhere; but it is worst in those whom the Lord loves best. If God sees pride in a David he will smite him till he ceases from his high thoughts; or if it be in a Hezekiah he will abase him; and be you sure that if the Lord sees pride in you he will smite you; ay, smite you again and again till you wait humbly at his feet.

All this I have given by way of preface, but I think it is also an argument which may run before the words of the text, and strengthen them, "Humble yourselves *therefore* under the mighty hand of God."

I shall handle the text, not at any great length, but for practical purposes, in three or four ways. May the Holy Spirit bless the discourse.

I. First, our text is evidently intended to bear upon us IN OUR CHURCH LIFE.

We will use it in that respect. Observe that Peter has been speaking to the elders, and telling them how they should behave themselves in the flock over which they are set as overseers. Then he speaks to the younger members, and he says, "Sumbit yourselves unto the elder." He says to all church-members, "all of you be subject one to another, and be clothed with humility"; and it is in the same context that he writes, "Humble yourselves therefore under the mighty hand of God." I am, as a member of a church, not to seek honor to myself, but I am to walk humbly. I am not to make it in any respect the object of my Christian life to be esteemed among my fellow-Christians so as to have influence over them, and to take the lead among them. I am to have far humbler motives than that. I am to think very little of myself, and to think so much of others that I admire all that I see of God's grace in them, and am glad to learn from them as well as to help them in their progress to heaven. Each one of us should think little of himself and highly of his brethren. I cannot say that all of us as Christians are clothed with humility as we should be. I am afraid that, from the preacher down to the most obscure member, we may, every one of us, listen with awe to the injunction, "Humble yourselves under the mighty hand of God," and confess that we fall short of this command. Yet I may honestly add that in this church I have seen more submissiveness, and deference to others, and less of ambitious self-esteem than anywhere else in the world. I have spoken nothing less than bare justice when I have said this. Let all the world know that as a pastor I can in this point praise the people of my charge beyond any that I have ever heard of. I am not apt to judge too favorably; I speak as I have seen, and this is my honest testimony. We owe our union and prosperity under God to the readiness of most of the brethren to do anything and everything for Christ without considering ourselves.

Now, true humility in our church relationship will show itself in our *being willing to undertake the very lowest offices for Christ*. Some cannot do little things: they must be ordained to great offices, or they will sulk in indolence. Genuine humility makes a man think it a great honor to be a doorkeeper in the house of God, or to be allowed to speak a word to a little child about Jesus, or even to wash the saints' feet. I am sure, brethren, that those who are not willing to fulfil the lesser offices will never be used by Christ to mind the greater duties. Humility is a qualification for greatness. Do you know how to be little? You are learning to be great. Can you submit? You are learning to rule. My symbolic sketch of a perfected Christian would be a king keeping the door, or a prince feeding lambs, or, better still, the Master washing his disciples' feet.

The next point of humility is, that *we are conscious of our own incompetence to do anything aright.* He who can do all things without Christ will end in doing nothing. The man who *can* preach without divine aid cannot preach at all. The woman who *can* teach a Bible-class cannot teach a Bible-class. Human ability without the grace of God is only puffed-up inability. Those of you who, apart from supernatural help, feel quite sufficient for any kind of holy service are miserably deluded. Self-sufficiency is inefficiency. The fulness of self is a double emptiness. He that has no sense of his weakness has a weakness in his sense. I believe, brethren and sisters, that any man whom God uses for a great purpose will be so emptied out that he will wonder that ever God uses him in the least degree; and he will be ready to hide his head, and long to get out of public notice, because he will feel himself to be utterly unworthy of the favor which God manifests towards him. I do not believe that God ever fills a cup which was not empty; or that he ever fills a man's mouth with his word while that man has his mouth full of his own words. Humble yourselves *therefore* under the mighty hand of God: if you desire that the Holy Spirit should bless you, be purged from your own spirit. The way to rise into God is to sink in your own self: as our Lord Jesus descended into the depths, that he might rise above all things and fill all things, so we, in our imitation of him, must descend to the uttermost that we may rise to the highest.

This humility will show itself, next, in this—*that we shall be willing to be ignored of men.* There is a craving in the heart of many to have what they do written upon tablets, and set up in the market-places. I once heard a professing Christian complain bitterly that he had been ignored. He had been a Sunday-school teacher for years, and yet he had never been publicly mentioned by any-one. Did he make that a complaint? He might far rather have rejoiced in his quietude. The fierce light of public notoriety is not much valued by those upon whom it falls. I wish some people would ignore *me*—at least, all next week, so much at least as not to call to see me, or write me a letter, or name me in the papers. I would be happy as all the birds in the air to be ignored, if I might be let alone, and allowed peacefully to work for God with his sweet smile to cheer me in my loneli-ness. Oh, to be a little ant, allowed to labor on at God's bidding, receiving nothing of men but the high privilege of being let alone! A saintly soul was wont to pray, "Grant me, O Lord, that I may pass unnoticed through the world!" It seems to me to be one of the highest delights of life for people to permit you to work for God without being interrupted by their praises or censures. When I have seen a certain great artist at work, I have only peeped at him from a corner, and have kept out of his sunshine: I am quite sure that he did not want me to express my valueless opinion about his glorious crea-tions. To have people for ever talking about you, for you, and against you is one of the wearinesses of mortal life; and yet some people sigh for the fuss that others would be glad to be rid of. Yes, so it is. It is but a little thing that certain friends have done, but they would like much made of it: their slender alms must be pub-lished at the corners of the streets, their prosy speech must be reported in all papers. Oh, brothers, do not let us care about its being known that we have done our part. Let it be done as to God, and in God's sight; and then, as to what our fellow-mortals shall say, let us have scant concern; for, if we live on human praise, we shall grow not only proud, but vain, which, if it be not more wicked, is certainly more silly. Serve God, and do not wish to have a trumpet blown before you. Never cry with Jehu, "Come, see my zeal for the Lord of hosts." Go on serving God year after year, though you be altogether unknown, feeling it quite sufficient that you have by the grace of God served your generation and honored your Redeemer. This would be a great attainment in our church life if we could reach to it.

Brethren, we want humility, all of us, in our church life, in the sense of *never being rough, haughty, arrogant, hard, domineering, lordly;* or, on the other hand, factious, unruly, quarrelsome, and unreasonable. We should endeavor to think very carefully of those who are poorest, for fear we should hurt their feelings; and very noticeably of those who are obscure, lest we should seem to despise them. It is ours never to take offence, and to be most cautious never to cause it even by inadvertence. He that is set as a leader in the church of God, let him be the person that is most ready to bear blame, and least ready to give offence: let him say, "You may think what you please of me, but I shall lay myself out to do you good, and to be your servant for Christ's sake." The lower you can stoop the greater is your honor. In the eye of wisdom no piece of furniture in the house of God has greater dignity than the doormat. If you are willing to let others wipe their feet on you, then shall Christ Jesus take pleasure in you, for you are a partaker of his lowly mind. Even for your own sake it will be wise to occupy a humble place, for in the vales the streams of peace are flowing. The mountains are the playground of the storm, but in the quiet villages the dove finds her shelter. If you would escape from ill-will, and live peaceably with all men, practice the maxims of an influential man, who, when asked after the Revolution how he managed to escape the executioner's axe, replied, "I made myself of no reputation, and kept silence."

I am speaking to a number of young men who have begun to speak for Jesus Christ in the church; let me earnestly entreat them to take great notice of my text, —" Humble yourselves under the mighty hand of God." Recollect, you cannot do any good except " the mighty hand of God " be with you; therefore be humble, and look to that hand for all success. Feel it to be a wonderful thing that the mighty hand of God should ever use *you;* therefore lie very low in that hand, and beneath that hand, for thus you may claim the promise that he will exalt you in due time. If you are willing to look after a few poor people in a village, and to do your duty thoroughly well among a lowly company, you shall have a larger sphere ere long. If you are satisfied, young brother, to stand in the corner of the street and talk about Jesus Christ to a few rough folk, you shall find hundreds of hearers by-and-by. If you are willing to be nothing, God will make something of you. The way to the top of the ladder is to begin at the lowest round. In fact, in the church of God, the way up is to go down; but he that is ambitious to be at the top will find himself before long at the bottom. "He that exalteth himself shall be abased; but he that humbleth himself shall be exalted." Suffer, my younger brethren, the word of exhortation.

II. And now, secondly, I will use the text in quite another way—in reference to OUR BEHAVIOR IN OUR AFFLICTIONS. Here let every tried believer listen to the counsel of the Holy Ghost.

Certain of us are never long together without affliction and trial: like salamanders, we live in the flame, passing from fire to fire. As by a succession of shafts we descend into the heart of the earth, going down from woe to woe; we had need learn the way of these dark places. Frequently our heavenly Father's design in sending trial to his children is to make and keep them humble; let us remember this, and learn a lesson of wisdom. The advice of Peter is that we should humble ourselves. Many people have been often humbled, and yet they have not become humble. There is a great difference between the two things. If God withdraws his grace and allows a Christian man to fall into sin, that fall humbles him in the esteem of all good men; and yet he may not be humble. He may never have a true sense of how evil his action has been; he may still persevere in his lofty spirit, and be far from humility. When this is the case the haughty spirit may expect a downfall. The rod will make blue wounds when pride abates not at gentler blows. The most hopeful way of avoiding the humbling affliction is to humble yourself. Be humble that you may not be humbled. Put yourself into a humble attitude, and draw near to God in a lowly spirit, and so he will cease from his chiding.

And do this, first, by *noticing whether you have been guilty of any special sin of pride*. You are suffering: let the rod point out to you wherein you have erred through pride. I believe that David was afflicted in his children because he had been proud of his children, and had indulged them. When there is a breakage in the house, it is generally the idol that is broken. Usually our sins lie at the roots of our sorrows. If we will repent of the sin, the Lord will remove the sorrow. Have you been tried in your worldly possessions? Were you ever puffed up by them? Is your health failing? Did you never glory in your bodily strength? Are you deceived? Were you never boastful of your own wisdom? Are you mourning over a failure in character? Did you not once dream that you were past temptation? Look into your affliction till you see, as in a glass, what was the thing you were proud of, and then take the idol down from its pedestal, humble yourself before God, and henceforth worship him alone.

In your affliction humble yourself by *confessing that you deserve all that you are suffering.* Is it poverty?—then, dear child of God, own that you deserve poverty because of your love of the world. Is it physical pain? Then own how every erring member deserves to smart. It is a great thing to have wrung out of us the confession that our chastisement is less than our deservings, and that the Lord is not dealing with us after our sins, nor rewarding us according to our iniquities. Is there a bereavement in the house? Then, I pray you, acknowledge that if God were to visit you, as he did Job, and take all your children away at a stroke, yet still you deserve it at his hands. Confess that the chastening hand is not dealing too severely with you. Humble yourself, and then you will not quarrel with your grief.

But, more than that, humble yourself so as to *submit entirely to God's will.* Ask the Holy Spirit to help you in this act of self-humiliation while you meekly kiss the rod. Bow yourself before the mighty hand of God, ready to receive yet harder blows if God so pleases; for when your will entirely yields to the will of God, it is highly probable that either the affliction will be removed, or else the sting of it will be taken away. Down, brother, down in the dust as low as ever you can get. God is evidently dealing with you as with a son; and a son's wisdom lies in cheerful submission to parental discipline. When a child is under his father's chastening hand, it will not help him to kick, and quarrel, and say ill words: his best hope lies in submitting absolutely to his father's good pleasure. When that is done the chastisement will soon end. Humble yourself therefore under the mighty hand of God. Yield up your will so as to have no suit-in-law against the Lord, no difference as to his goodness, not even if the evil you dread should actually come, and come in the worst form. Submit to the Lord's will as the rush bends to the wind, or as the wax yields to the seal. Pray against the calamity which moves you to fear, but let your petition always end with "Nevertheless, not as I will, but as thou wilt." Ask that you may not be obliged to drink the bitter draught, but do not upset the cup, nor push it away. There let it stand, while you for the moment supplicate for its removal; and when there comes no answer to your prayer, then take it up meekly, put it to your lips resolutely, and drink right on, even as your Master drank his cup and drained it to the dregs. This needs the help of the Holy Spirit, and truly he waits to help us: he delights to aid us in such holy acts of submission. Nothing is better for us in our time of tribulation than to bow ourselves in lowliest obeisance before the hand of God.

Dear friend, what can be the use of striving against the hand of the Lord? It is a mighty hand: we cannot resist it, even if we are wicked enough to attempt rebellion. If affliction is to come it will come, and come with all the greater sharpness because we refuse to yield. If God appoints a trial, we cannot escape it. What can be the use of our striving against divine decrees? It will only make our sorrow the more severe. When the ox kicks out against the goad the iron enters the deeper into its flesh; but when the bullock hastens on its way, sensitive to the least touch, the driver scarcely urges it again. The tender, sensitive horse scarcely receives a stroke from the whip; he feels it too much: but the mule that will not move is struck again and again for his obstinacy. So will it be with us. We can make rods for ourselves by wilfulness. Oh foolish fingers, which prepare prickles for our own pillows! Humble yourself, therefore, under the mighty hand of God, and by-and-by, brother, you shall be exalted to consolation and prosperity. Your affliction shall bring forth the comfortable fruits of righteousness. You shall come out of the furnace purified and refined. You shall have more knowledge, more grace, more zeal, more of every excellence, as the result of sanctified trial; but all this must come by obedient resignation. A rebellious heart comes out of affliction worse rather than better. Submit, and you shall be so exalted by your affliction that you shall bless God for it, and feel that you would not have missed the trouble for ten thousand pounds if you could have done so. Heavy tribulation shall bring with it unspeakable preferment. You shall be exalted to a higher degree in the peerage of Christianity by battling with adversities. Therefore, I pray you, humble yourselves under the hand of God.

III. Thirdly, I am going to use the text in another way. IN OUR DAILY DEALINGS WITH GOD, whether in affliction or not, let us humble ourselves under his hand, for so only can we hope to be exalted.

It is a blessed thing whenever you come to God to come wondering that you are allowed to come, wondering that you have been led to come; marvelling at divine election, that the Lord should ever have chosen you to come; wondering at divine redemption, astonished that such a price should have been paid that you might be brought nigh to God. It is well to draw near to God weighed down with gratitude that ever the Holy Spirit should have deigned to work effectual calling upon you. Humble yourself under the mighty hand of divine grace, which has brought you into the family of love, and constantly say, "Why me, Lord? Why me?" A grateful walk is a gracious walk, and there is no gratitude where there is no humility. Never trace the difference between yourself and others to your own free-will, nor to any betterness of your natural disposition, but entirely to the mercy and grace of God, which have been freely bestowed on you. Let grace be magnified by your grateful heart!

When you are doing this be very humble before God, because you have not made more improvement of the grace that he has given you. You are chosen, but you are not as choice as you ought to be; you are redeemed, but you are not so much your Lord's as you ought to be; you are called, but you are still too deaf to the divine call; you are blessed, enriched, instructed, adopted, comforted, with heaven before you and everything prepared on the road thither; but what a poor return have you made! Always feel thus humbled in reference to your God and his grace. When you are doing most, and God is using you most, always feel that if you had been fit for it he might have done much more by you—that if you had been meet to be used he might have used you far more extensively. Thus you will always see cause for humility even when you discern abounding reason for gratitude. Walk always so with God that when you stand on the highest point you still feel, "I might have been higher but for my own fault. I have not, because I have not asked, or because I have asked amiss. I have not become as rich as I might have been in **spiritual** things, because I have not been as diligent in my Lord's business, or as fervent in Spirit, or as abundant in serving God as I ought to have been.

Next, humble yourself, dear brother, under the hand of God by feeling your own want of knowledge whenever you come to God. Do not think that you understand all divinity. There is only one body of divinity, and that is Christ himself; and who knoweth him to the full? When even his love, which is the plainest point about him, passeth knowledge, who shall know Christ in all his fulness? Come before God to be instructed in the knowledge of your God and Saviour. Do not think that you understand providence, for I am sure that none of us do. We sometimes think that we could manage things a great deal better than they are managed. Many farmers would not have appointed that heavy shower for this afternoon, and yet that downpour was essential to the general well-being of the universal kingdom. I cannot tell why, but it was so. Everything that comes by God's appointment is a cog in the wheel of providence, and if that cog were gone, the machinery would be out of order. The Lord does all things wisely: only a vile pride will suspect otherwise. Consider, O man, that you do *not* know: God only knows. Little children sometimes think they are wise, but they know nothing: wisdom is with their father, not with them. Let us be content to humble ourselves under the hand of God as poor know-nothings, satisfied that he knows what is best for us. This humility is the vestibule of knowledge, the corner-stone of true philosophy. Commence with a confession of ignorance, or you will never be taught of the Lord. It cannot be hard to confess this when the mighty hand of the Lord is seen and felt.

One point concerning which I should like every one of us to humble ourselves under the hand of God is about our little enjoyment of divine things. The elder brother in the parable said, "Lo, these many years do I serve thee, neither transgressed I at any time thy commandment: and yet thou never gavest me a kid, that I might make merry with my friends." So have I known certain sincere Christian men fall into a horribly legal state of mind. They have always been very regular in their living, constant in their religious observances, and persevering in their prayers, and yet they have never had much joy: but they see a poor soul, just saved from sin, full of delight, and they envy him, and cry out, "Why is a fuss made over such a sinner, when I have been all these years a Christian, and my brethren have never made any rejoicing over me? There is no music and dancing about me! Thou never gavest me a kid that I might make merry with my friends." I do not know how we could make a fuss over some of the elder brothers: they would not bear it, they would be angry, and enquire, in hard and surly tones, what these things meant. Music and dancing are things too trivial for their solid souls. They stand outside and grumble, and we cannot warm them into a revival spirit. They are freezing outside the door of our happy home. Must they always stand there? How divinely sweet was the father's answer to that naughty elder brother! He said to him, "Son, thou art ever with me, and all that I have is thine." That is to say, "You live in my house. You are with me as my own dear son. Everything I have is yours by heirship. Your brother had his portion, and he spent it, but all that remains to me is yours." Hence his short commons had been of his own appointing. If he had not made merry with his friends it was his own fault. Is it not much the same with us if we have been dull and melancholy; I mean those of us who are believers? Are not all things ours? Come, let us humble ourselves under the hand of God, because we have not made merry with our friends. You growling Christians—if you growl it is because you *will* growl; there is nothing to murmur at. You who never have a happy day, who never have any of the fervors and enthusiasms of young beginners: whose fault is that? It is your own. You might have anything in the Father's house. You have a right to rare music and dancing, for you are ever with God, and all that he has is yours. It is meet that we should make merry and be glad; and if we are dull at the business of holy merry-making, let us humble ourselves under the hand of God because of our despondencies and mistrusts. O my soul, if thy ceilings are painted with black instead of vermilion, blame thyself alone, and not thy God.

I am sure, dear friends, if any of us will go over our daily lives we shall find plenty of reasons for humbling ourselves under the hand of God. It is really dreadful how a man can serve God nobly and do great things and yet in a certain matter he may fail sadly. A grand old prophet is that Jonah, going through the streets of Nineveh, and bravely delivering the Lord's warning. Who ever did the like? "Yet forty days and Nineveh shall be overthrown" is the word which he hurls into the face of princes. Grand man! One, yet a conqueror of myriads! Yes! But look at him a day or two after! Call that a grand man, sitting there crying because the cucumber that grew up over his head is withered! fretting because a worm has devoured a gourd! He is angry, and he says that he does well to be angry about a bower of melon-leaves. Dear me, that a man can be so great in noble things and so little in a trifling matter! How many have like cause to be humble before God! Observe that good man: he bore the loss of his property with holy resignation, but he lost his temper because a button was gone from his linen. Such a thing has often happened. Do I put it so that you smile at it? It would be better to weep over it. As you think about yourselves, my brethren, recollect the causes that you have to be humble under the hand of God because of the gross weakness by which you have shown the natural depravity of your heart, and the faultiness of your nature apart from the strengthening Spirit of God.

Humble yourselves therefore under the hand of God as creatures under the hand of the Creator. We are the clay, and thou our potter, O Lord: it becomes us to be lowly. Humble yourselves under the hand of God as criminals under the hand of their judge. Cry, "Against thee, thee only, have I sinned, and done this evil in thy sight: that thou mightest be justified when thou speakest, and be clear when thou judgest." Humble yourselves under the hand of God—as chastened children under a father's rod—for he chastens us for our profit, and right well do we deserve each smarting blow. Humble yourselves under the mighty hand of God, lastly, as servants under their Lord's word. Ask no questions about your Master's command, but go and do it; and when he rebukes you for shortcomings answer not again, but accept the reproof with bowed head and tearful eye, acknowledging that his rebuke is well deserved. Humble yourselves thus, dear brethren, in your daily lives, and God will exalt you in due time.

IV. I finish by using my text with all the earnestness my soul can feel in reference to the unconverted part of this audience IN OUR SEEKING FORGIVENESS AS SINNERS. Oh, tender Spirit of God, help me now.

The text was not originally meant for the ungodly, but it may fitly be applied to them. If you would find grace in God's sight and live, dear unconverted hearers, you must humble yourselves under the mighty hand of God. So you want to be saved, do you? The way of salvation is, " Believe in the Lord Jesus Christ." " But," you say, " I cannot understand it." Yet it is very simple: no hidden meaning lies in the word: you are simply bidden to trust Jesus. If, however, you feel as if you could not do that, let me urge you to go to God in secret and own the sin of this unbelief; for a great sin it is. Humble yourself. Do not try to make out that you are good. That will be fatal, for it will be a falsehood which will shut the gate of grace. Confess that you are guilty. When a man is clearly and manifestly guilty it is of no use his standing before the judge and beginning to urge his own merit: his best course is to cast himself upon the mercy of the court. It is *your* only course, dear soul, the only one that can avail you. Know that you have transgressed, and feel that it is so. Sit down and think over the many ways in which you have done wrong, or failed to do right. Pray God to break you down with deep penitence. It is no waste of time to dig out foundations when you build a house, and it is no superfluity to labor after a deep sense of sin.

When your sin is confessed, then acknowledge that if justice were carried out towards you, apart from undeserved grace, you would be sent to hell. Do not cavil at that fact. Do not entertain sceptical questions as to whether there is a punishment for sin, and as to what it will be; but own that, whatever it is, you deserve it. Do not fence with God or quarrel with Scripture; but as his word declares that the wicked shall be cast into hell with all the nations that forget God, own that you deserve to be so dealt with; for you *do* deserve it. When this is acknowledged you are on the road to mercy. You have almost obtained mercy when you have fully submitted to justice. You have in a measure received grace when you are brought to own your sin and the justice of its penalty.

Then, next, accept God's mercy in his own way. Do not be so vain as to dictate to God how you ought to be saved. Be willing to be saved by free grace through the blood of Jesus Christ; for that is God's way. Be willing to be saved by faith in Jesus Christ, for that also is God's way. If your unbelief begins to ask, "How can it be, and why should it be?" cease from such questions. Humble yourself and say, "God says it is so, and therefore it must be so;" if God says, "Believe, and be saved," I will believe and be saved; and if he says, "Trust Christ, and live," I will trust Christ and live. If a man had forfeited his life, but should be told by the court that he shall have pardon freely given to him if he will freely accept it—he would be a fool if he began to enquire, "But is this according to law? Is this according to precedent? What may be the effect of this pardon?" and so on. These enquiries are for the court, not for the prisoner. My dear man, you do not want to hang yourself, do you? Yet some men argue against their own souls, and labor to find out reasons why they should not be saved. If this perverse ingenuity could but be taught right reason, and men would strive to find out why they should at once yield themselves to God's way of salvation, they might enter into comfort and rest much sooner. O cavilling sinner, let thy artful doubts and reasonings be nailed with Jesus to the tree. Be a little child, and come and believe in the salvation which is revealed in Jesus Christ. Trust Christ to save you, and he will do it, as he has saved so many of us, to the praise of the glory of his grace.

"Ah," say you, "I have done this, but I cannot get peace." Then, dear friend, sink lower down! sink lower down! Did I hear you say, "Alas, Sir, I want to get comfort." Cease from that. Do not ask for comfort; ask for forgiveness, and that blessing may come through your greater discomfort. Sink lower down! Sink lower down! There is a point at which God will surely accept you, and that point is lower down. "Oh," you say, "I think I have a due sense of sin." That will not do. I want you to feel that you have *not* a due sense of sin, and come to Jesus just so. "Oh, but I do think that I have been brokenhearted." I should like to see you lower than that, till you cry, "I am afraid I never knew what it is to be brokenhearted." I want you to sink so low that you cannot say anything good of yourself; nay, nor see an atom of goodness in yourself. When you look inside your heart and can see nothing but that which would condemn you; when you look at your life and see everything there that deserves wrath; then you are on the road to hope. Come before God a criminal, in the prison dress, with the rope about your neck. You will be saved, then. When you confess that you have nothing of your own but sin—when you acknowledge that you deserve to die, and to be cast away for ever— God in infinite pity will let you live through faith in Christ Jesus. Many years ago a certain prince visited the Spanish galleys, where a large number of convicts were confined, chained to their oars, to toil on without relief; —I think nearly all of them condemned to a life sentence. Being a great prince, the King of Spain told him that he might in honor of his visit set free any one of the galley-slaves he chose. He went down among them to choose his man. He said to one, "Man, how did you come here?" He replied that false witnesses swore away his character. "Ah!" said the prince and passed on. He went to the next, who stated that he had done something that was wrong, certainly, but not very much, and that he never ought to have been condemned. "Ah!" said the prince, and again passed on. He went the round, and found that they were all good fellows—all convicted by mistake. At last he came to one who said, "You ask me why I came here. I am ashamed to say that I richly deserve it. I am guilty, I cannot for a moment say that I am not: and if I die at this oar, I thoroughly deserve the punishment. In fact, I think it a mercy that my life is spared me." The prince stopped and said, "It is a pity that such a bad fellow as you should be placed amongst such a number of innocent people. I will set you free." You smile at that; but let me make you smile again. My Lord Jesus Christ has come here at this time to set somebody free. He has come here at this time to pardon somebody's sins. You that have no sins shall have no pardon. You good people shall die in your sins. But, oh, you guilty ones, who humble yourselves under the hand of God, my Master thinks that it is a pity that you should be among these self-righteous people. So come right away, and trust your Saviour, and obtain life eternal through his precious blood; and to him shall be glory for ever and ever. Amen.

XVI.

THE LUTHER SERMON AT EXETER-HALL.

November 11, 1883.

"For in Jesus Christ neither circumcision availeth anything, nor uncircumcision; but faith which worketh by love."—GALATIANS v. 6.

PAUL makes a clean sweep of that trust in the externals of religion which is the common temptation of all time. Circumcision was a great thing with the Jew, and oftentimes he trusted in it; but Paul declares that it availeth nothing. There might be others who were glad that they were not Jews, but Paul declares that their uncircumcision availeth no more than its opposite. Certain matters connected with godliness are external, and yet they are useful in their places: especially is that the case with baptism and the Lord's supper, the assembling of ourselves together, the reading of the word, and public prayer and praise. These things are proper and profitable; but none of them must be made in any measure or degree the ground of our hope of salvation; for this text sweeps them all away, and plainly describes them as availing nothing if they are made to be the foundations of our trust.

In Luther's day superstitious confidence in external observances had overlaid faith in the gospel; ceremonies had multiplied excessively under the authority of the Pope, masses were said for souls in purgatory, and men were actually selling indulgences for sin in the light of day. When God raised up Martin Luther, who was born four centuries ago, he bore emphatic testimony against salvation by outward forms and by the power of priestcraft, affirming that salvation is by faith alone, and that the whole church of God is a company of priests, every believer being a priest unto God. If Luther had not affirmed it, the doctrine would have been just as true, for the distinction between clergy and laity has no excuse in Scripture, which calls the saints, "God's *kleros*"—God's clergy, or heritage. Again we read, "Ye are a royal priesthood." Every man that believes in the Lord Jesus Christ is anointed to exercise the Christian priesthood, and therefore he need not put his trust in another, seeing the supposed priest is no more than any other man. Each man must be accountable for himself before God. Each one must read and search the Scriptures for himself, and must believe for himself, and when saved, he must offer up himself as a living sacrifice unto God by Jesus Christ, who is the only High Priest of our profession. So much for the negative side of the text, which is full of warning to this Ritualistic age.

The chief testimony of our great Reformer was to the justification of a sinner in the sight of God by faith in Jesus Christ, and by that alone. He could fitly have taken this for his motto, "In Jesus Christ neither circumcision availeth anything, nor uncircumcision; but faith which worketh by love." He was in the Augustinian monastery at Wittenberg troubled and perturbed in mind; and he read there, in an old Latin Bible, this text,—"The just shall live by faith." It was a new idea to him, and by its means spiritual light entered his soul in some degree; but such were the prejudices of his up-bringing, and such the darkness of his surroundings, that he still hoped to find salvation by outward performances. He therefore fasted long, till he was found swooning from hunger. He was exceedingly zealous for salvation by works. At last he made a pilgrimage to Rome, hoping to find there everything that was holy and helpful: he was disappointed in his search, but yet found more than he looked for. On the pretended staircase of Pilate, while in the act of climbing it upon his knees, the Wittenberg text again sounded in his ear like a thunder-clap: "The just shall live by faith." Up he started and descended those stairs, never to grovel upon them again. The chain was broken, the soul was free. Luther had found the light; and henceforth it became his life's business to flash that light upon the nations, crying evermore, "The just shall live by faith." The best commemoration which I can make of this man is to preach the doctrine which he held so dear, and you who are not saved can best assist me by believing the doctrine, and proving its truth in your own cases. May the Holy Ghost cause it to be so in hundreds of instances.

I. First, let us inquire WHAT IS THIS FAITH? We are always talking about it; but what is it? Whenever I try to explain it, I am afraid lest I should confuse rather than expound. There is a story told concerning John Bunyan's "Pilgrim's Progress." Good Thomas Scott, the Commentator, wrote notes to it: he thought the "Pilgrim's Progress" a difficult book, and he would make it clear. A pious cottager in his parish had the book, and she was reading it when her minister called. He said to her, "Oh, I see, you are reading Bunyan's 'Pilgrim's Progress.' Do you understand it?" She answered innocently enough, "Oh, yes, sir, I understand Mr. Bunyan very well, and I hope that one day I shall be able to understand your explanations." I am afraid lest you should say when I have done, "I understand what faith is, as I find it in the Bible, and one day, perhaps, I may be able to understand the preacher's explanation of it.' Warned by this, I will speak as plainly as I can.

And first, it is to be remembered that faith is not a mere creed-holding. It is very proper to say, " I believe in God the Father Almighty, Maker of heaven and earth," and so forth; but you may repeat all that and be no "believer" in the Scriptural sense of that term. Though the creed be true, it may not be true to you; it would have been the same to you if the opposite had been true, for you put the truth away like a paper in a pigeon-hole, and it has no effect upon you. "A very proper doctrine," you say, "a very proper doctrine," and so you put it to sleep. It does not influence your heart, nor affect your life. Do not imagine that the professing an orthodox creed is the same thing as faith in Christ. A truthful creed is desirable for many reasons; but if it be a dead, inoperative thing, it cannot bring salvation. Faith is belief of the truth; but it is more.

Again, faith is not the mere belief that there is a God, though that we must have, for we cannot come to God except we "believe that he is, and that he is a rewarder of them that diligently seek him." We are to believe *in* God—that he is good, blessed, true, right, and therefore to be trusted, confided in, and praised. Whatever he may do, whatever he may say, God is not to be suspected, but believed in. You know what it is to believe in a man, do you not? to believe in a man so that you follow him, and confide in him, and accept his advice? In that same way faith believes in God—not only believes that he is, but finds rest in his character, his Son, his promise, his covenant, his word, and everything about him. Faith livingly and lovingly trusts in her God about everything. Especially must we believe in what God has revealed in Scripture—that it is verily and indeed a sure and infallible testimony to be received without question. We accept the Father's witness concerning Jesus, and take heed thereto "as unto a light that shineth in a dark place."

Faith has specially to believe in him who is the sum and substance of all this revelation, even Jesus Christ, who became God in human flesh that he might redeem our fallen nature from all the evils of sin, and raise it to eternal felicity. We believe *in* Christ, *on* Christ, and *upon* Christ; accepting him because of the record which God has given to us concerning his Son, that he is the propitiation for our sins. We accept God's unspeakable gift, and receive Jesus as our all in all.

If I wanted to describe saving faith in one word, I should say that it is *trust*. It is so believing God and so believing in Christ that we trust ourselves and our eternal destinies in the hands of a reconciled God. As creatures we look up to the great Father of spirits; as sinners we trust for the pardon of our sins to the atonement of Jesus Christ; as being weak and feeble we trust to the power of the Holy Spirit to make us holy and to keep us so; we venture our eternal interests in the vessel of free grace, content to sink or swim with it. We rely upon God in Christ. The word employed to set forth faith in the Scriptures sometimes signifies to lean. We lean with all our weight upon our God, in Jesus Christ. We hang upon Christ as a vessel hangs upon the nail. "Recumbency" was a term by which the old Puritans used to describe faith—a lying, or leaning upon, something out of ourselves. Guilty as I am, I believe God's word, that "the blood of Jesus Christ his Son cleanseth us from all sin:" trusting to that blood I know that I am cleansed from all sin. God sets forth Christ to be a propitiation; we believe that he is a propitiation, and we take him to be *our* propitiation: by that appropriation our sin is covered and we are free. Faith is the grasping, the appropriating, the receiving into one's self, of the Lord Jesus Christ. I sometimes illustrate it by that passage of Paul where he says, "The word is nigh thee, even in thy mouth." When a morsel is in your mouth, if you desire to possess it so as never to lose it, what is the best thing to do? *Swallow it.* Let it go down into the inward parts. Now the word that we preach is, according to the Apostle, "in thy mouth"; suffer it then to go down into thy heart, and thou shalt find it true that "with the heart man believeth unto righteousness; and with the mouth confession is made unto salvation." This is the faith which saves the soul.

II. In the second place we will consider, WHY FAITH IS SELECTED AS THE WAY OF SALVATION?

I would remind you that if we could not answer this question it would not matter; for since the Lord has appointed believing as the way of grace it is not ours to challenge his choice. Beggars must not be choosers: let us trust, if so the Lord ordains.

But we can answer this question in a measure. First, it is clear that *no other way is possible.* It is not possible for us to be saved by our own merits, for we have broken the law already, and future obedience, being already due, cannot make up for past defects.

> "Could my tears for ever flow,
> Could my zeal no respite know,
> All for sin could not atone:
> Thou must save, and thou alone."

The road of good works is blocked up by our past sins, and it is sure to be further blocked up by future sins:

we ought therefore to rejoice that God has commended to us the open road of faith.

God has chosen the way of faith *that salvation might be by grace.* If we had to do anything in order to save ourselves, we should be sure to impute a measure of virtue to our own doings, or feelings, or prayers, or almsgivings, and we should thus detract from the pure grace of God. But salvation comes from God as a pure favor—an act of undeserved generosity and benevolence, and the Lord will, therefore, only put it into the hand of faith since faith arrogates nothing to herself. Faith, in fact, disowns all idea of merit, and the Lord of grace therefore elects to place the treasure of his love in the hand of faith.

Again, it is of faith *that there may be no boasting;* for if our salvation be of our doings or feelings, we are sure to boast; but, if it be of faith, we cannot glory in self. "Where is boasting then? It is excluded. By what law? of works? Nay: but by the law of faith." Faith is humble, and ascribes all praise to God. Faith is truthful, and confesses her obligation to the sovereign grace of God.

I bless the Lord that he has chosen this way of faith, because *it is so suitable for poor sinners.* Some among us to-night would never have been saved if salvation had only been prepared for the good and righteous. I stood before my God guilty and self-condemned. No youth ever had a keener sense of guilt than I had. When I was convinced of sin I saw my thoughts and desires to be vile in the sight of God, and I became vile in my own eyes also. I was driven to despair; and I know that I could never have been cheered by any plan of salvation except that which is of faith. The covenant of works by reason of our weakness affords us no suitable way of hope at any time, but under certain circumstances we see this very vividly. Suppose that you were in the last article of death, what good works could you do? Yonder dying thief found it a happy thing that by faith he could trust the Crucified One, and before set of sun could be with him in Paradise. Faith is a way suitable for sinners, and especially for sinners who are soon to die; in some sense we are all in that condition, and some of us peradventure are especially so; for what man among us knows that he will see to-morrow's dawn?

I bless God again that the way of salvation is by faith, because *it is a way open to the most unlearned*. What fine theology we get nowadays—deep thinking they call it. The men go down so deep into their subjects, and so stir the mud at the bottom, that you cannot see them and they cannot see themselves. I apprehend that teachers of a certain school do not themselves know what they are talking about. Now, if salvation were only to be learned by reading through huge folios, what would become of multitudes of poor souls in Bow, and Bethnal Green, and Seven Dials? If the gospel had consisted of a mass of learning, how could the unlearned be saved? But now we can go to each one of them and say, "Jesus died."

> "There is life in a look at the Crucified One;
> There is life at this moment for thee."

However little you may know, you know that you have sinned; know, then, that Jesus has come to put away sin, and that whosoever believeth in him is immediately forgiven, and enters into life eternal. This brief and blessed gospel is suitable to all cases, from princes to peasants, and we wonder not that faith was selected as the way of salvation.

III. But now, thirdly, I want to say a good deal to-night upon another question, How DOES FAITH OPERATE? For according to our text, it is "Faith *which worketh by love.*" It is a living, laboring, loving faith which alone saves the soul. I cannot tell you what hard things I have heard about this doctrine of salvation by faith. They say that it is immoral. I have heard immoral men say so, and surely they ought to know. They say that it will lead to sin; and those who say so would, I should think, be rather pleased with it for that reason if they believed their own statement. I have never heard a holy man charge faith with leading him into sin. I know no man that follows after God and lives near to him who is under fear that faith in God will tempt him to transgress. The fact is, faith does nothing of the kind; its action is most distinctly the reverse. Like the prudent wife in the Proverbs, faith will do a man good and no harm all the days of his life.

First, *it touches the mainspring of our nature by creating love within the soul.* What is wanted now for the degraded classes in London? Sanitary regulations? Certainly, if they are not allowed to be a dead letter for the want of some one to carry them out. New houses? By all manner of means: the more the better. Lower rents? Assuredly, for no one has a right to get an excessive rent for unhealthy accommodation. Higher wages? Certainly, we could all of us do with a little more. Many other things are wanted. While yonder gin-palaces remain at the corners of the streets you will not make much headway in uplifting the masses; and I suppose the drink-shops will always flourish while the taste for drink remains. Suppose the licensed poison-shops were shut up, would that suffice? I think not. There are men and women in London, and thousands of them, who, if they were put into the cleanest houses, and were a mile off a gin-shop, would still drink and still turn their houses into piggeries. What is wanted? Oh, if you could make Christians of them! Suppose they could be born again. Suppose they could be made to love the things which they now hate, and hate the things which they now love. New hearts and right spirits are the need of London's outcasts. How can these be produced? In the hand of God the Holy Ghost, this is exactly what faith works in the heart. Here is a watch. "It wants cleaning." Yes, clean it. "It does not go now. It wants a new glass." Well, put in a new glass. "It does not go any the more. It wants new hands." Get new hands by all means. Still it does not go. What is the matter with it? The maker says that it needs a mainspring. There's the seat of the evil: nothing can be right till that is rectified. Set all other matters going, but do not forget that the mainspring is the chief part of the business. Faith supplies the soul with a powerful spring of action. It says to the man, "Thou art forgiven through the blood of Christ who died for thee: how dost thou feel towards him?" The man replies, "I love the Lord for redeeming me." Loving Jesus, the man has now within his soul the seed of every good. He will become a holier and a better being; for he has begun to love, and love is the mother of holiness. Is any service in the world like the service of love? You have a servant in your house, fawning and obsequious; but if you were to reduce his wages, he would show you the rough side of his tongue and seek another situation. You do not expect any more of him than that, and if you did, you would not get it. How different was an old servant I have heard of, who, when his master went down in the world, was content with half-pay; and when he was sorrowfully told that he must go, for his master could not afford him clothes, he made his old ones last him, for he would not leave his master in his old age. He would rather have earned bread for his old master than have left him. He was an attached servant worth his weight in gold: there are few such servants nowadays, for there are not many such masters. This kind of service cannot be purchased; but its price is above rubies. When the Lord leads us to believe in Jesus, we become henceforth his loving servants, and serve him not for reward, but out of gratitude. It is no longer with us so much work and so much pay; we do not fear the threat of hell for disobedience, nor do we look to heaven as won by works. No, no; our salvation is a free gift. It is furnished for us through infinite love and supreme compassion, and therefore we return our heart's warmest affection. Our heart clings to that dear side which was opened for us. We feel a tender love to those dear pierced feet; we could kiss them every day. Those blessed hands of the Crucified! If they do but touch us, we are strengthened, honored, comforted. Jesus is altogether lovely to us, our bosom's lord. Faith, instead of being a poor, paltry thing, as some imagine, is the grandest cause of love, and so of obedience and holiness.

Know, again, that *faith puts us into a new relation.* We are bound by nature to be the servants of God; but faith whispers in our ear, "Say 'Our Father,'" and when the heart has received the Spirit of adoption, the aspect of service is entirely changed; mercenary service is succeeded by loving obedience, and our spirit is altered. To become an heir of God, a joint-heir with Jesus, is to elevate work into delight, labor into fellowship with God. The law is no fetter to a child of God: it is his delight.

Faith removes from the soul that form of selfishness which aforetime seemed necessary. So you hope to be saved by what you do, do you? May I ask you, friend, whom you are serving in all this? I will tell you. You are serving yourself. All that you do is to win happiness for yourself. How, then, are you serving God? You are living a selfish life, though it be tinged with the color of spirituality. What is done by you in the matter of religion has no object but that *you* may be saved, and go to heaven. Your most zealous work is all for self. Suppose I say to you, "I know that I am saved: I know that Jesus has put away my sin: I know that he will not permit me to perish;"—why, then there is room in my case for the service of the Lord because of what he has done for me. Now I have not myself to save, I have Christ to serve. Gratitude is the motive of the gospel, and under its power unselfish virtue is possible, but not upon the ground of legal service. Pure virtue, it seems to me, is a sheer impossibility till a man is saved, because it always must partake till then of the low and grovelling view of benefiting himself by what he is doing. When once the great transaction is done, and you are saved, then you are lifted up into a nobler sphere, and you say,

> "Then why, O blessed Jesu Christ,
>   Should I not love thee well?
> Not for the hope of winning heaven
>   Nor of escaping hell;
>
> "Not with the hope of gaining aught,
>   Not seeking a reward:
> But as thyself hast lovéd me,
>   O ever-loving Lord,

> "So would I love thee, dearest Lord,
>   And in thy praise will sing;
> Solely because thou art my God,
>   And my Eternal King."

Hence faith inspires us with a higher motive than the law can suggest.

Faith soon creates love to man; for, if the Lord Jesus has saved you, my brother, you will speedily desire that others may be saved also. You have tasted of this honey, and the sweetness upon your own tongue constrains you to invite others to the feast. He who has been brought into the liberty of free grace would set free every captive sinner if he could.

When well worked out, *faith means harmony with God.* It creates an agreement with the divine will, so that whatever pleases God pleases us. If the Lord should set the believer on a dunghill with Job, he would still bless his name. Faith agrees with the divine precept which it desires to obey, with the divine doctrine which it desires to know and publish; yea, whatsoever is of God faith saith, "It is the Lord, let him command, teach, or do what seemeth him good."

I have shown you that faith is not the trifling principle which its deprecators describe as "Only believe." Oh, that they knew what it is only to believe. It is the setting free of the mind from fetters. It is the dawn of heaven's own day. It is a lifelong struggle, this "Only believe." It is "the work of God, that ye believe on him whom he hath sent."

Brethren, I believe that *a humble, persevering faith in God is one of the highest forms of adoration that ever reaches the throne of God.* Though cherubim and seraphim salute the Lord with their "Holy, holy, holy"; though the whole host of shining ones surround the throne with perpetual hallelujahs, there is no more hearty reverence given to God thereby than when a poor sinner, black as night, cries believingly, "Wash me, and I shall be whiter than snow." To believe in the pardon of sin is a wonderful adoration of the mercy and power of God. To believe in a constant providence is a sweet way of worshipping God in his power and goodness. When a poor laborer in his cottage, needing bread for his children, kneels down and cries, " Lord, it is written 'Thy bread shall be given thee, and thy water shall be sure,' I believe thy word, and therefore I look to thee in my necessity," he renders a homage to the truth and faithfulness of God such as Gabriel could not give, for he never knew the pinch of hunger. To believe that God will keep us to the end and raise us to his glory is more honoring to God than all the hymns of the glorified. From us dying sons of earth, when we confide in his promise, there arises up to heaven incense of a sweet smell, acceptable to God by Jesus Christ.

To my mind there is also this about faith—that it has a marvellous power over God. Do you ask me to retract that expression? Let it stand. I will explain it. Faith overcomes the Highest upon his throne. Faith in an inferior can hold a superior fast. Some years ago I was walking in the garden one evening, and I saw a stray dog about whom I had received information that he was in the habit of visiting my grounds, and that he did not in the least assist the gardener, and therefore his attentions were not desired. As I walked along one Saturday evening meditating upon my sermon, I saw this dog busily doing mischief. I threw my stick at him, and told him to go home. But what do you think he did? Instead of grinding his teeth at me, or hurrying off with a howl, he looked at me very pleasantly, took up my stick in his mouth, and brought it to me, and then, wagging his tail, he laid the stick at my feet. The tears were in my eyes: the dog had beaten me. I said, "Good dog! Good dog; you may come here when you like after that." Why had the dog conquered me? Because he had confidence in me, and would not believe that I could mean him any hurt. To turn to grander things: the Lord himself cannot resist humble confidence. Do you not see how a sinner brings, as it were, the rod of justice to the Lord, and cries, "If thou smite me, I deserve it, but I submit to thee." The great God cannot spurn a trustful heart. It is impossible. He were not God if he could cast the soul away that implicitly relies on him. This is the power of faith, then, and I marvel not that the Lord should have chosen it, for believing is a thing most pleasing to God. O that you would all trust him! God lifts his sword against you—run into his arms. He threatens you—grasp his promise. He pursues you—fly to his dear Son. Trust at the foot of the cross in his full atonement, and you must be saved.

IV. Now, I am going to finish in a way suitable to this Luther memorial. You have heard a great deal about Luther's preaching salvation by faith alone. Now LET US TURN TO LUTHER'S LIFE, and see what Luther himself meant by it. What kind of faith did Luther himself exhibit by which he was justified?

First, in Luther's case, faith led him to *an open avowal of what he believed*. Luther did not mean to go up to heaven by the back stairs, as many young men hope to do. You wish to be Christians on the sly, so as to escape the offence of the cross. Luther did not refuse to confess Christ and take up his cross and follow him. He knew that he who with his heart believeth, must also with his mouth make confession, and he did so right nobly. He began teaching and preaching the truth which had enlightened his own soul. One of his sermons displeased Duke George of Saxony; but as it saved a lady of high rank Luther did not fret. He was not the man to conceal truth because it was dangerous to avow it. Tetzel came with his precious indulgences, and his releases for souls in purgatory. Thousands of good Catholics were indignant; but no one would bell the cat. Luther called Tetzel "servant of Pope and of the devil," and declared, "As he came among us practicing on the credulity of the people, I could not refrain from protesting against it, and opposing his odious career." Without mincing words, or attempting to speak politely, Luther went at him fearless of consequences. He believed in the blessings of grace "without money and without price," and he did not conceal his convictions. He nailed his theses to the church door where all might read them. When astronomers require a new constellation in the heavens let it be "the hammer and nails." O you who make no profession, let this man's outspoken faith rebuke you!

His *dauntless valor for truth* caused him to be greatly hated in his own day with a ferocity which has not yet died out. Luther is still the best hated man in certain quarters. Witness the vile tracts which have been produced during the last fortnight, to the disgrace of the press which they defile. I can say no worse nor better of them than that they are worthy of the cause in whose interest they are issued. Mention the name of Luther and the bond-slaves of Rome gnash their teeth. This intense ill-feeling proves Luther's power. Young men, I do not know what your ambition may be; but I hope you do not wish to be in this world mere chips in the porridge, giving forth no flavor whatever. My ambition does not run in that line. I know that if I have no intense haters, I can have no intense lovers; and I am prepared to have both. When right-hearted men see honest love of truth in a man, they cry, "He is our brother. Let him be our champion." When the wrong-hearted reply, "Down with him!" we thank them for the unconscious homage which they thus pay to decision of character. No child of God should court the world's approbation. Certainly Luther did not. He pleased God, and that was enough for him.

His faith was of this kind also—that it moved him to *a hearty reverence for what he believed to be Holy Scripture.* I am sorry that he was not always wise in his judgment of what the Bible contains; but yet to him Scripture was the last court of appeal. If any had convinced Luther of error out of that book, he would gladly have retracted; but that was not their plan, they simply said, "He is a heretic: condemn him or make him retract." To this he never yielded for an instant. Alas, in this age numbers of men are setting up to be their own inspired writers. I have been told that every man who is his own lawyer has a fool for his client: and I am inclined to think that, when any man sets up to be his own Saviour and his own revelation, much the same thing occurs. That conceited idea is in the air at this present: every man is excogitating his own Bible. Not so Luther. He loved the sacred book! He fought by its help. It was his battle-axe and his weapon of war. A text of Scripture fired his soul; but the words of tradition he rejected. He would not yield to Melancthon, or Zwingle, or Calvin, or whoever it might be, however learned or pious; he took his own personal faith to the Scripture, and according to his light he followed the word of the Lord. May many a Luther be in this place!

The next thing I note was *the intense activity of his faith*. Luther did not believe in God doing his own work, so as to lie by in idleness himself. Not a bit of it. A disciple once said to Mahomet, "I am going to turn my camel loose, and trust in providence." "No," said Mahomet, "trust in providence, but tie up your camel carefully." This resembled Oliver Cromwell's Puritan precept, "Trust in God, but keep your powder dry." Luther believed above most men in keeping his powder dry. How he worked! By pen, by mouth, by hand; he was energetic almost beyond belief. He seemed a many-handed man. He did works which would have taxed the strength of hundreds of smaller men. He worked as if everything depended upon his own activity, and then he fell back in holy trust upon God as though he had done nothing. This is the kind of faith which saves a man both in this life and in that which is to come.

Again, *Luther's faith abounded in prayer*. What supplications they were! Those who heard them tell us of his tears, his wrestlings, his holy arguments. He would go into his closet heavy at heart, and remain there an hour or two, and then come forth singing, "I have conquered, I have conquered." "Ah," said he one day, "I have so much to do to-day that I cannot get through it with less than three hours' prayer." I thought he was going to say, "I cannot afford to give even a quarter of an hour to prayer;" but he increased his prayer as he increased his labor. This is the faith that saves—a faith that lays hold on God and prevails with him in private supplication.

His was a faith that *delivered him entirely from the fear*

of man. Duke George is going to stop him. "Is he?" said Luther. "If it were to rain Duke Georges I would go." He is exhorted not to go to Worms, for he will be in danger. If there were as many devils in Worms as there were tiles on the house-tops he would be there. And he was there, as you all know, playing the man for the gospel and for his God. He committed himself to no man, but kept his faith in God pure and unmingled. Popes, emperors, doctors, electors were all as nothing to Luther when they stood against the Lord. Be it so with us also.

His was a faith that made him risk all for the truth. There seemed no hope of his ever coming back from Worms alive. He was pretty sure to be burned like John Huss; and the wonder is that he escaped. His very daring brought him safety from peril. He expressed his regret that the crown of martyrdom would, in all probability, be missed by him; but the faith which is prepared to die for Jesus was within him. He who in such a case saves his life shall lose it, but he that loses his life for Christ's sake shall find it unto life eternal.

This was the faith that made Luther a man among men, and *saved him from priestly affectations.* I do not know whether you admire what is thought to be very superior religion: it is a thing of beauty, but not of use; it ought always to be kept in a glass case; it is made up for drawing-rooms and religious meetings, but would be out of place in a shop or on a farm. Now, Luther's religion was with him at home, at the table as well as in the pulpit. His religion was part and parcel of his common life, and that life was free, open, bold, and unrestrained. It is easy to find fault with him from the superfine standpoint, for he lived in an honest unguardedness. My admiration kindles as I think of the hearty openness of the man. I do not wonder that even ungodly Germans revere him, for he is all a German, and all a man. When he speaks he does not take his words out of his mouth to look at them, and to ask Melancthon whether they will do; but he hits hard, and he has spoken a dozen sentences before he has thought whether they are polished or not. Indeed, he is utterly indifferent to criticism, and speaks what he thinks and feels. He is at his ease, for he feels at home: is he not everywhere in his great Father's house? Has he not a pure and simple intent to speak the truth and do the right?

I like Luther with a wife and children. I like to see him with his family and a Christmas-tree, making music with little Johnny Luther on his knee. I love to hear him sing a little hymn with the children, and tell his pretty boy about the horses in heaven with golden bridles and silver saddles. Faith had not taken away his manhood, but sanctified it to noblest uses. Luther did not live and move as if he were a mere cleric, but as a brother to our common humanity. After all, brethren, you must know that the greatest divines have to eat bread and butter like other people. They shut their eyes before they sleep, and they open them in the morning, just like other folks. This is matter of fact, though some stilted gentlemen might like us to doubt it. They feel and think like other men. Why should they seem as if they did not? Is it not a good thing to eat and drink to the glory of God, and show people that common things can be sanctified by the word of God and prayer? What if we do not wear canonicals, and so on? The best canonicals in the world are thorough devotion to the Lord's work; and if a man lives aright, he makes every garment a vestment, every meal a sacrament, and every house a temple. All our hours are canonical, all our days holy days, every breath is incense, every pulse music for the Most High.

They tell us that Luther ignored good works. It is true he would not allow good works to be spoken of as the means of salvation; but of those who professed faith in Jesus he demanded holy lives. *Luther abounded in prayer and charity.* What an almsgiver Luther was! I fear he did not at all times duly regard the principles of the Charity Organization Society. As he goes along, if there are beggars he empties his pockets for them. Two hundred crowns have just come in, and, though he has a family about him, he cries, "Two hundred crowns! God is giving me my portion in this life." "Here," says he to a poor brother minister, "take half. And where are the poor? Fetch them in. I must be rid of this!" I am afraid that his Catherine was forced at times to shake her head at him; for, in truth, he was not always the most economical husband that might be. In almsgiving he was second to none, and in all the duties of life he rose far beyond the level of his age. Like all other men he had his faults; but as his enemies harp on that string, and go far beyond the truth, I need not dwell upon his failings. I wish that the detractors of Luther were half as good as he. All the glory of his grand career be unto the Lord alone.

Lastly, Luther's faith was a faith that *helped him under struggles that are seldom spoken of.* I suppose that never man had greater soul-conflict than Luther. He was a man of heights and depths. Sometimes he went up to heaven and he sang his hallelujahs; and then he went down again into the abyss with his "misereres." I am afraid that, great, vigorous man that he was, he had a bad liver. He was grievously afflicted in body in ways which I need not mention; and he was sometimes laid aside for months together, being so racked and tortured that he longed to die. His pains were extreme, and we wonder how he endured them so well. But ever between the attacks of illness Luther was up again preaching the word of God. Those desperate struggles with the devil would have crushed him but for his faith. The devil seems to have been constantly assailing him, and he was constantly assailing the devil. In that tremendous duel he fell back upon his Lord, and, trusting in Omnipotence, he put Satan to rout.

Young men, I pray that a Luther may spring up from your ranks. How gladly would the faithful welcome him! I, who am more a follower of Calvin than of Luther, and much more a follower of Jesus than of either of them, would be charmed to see another Luther upon this earth.

God bless you, brethren, for Christ's sake. Amen.

XVII.

BLESSED PROMISES FOR DYING OUTCASTS.

December 2, 1883.

"For I will restore health unto thee, and I will heal thee of thy wounds, saith the Lord; because they called thee an Outcast, saying, This is Zion, whom no man seeketh after."—JEREMIAH xxx. 17.

The promises of this verse will be exceedingly sweet to those who feel their personal need of them; but those who boast that they are neither sick nor wounded will take no interest in this comfortable word. Those who are charmed with themselves will see no charm in the beloved Physician. I have heard of certain hungry travellers, who were lost in the wilderness, and came upon a bag which they longingly hoped might yield them a seasonable supply of food. They were near to death's door by starvation, and eagerly opened the bag, but, alas! it contained nothing but pearls, which they poured out contemptuously upon the desert sand as things of no use to them. Even so, when a man is hungering and thirsting after the things of this life, and all his thoughts are taken up with carnal appetites, carnal sorrows, and carnal joys, he will reject as worthless the priceless promises of God, for he considers that they are of no immediate use to him. Let his hunger be of another sort, let his heart hanker after unsearchable riches, let his soul pine for eternal love, then are his views of things entirely changed, and to buy the pearl of great price he would gladly sell all that he has. Oh, you that are sick at heart, here is a word for you from the God of all grace: Jehovah Rophi himself says, "I will restore health unto thee." Oh, you that have felt the shafts of God pierce your inmost souls, here is a word from him who healeth the broken in heart, and bindeth up their wounds: "I will heal thee of thy wounds, saith the Lord." Here is music for your ear, honey for your mouth, comfort for your heart. But if you feel you have no sickness and no wound, no weakness and no spiritual need, then the words of sacred consolation will pass over your ear as a meaningless sound, having no voice for you. Neither shall we wonder at this, for the whole have no need of a physician, but they that are sick: healthy men care not to hear of medicines and remedies, for they feel no need of them. This thins my audience, but improves it; for, while it drives away the conceited, it draws the needy to a more careful listening.

Our text describes *a serious plight*, mentions *a special interference*, and records *a singular reason* for that interference. When we have spoken upon each of these, we shall close by giving you *a suitable advice*. May the Spirit of God bless the discourse.

I. First, then, taken in connection with the verses which precede it, our text describes a class of men and women who are in A SERIOUS PLIGHT.

These people suffer under two evils. First, they are sick through sin: for they need to have their health restored; and, secondly, they are wounded for their sin by the chastisements of the Lord, so that there is necessity for their wound to be healed. They are afflicted with the distemper of evil, and also by dismal disquietude of conscience. They have broken God's commandments, and now their own bones are broken.

They have grieved their God, and their God is grieving them.

Let us carefully look at the first part of their sad condition: *they are sick with sin*, and that disease is one which, according to the fifth and sixth verses, brings great pain and trouble into men's minds when they come to their senses, and know their condition before God. At first, iniquity numbs the conscience, and its tendency is to sear it as with a hot iron. It may be compared to a stroke of paralysis, which, when it falls upon a man's body, takes away from him all pain, and makes him as one dead in the parts which it affects. Sin paralyzes the consciences of the ungodly. At first they do not know it to be an exceeding great evil; they trifle with it; it is a basilisk, whose very look is poisonous, and yet they sport with it as though it were a bird. It is a deadly disease, causing the soul to be full of leprosy, and yet men will exhibit the marks of it as though they were the spots of God's children. But after a while, when the conscience is awakened by judgments, or aroused by God's word, then this disease ceases to stupefy, and becomes the source of intolerable pain. Read these words: "For thus saith the Lord; We have heard a voice of trembling, of fear, and not of peace. Ask ye now, and see whether a man doth travail with child? wherefore do I see every man with his hands on his loins, as a woman in travail, and all faces are turned into paleness?" The fiercest form of bodily pain is here selected as the type of the anguish caused by strong conviction of sin. Believe me, there can be nothing in the world so terrible as to feel sin without feeling pardon; to know yourself to be guilty, and not to know how to get the guilt removed. Conviction without faith is an earthly hell. Brethren, you have many of you felt it, and you know that death itself, if there were no hereafter, would be preferable to life under the pressure of guilt. "The spirit of a man will sustain his infirmity; but a wounded spirit who can bear?" Sin is a disease of the spirit, which embitters the central fountain and well-spring of our life, till gall and wormwood flavor all things. Sin felt and known is a terrible kill-joy: as the Simoom of the desert smites the caravan with death, and as the Sirocco withers every herb of the field, so does a sense of sin dry up peace, blast hope, and utterly kill delight. If those who hear me are oppressed with the disorder of sin, they will rejoice greatly as they dwell upon the words of our text, "I will restore health unto thee, and I will heal thee of thy wounds."

This disease, moreover, is not only exceedingly painful when the conscience is smarting, but it is altogether incurable, so far as any human skill is concerned. We are told in the twelfth verse, "Thus saith the Lord, Thy bruise is incurable, and thy wound is grievous." It would be much easier to heal a man's body of leprosy than to heal a man's soul of sin. It is a disease which takes such fast hold upon the nature, and so entirely impregnates the mind with a deadly virus, that it abides in the very essence of manhood, and can only be removed by a miracle. It is far more possible for the Ethiopian to change his skin, or the leopard his spots, than for a man who is accustomed to do evil to learn to do well; especially to love to do well, and find a pleasure in it. If this were a matter of custom, or practice only, it might be fought with and overcome, but inasmuch as it is a matter of nature, and the whole head is sick, and the whole heart faint with it, no human power can possibly effect a cure. Some have wept over sin, but tears are a poor lotion for a disease which penetrates to the core of the heart. Others have shut themselves up alone, and retired as hermits to escape from evil by solitude; but they have found no secret place which evil could not enter. Whither shall we flee from the presence of sin? When it has once laid hold upon our nature, if we take the wings of the morning, and fly to the uttermost parts of the sea, our depravity will still be with us. If we cover ourselves with multiplied midnights, sin will only be the more completely in its element. Where can we fly, and what can we do, to escape from this terrible force, this ever-present mischief? This poison has penetrated all our nature, so that we must confess:—

> "It lies not in a single part,
> But through my frame is spread;
> A burning fever in my heart,
> A palsy in my head."

Neither body, soul, nor spirit is free from its taint. At all hours it is our curse and plague; over all places it casts its defiling influence; in all duties it injures and hinders us. To those who know this there is a music sweeter than marriage-bells in these words,—" I will restore health unto thee, and I will heal thee of thy wounds." The incurable shall be cured; the insatiable malady shall be stayed.

Further on we are told that this disease is one for which there is neither surgeon nor medicine:—"There is none to plead thy cause, that thou mayest be bound up: thou hast no healing medicines. Why criest thou for thine affliction? thy sorrow is incurable for the multitude of thine iniquity; because thy sins were increased, I have done these things unto thee." What a disease this must be for which there is no physician, since the direst forms of human disease have found each one its specialist, who has at least attempted to perform a cure; but here is a sickness for which there is no physician. Bad men do not pretend to heal the disease of sin; they do not even consider it to be a disease, and they care not to make men holy. Good men are very far from thinking that they can conquer sin in others, for they cannot even overcome it in themselves, and therefore they never set up to be physicians in such a case as this. No human hand can bind up this wound: no earthly skill can touch this deeply-seated complaint: it is past all mortal surgery. Yea, and the prophet adds, "There is no healing medicine": none has ever been known. The question is often asked, "Is there no balm in Gilead? Is there no physician there?" The answer to that question is, No, there is no balm in Gilead; there never was. Balms for soul-mischiefs do not grow in the fields of Gilead, nay, nor on Carmel and Sharon. Physicians of sin-sick souls are not to be found beneath the skies: the other question proves it,—" Why then is not the health of the daughter of my people recovered?" If there were balms and physicians for her disease she would have been healed long ago; but neither salve nor surgeon can be found among the sons of men. Search through all the lore of the ancients, and you shall discover no remedy for sin; examine all the inventions of the moderns, and you shall light upon no physic for the love of evil. Nothing can touch it save one thing, and that is not of earth. The Lord from heaven, upon the cross, did bleed a balm that can cure this wound, and by his death he was the death of this disease; but apart from him no one can bind up our wounds, or mollify them with ointment. He is the one and only good Samaritan for the spiritually bruised: he alone hath wine and oil suitable for our wounds. Are my hearers brought to feel this? Are there any here who have not yet found out God's way of salvation, but still are well aware that they have none of their own? I am thankful you are brought so far; may you not be long before you go much further, and find the Lord Jesus able to heal you of every disease. You are for ever lost unless you go to him, for your sickness is unto death, your wound is breeding corruption, and none can give you health for your sickness, or healing for your wound, but the Lord Jesus, who is able to save unto the uttermost.

> "When wounded sore the stricken soul,
> Lies bleeding and unbound,
> One only hand, a pierced hand,
> Can salve the sinner's wound."

This disease is exceeding dangerous, because it insinuates itself into the heart, and takes up its abode there. If apparently it be for a time driven out, it returns when we least expect it. Like the tree which is cut down, it will sprout again; at the scent of water it will bud. It annoys us in every way; it hinders our aspirations, for how to perform that which we would, we find not; it robs us of comfort, and makes us groan, being burdened; it enters into our holiest things, chills our prayers, freezes our praise, and hampers our usefulness. It is evil, only evil, and that continually. How gracious is it on God's part, to pity a creature infested with this vile distemper! How good of him to regard our iniquity rather as a sickness to be healed than as a crime to be punished!

I told you of a double mischief in this plight, and the second mischief is that this person *has been wounded for his sin.* His wounds are of no common sort, for we are told in the fourteenth verse that God himself has wounded him. The Lord says, "I have wounded thee with the wound of an enemy, with the chastisement of a cruel one, for the multitude of thine iniquity; because thy sins were increased." God in infinite mercy determines to make the sinner see and feel the evil consequences of his sin; and in doing this he makes deep wounds, such as an enemy would give who felt no pity, but only wished to cause pain. The Lord knows that in this work slightness is of no avail, and therefore he strikes home, and cuts deep. He does not play with consciences, but his chastisement is so severe that men think him cruel. There is such a thing as cruel kindness, and the opposite to it is a loving cruelty, a gracious severity. When the Lord brings sin to remembrance, and makes the soul to see what an evil it has committed in transgressing against God, then the wound bleeds, and the heart breaks. You could not tell the blows of our greatest Friend from those of our worst enemy if you only judged by present feeling. Under the Lord's hand the soul is well-nigh driven to despair. Vain hopes are dashed in pieces like potsherds, false lights are quenched in gloom, and joys are ground to powder. It is in love that the Lord thus judges us, and chastens us that we should not be condemned with the world. The smart is sharp, but salutary. The Lord wounds that he may heal, he kills that he may make alive. His storms wreck us upon the rock of salvation, and his tempests drive us into the fair havens of lowly faith. Happy are the men who are thus made unhappy; but this for the present they know not, and therefore they need the promise, "I will heal thee of thy wounds, saith the Lord."

The blows are not only on the conscience, but when God is in earnest to make men flee from their sins, he will smite them anywhere and everywhere. He takes away the delight of their eyes with a stroke; the child, the husband, the wife, or the friend is laid low; for the Lord will fill our houses with mourning sooner than leave us in carnal security. He takes away the silver and the gold, for he will make us beggars sooner than leave us to worship the idols of the world. The oil vat is burst, and the barn is burned; for he will not permit us to bury our souls in earthly things. He brings the body into sickness, and the mind into distress; health departs, and the robust worker is stretched upon a sick bed; he groans and moans under the hand of God. God is in all this smiting most cruelly, according to the short-sighted judgment of men; but in very truth he is tender and gracious, and is working out the eternal good of the sufferers. Like as the surgeon uses a sharp knife, and cuts far down into the flesh when he would eradicate some deadly ulcer, even so does the Lord in true severity wound the heart until he gets at the roots of our self-love.

Surely, a man is in a wretched plight when he is diseased with sin, and then bruised by divine chastisement, but, it may be, he adds to this wounds inflicted by himself, for falls into sin are falls that break the bones. Many a man will have to go limping to his grave because of his transgressions. Doubtless David did so; he never recovered what he lost when he sinned with Bathsheba. Much pain comes of broken bones, especially when you have broken them yourself, through your own folly. When you cannot trace an affliction to second causes, nor look upon it as an affliction from God, but when you hear conscience whisper, "Thou hast procured this unto thyself," then the wormwood is mixed with gall, and the suffering knows no solace. If thou be poor because thou hast squandered thy substance; if thou be sick because thou hast indulged thine appetites or passions, who can say thee a word of cheer? If thou hast lost godly friends whom thou didst once despise, if thou art by sore sickness prevented from going up to the house of the Lord, which was formerly a weariness to thee, is there not a special sharpness in thy grief?

Now, put these three things together—bones broken through thine own sin, God dealing with thee in the way of chastisement, and sin felt in the conscience like a grievous disease; and I think I said not too much when I described the soul as in a serious plight. God help the man who is in such a case, for none else can. The comfort is that the Lord Jesus does help such, for so his gracious promise runs, "I will restore health unto thee, and I will heal thee of thy wounds." May the Holy Spirit bless this first head to many of you!

II. Our second consideration fitly falls under the title of A SPECIAL INTERFERENCE. The poor creature is in desperate dolor; but the God of pitying love comes in, and I beg you to notice the result.

This interference is, first of all, *divine*. "I will restore health unto thee, and *I* will heal thee of thy wounds." The infinite Jehovah alone can speak with that grand *Ego*, and say, "I will," and again, "I will." No human physician who was worthy of the name would speak thus. He would humbly say, "I will attempt to give you health; I will endeavor to heal your wounds;" but the Lord speaks with the positiveness of omnipotence, for he has the power to make good his words. All others fail; but the Lord will do it. Thou canst not heal thyself; but the Lord will heal thee. And who is this great "I" that speaks so exceeding boldly? It is none other than he that made the heavens and the earth, and sustaineth all things by the power of his hand; it is the "I AM," the everlasting Jehovah, whose word has boundless power in it. He appears in the moment of man's extremity, and when there is no helper, his own arm brings salvation. Blessed be the Lord who forgiveth all our iniquities, who healeth all our diseases.

Note, that since this interference is divine it is *effectual*. The Lord effectually heals all those on whom he lays his hand. How could it be otherwise? What can baffle the Lord? Can anything perplex infinite wisdom? Is anything difficult to almighty power? "If it be marvellous in thine eyes, should it also be marvellous in mine eyes? saith the Lord of hosts." He speaks, and it is done; he commands, and it stands fast. When therefore God says, "I will restore health unto thee," health will visit the wretch who lies pining at death's door. When he says, "I will heal thee of thy wounds," the deep cuts and gashes are closed up at once. Glory be to the name of the Beloved Physician! Poor, troubled heart, where are you this morning? Do you say, "Nobody can cure me?" Thou sayest truly if thou wilt make one exception, and that exception is thy God. I tell thee he can heal thee now, so that the bones which he has broken shall rejoice. He can take away this disease of yours, and give you back wholeness as though your flesh were the flesh of a little child, and you shall be clean; only have faith in him. He that made you can make you anew. Do you believe this?

Observe that this interposition performs a work which is most *complete*, for it meets the two-fold mischief. "I will restore health unto thee:"—That is a great matter. When a man grows healthy he can bear a wound or two without being too much overburdened; but God does nothing by halves, for having restored health he then adds "I will heal thee of thy wounds." He will heal both disease and wound. There is no condition into which the heart can sink but what the Lord is equal to the raising of it from the depths. If thou art in the borders of Hades, and on the verge of hell, yet as long as thou hast not passed the iron gates of death thy salvation is possible with God, ay, simple and sure with God if thou wilt but trust in his well-beloved Son. What a mercy it is that the Redeemer does not half save us, and leave us to finish the work! He does not commence and do a part of the cure, and then say, "I must leave nature to work out the rest." No; the cure is absolutely complete: "I will restore health unto thee, and I will heal thee of thy wounds." Oh, sick and wounded one, go just as thou art, and throw thyself at Jesus' feet, and say unto him, "Keep thy promise, Lord: I am come with thy word in my mouth and in my heart; be as good as thine own declaration, and restore health to *me*, and heal *me* of my wounds."

Notice, too, how sovereignly *free* this promise is. It does not say, "I will restore health unto thee if——." No, there is no "if;" and there is no mention of a fee. Here is healing for nothing. Jesus comes to give us health without money and without price, without pence or penance, without labor or merit. I admire for my part the splendid, unconditional character of this promise made by Jehovah to his covenant people. Its tenor is, "I will." There is no sort of condition or demand. "Perhaps" is banished: "peradventure" is not so much as hinted at. Come, poor guilty soul, thou who hast no claim on God, come and plead the divine "I will." Thou canst not have a better hand-hold of the covenant angel in wrestling with him. God's promise is an unconquerable plea: to use it well will put thee among the invincibles. Come then, I pray thee, and just say, "Lord, it is so written in thy word; therefore, write it, I pray thee, on the page of my experience."

Notice that, although it be thus free and unconditional, yet it is now a matter of covenant *certainty*, for God has made the promise, and he cannot turn from it. To every guilty sinner, conscious of his guilt, who will come and confess it before God, this promise is made to-day, "I will restore health unto thee, and I will heal thee of thy wounds." To you, dear fellow-sinners, as much as unto Judah and Israel of old, is this promise sent: if you will bring your sorrow and your sin before the eye of the all-merciful Father, and plead the precious blood of Christ. No sick one shall be shut out from this hospital of love. If, like Job, the sinner is covered with sores from head to foot; and if he only feels at home when he sits on a dunghill, and begins to scrape himself with a potsherd, yet the Lord says, "I will heal thee." If thy sin has made thee loathsome to thyself, till thou criest out with one of old, "My wounds stink and are corrupt," still is the Lord Jesus able to save thee; nay, he promises to save thee. Grasp thou the promise by the hand of faith, and thou shalt be made whole. All manner of sin and of iniquity shall be forgiven unto men; ay, and all tendencies to sin, and all taint of iniquity, shall be removed from men if they will trust the power and promise of the faithful Lord. Sinner, his touch can make thee clean at once. Trust thou that hand, I say, and the miracle shall be wrought.

III. But now I come to a third point, which is this— A SINGULAR REASON. "I will restore health unto thee, and I will heal thee of thy wounds, saith the Lord; *because they called thee an Outcast, saying, This is Zion, whom no man seeketh after.*" God never finds a reason for mercy in the sinner's supposed goodness. He looked upon this sick one, and he could not find a redeeming feature of beauty by which the blessing might be won; therefore, he did not look at the sinner at all, except to pity him. Is it not a singular thing that the Lord will sooner *find a reason for mercy in the lying mouths of the wicked* than he will attempt to find it in the supposed righteousness of those who count themselves righteous? He says not " Because you were holy " or " Because you had good desires ;" but " Because *they* called thee an outcast." Who were they ? Why, the jeerers, and mockers, and blasphemers: the Lord actually transforms the venom of asps, which was under the tongues of the malicious, into a reason for his mercy. This clearly shows how God hates the very notion of man's merit; but it also shows that he will find a reason for mercy somewhere. They called poor Zion, when God seemed to have given her up, "an outcast ;" they said, " Nobody goes to Jerusalem now: there was a temple there once, but it is a wretched heap now: princes dwelt there once, but now the inhabitants of Jerusalem are a set of beggars; no man cares to mix with them; they are the world's castaways." *This roused the Lord's pity.* " Oh," he said, " has it come to this ? Have they dared to call my beloved 'an outcast,' and say that no man seeketh after her ? Then I will seek her, and heal her, and restore her, for I cannot endure such tauntings." Now, if there is a poor sinner in the world, upon whom other sinners, who are just as bad in their heart, begin to vent their scorn, and say, " She is an outcast ;" then the God of mercy seems to say, " Who are you that you should talk like this ? You are as vile yourselves, and yet you dare to look down upon this poor, selected one, as if she were so much worse than you. Therefore, I will save that despised one, and will have mercy upon the rejected." God's tastes and man's differ very much. Whom man despises God delights in; and whom man delights in God despises. It often happens that when a transgressor has been put out of the synagogue Jesus finds him directly. When certain offenders happen to transgress in a particular way, which particular way is scouted and denounced by the bulk of ungodly people, then like so many hounds they unite to hunt the wretched being to death, but the Lord Jehovah interposes to save; as if he would say, "Why do you this, ye hypocrites? Wherefore do ye denounce those whose sins are no viler than your own?" I believe the Lord Jesus often stands as he did with the woman taken in adultery, and cries, "He that is without sin among you, let him first cast a stone at her." Still he convicts men in their consciences, and still in sweetness of mercy turns to the poor, condemned one, and says, "Neither do I condemn thee; go, and sin no more." Where are you, poor hunted sinner? You are somewhere or other in the crowd, I know. They told you yesterday that they would never associate with you any more. You do not deny your wickedness: still, it is not for your fellow-sinners to be hard with you, for they are not your judges. By faith take this promise to thyself: "I will restore health unto thee, because they called thee an outcast." Thou mayest get a good deal out of it if thou hast but faith to do so. Now that the world has cast thee out, the church shall take thee in: now that the devil seems tired of thee, Christ shall begin with thee: now that the door is shut against thee by those who once delighted in thee, Christ's door is open to receive thee. "Because they called thee an outcast" *he* calls thee to approach him.

But this is not the full meaning of the text. I think it means that *God's jealousy is aroused* against those who despise his people, and speak ill of them. Whatever Zion might be, it was still the palace of God: however guilty Jerusalem might have become, it was still the holy city, the dwelling-place of the great King. The Lord, for a while, when he was very angry with Jerusalem, on account of its great *iniquity*, gave it over to the destroyer, and it was laid waste and burned with fire; but when he heard the heathen everywhere saying, "As for those people, they are outcasts, and as for that city, no man seeks after it:" then the Lord said to himself, "But they are my people, and I will not have them called outcasts; and this is my city, and I will not have it said that no man seeks after it. Her name shall be called Hephzibah, and her land Beulah, for the Lord delighteth in her." His love burned like fire, and kindled into a flame of jealousy, and he said, "I will restore health to her, and shut the mouths of her adversaries." It is one thing for a father to chasten his boy; but if, when he is out in the streets, a stranger begins to kick him, his father declares that it shall not be. He arouses himself to defend his child, the same child that just now he smote so heavily. A man might complain of his wife if she had vexed him, but I suppose the quickest way to put him in good temper with her would be for somebody else to find fault with her. "What business is that of yours?" says he; "I will not have my wife abused: no man shall speak against her in my presence." That is a fair parallel to the case of our God. He will chasten his people in measure, but the moment that their enemies call them outcasts he turns his anger another way and releases his people. Oh, how blessedly does good come out of evil! How graciously he causes the wrath of man to praise him. He restores health to Zion, and heals her wounds because she is called an outcast.

I always have great hope for the entire Church of Christ when the ungodly begin to rail and revile. They say, "Christianity has lost its power; the Church is an old effete institution; no people of culture and intelligence keep to the old book and the old faith. The religion of Jesus is a by-word and a proverb among learned men." Therefore, I am confident that God will return to his Church, and magnify his truth. As surely as he lives he will give us bright days and glorious days, because they call his true Church an outcast, whom no man seeketh after. I like to read in man's black book, for man's revilings will lead to the speedier fulfilment of God's glorious promises.

> "Let Zion's foes be fill'd with shame;
> Her sons are bless'd of God;
> Though scoffers now despise their name,
> The Lord shall break their rod.
>
> "Oh, would our God to Zion turn,
> God with salvation clad;
> Then Judah's harps should music learn,
> And Israel be glad."

Appropriate the text personally any of you who have been made to feel that you are outcasts. One said to me the other day, talking of her sin, and of her repentance, "Yet, sir, I am an outcast." That word pierced my heart like a dagger. I said, "Yes, but the Church of Christ was made on purpose to be a home for outcasts: here is a new household for you, new brothers and sisters for you, a new future for you; for now you are one of the solitary ones whom the Lord will set in families."

Some of us were never called outcasts by other people, but we thought ourselves such. I once felt like Cain, as if God had set a mark upon me never to bless me; like an outlaw, condemned, and cast away; but when I reached that point the Lord's mercy revealed itself to me. He seemed to say, "Because thou hast called thyself an outcast, therefore will I restore health unto thee, and I will heal thee of thy wounds."

I should like to say a word that would be comforting to poor hearts that are greatly down-trodden. I do not feel able to preach at all, for I am weak and weary; but I always find when I am weak the Lord says somewhat by me which is just the thing wanted by some poor devil-hunted soul that cannot find rest. I think the Lord puts the trumpet out of order on purpose to draw from it a different note from what it gives when it is in proper condition,—a note that may precisely suit some weary ear that could not hearken to any other sound. May the Holy Spirit cause it to be so now.

IV. I am going to finish in the fourth place, by giving A LITTLE SUITABLE ADVICE. I will suppose that I have those before me who have felt their disease and their wound, and have been healed by the God of mercy. I would recommend them to attend to certain matters. The first thing is, *take care that you live very near your Physician*. I notice that patients come up from the country when they are suffering with serious complaints, and they take lodgings near a medical man who is in high esteem for such cases as theirs. They leave the comforts of home, and let their business go, because life is precious, and they need a helper close at hand. No one blames them for this; in fact we count them wise; let us learn wisdom from their example. Now, the Lord has healed your wound, and restored health to you, therefore abide in him; never leave him, nor **live far away** from him, for this old disease of yours may break out on a sudden, and it will be well to have the Healer close at hand. It will be best to entertain him constantly beneath your roof, and within your heart; for his presence is the wellspring of health to the soul. Abide perpetually with Christ, and then the sun shall not smite you by day, nor the moon by night: dwelling in the secret place of the Most High, there shall no evil befall you, neither shall any plague come nigh your dwelling. This disease of sin may cause eruptions when we least expect it; when we suppose that the evil leaven will work no more it may suddenly gather force, and the whole body of our nature will be in a ferment with iniquity. The danger is near, abide therefore near your security. Live with him who renews your youth like the eagle's, and restores your souls.

I recommend you often to put yourself under his searching examination. Go to this great Physician, and ask him to look into your hidden parts, to search you, and try you, and see what wicked way may be in you, that he may lead you in the way everlasting. A man may have a deadly disease upon him and scarcely be aware of it, because no skilled person has looked upon him, and observed his symptoms: and in spiritual things this is a common mischief, to which multitudes fall a prey. Invite, therefore, the eyes of the Lord Jesus, for in our most honest searches we miss much, and we are naturally prejudiced in our own favor, so that we are pretty sure to give a verdict on our own side; and this may lead to final and fatal self-delusion. If we intrust the search to him whose eyes are as a flame of fire we shall not be deceived.

I recommend you from personal experience to consult

with this Doctor every day. It is a wise thing before you go downstairs into the world's tainted atmosphere to take a draught of his *Elixir Vitæ* in the form of renewed faith in him. I am sure at night it is an admirable thing to purge the soul of all the perilous stuff which has accumulated through the day by full confession and renewed confidence.

Lay bare your case before him; conceal nothing; beg of him to deal with you according to his knowledge of your case. Make a clean breast that Christ may make a sure cure. Conceal no symptom however threatening, but tell him all the truth. He cannot be deceived; do not attempt it, but unbosom every secret thing before his all-surveying gaze. Entreat him to search both thoughts and affections, designs and motives. The ill may gather in secret places unless his discerning eye shall detect the growing danger, and prevent it by immediate action.

Then I should very strongly recommend you always to *obey the prescriptions of the great Healer.* "Whatsoever he saith unto you, do it." Do not follow a part of his orders, and neglect the rest. The Lord Jesus must be received as a whole, or not at all. Say not "This is non-essential;" for such a speech is flat rebellion. I do not believe in any words of our Lord being non-essential. They may not be essential to our salvation, but every word of Christ is essential to our spiritual health; neither can we disregard the least of his precepts without suffering loss through our disobedience. Be very careful that you follow the Lamb whithersoever he goeth; no other kind of walking is safe in such a world as this. Do what he bids you, as he bids you, and it shall be well with you.

Take care also to *exercise great confidence in this Physician.* Rely upon him without stint or question. Your cure is working wondrously when you trust in Jesus heartily. Never doubt the Saviour's power to make you perfectly whole. Our Lord never can be baffled; though all diseases should meet in one person he would overcome them all. Stick to this with unyielding assurance. Let not the devil force you to doubt the boundless power of your Lord. When our Lord Jesus set up to be a Saviour, he understood the work upon which he entered. His is no 'prenticed hand. He has never had a failure yet. Never did a soul trust him for salvation and remain unsaved; and you shall not be the first to defeat his skill. Trust him with all your heart. There is no cause to doubt. Distrust is what you have to fear; faith is your strength.

When you are healed, as I trust you are already, *speak well of your Benefactor.* Make a point of going round to your neighbors, if you find them sick, and telling them how you have been healed; thus will you make to your Lord a name of honor and renown. Tell out among all men what the Lord has done for you. I know you can tell them that story though you are no orator. When you were restored from sickness the other day, you were quite able to inform your friends as to that new medicine which acted like a charm, and you found a tongue to speak well of your doctor; and I am sure you have ability enough to declare the wonderful works of the Lord in your case. "Oh, but I could not embellish the tale!" Do not attempt to embellish it; for that would only spoil it. Tell the story as simply as possible. I think it is of Mr. Cecil that I have read the following incident. A friend came from some distance to inform him of a medicine which was to relieve him of his disorder. This friend told him all about it, and having done so, entered into conversation upon the current matters of the day. The result was that Mr. Cecil was greatly interested in the talk, and when his friend was gone, he quite forgot every ingredient of the wonderful medicine. Beware of allowing the many things to drive the one thing needful out of your friend's mind. When we preach fine sermons our hearers say, "That was prettily put." They do not so much notice what we taught as how we taught it; and this is a great evil. Even so if you go and talk about your salvation to your neighbor, and narrate it eloquently, she will say, 'Mrs. So-and-so has been here, and told me about her conversion in such beautiful language; I do not know that I ever heard such elegant sentences; it was most delightful to hear her." What did she say? "I do not know what she said, but it was very beautiful." Thus many a sermon or Sunday-school address is overlaid and buried under its own robes. Pity that those we seek to bless should be more taken up with our pretty words than with our adorable Master. I hope I have not this morning fallen into the evil which I lament. Lest I should have done so in any measure I would make my text my banner, and display it again. The Lord has said, "I will restore health unto thee, and heal thee of thy wounds." I believed that word when I was sick and wounded, and "the Lord was ready to save me: therefore we will sing my songs to the stringed instruments all the days of our life in the house of the Lord."

530 Broadway, New York,
March, 1884.

ROBERT CARTER AND BROTHERS'

NEW BOOKS.

HANDS FULL OF HONEY, and other Sermons, preached in 1883, by C. H. Spurgeon. 12mo. $1.00.

THE PRESENT TRUTH. New Sermons by C. H. Spurgeon. 12mo. $1.00.

Sermons. 10 vols. 12mo . . $10.00	Commenting and Commentaries. 12mo $1.00
Any volume sold separately at $1.00.	
Morning by Morning. 12mo 1.00	John Ploughman's Talk . . .75
Evening by Evening. 12mo . 1.00	John Ploughman's Pictures.
Types and Emblems. 12mo . 1.00	16mo 75
Saint and Saviour. 12mo . 1.00	John Ploughman's Talk and
Feathers for Arrows. 12mo 1.00	Pictures 12mo 1.00
Lectures to Students. 12mo 1.00	Gleanings among the Sheaves.
Spurgeon's Gems. 12mo . . 1.00	18mo 60

THE LIFE AND WORKS OF THOMAS GUTHRIE, D.D. New, neat, and very cheap edition. 11 vols. $10.00.
Or, separately, as follows:—

Guthrie's Autobiography	Man and the Gospel, and
and Life. 2 vols. 12mo . $2.00	Our Father's Business.
The Gospel in Ezekiel. 12mo 1.00	In 1 vol. 12mo $1.00
The Saint's Inheritance . . 1.00	Speaking to the Heart. 12mo 1.00
The Way to Life. 12mo. . 1.00	Out of Harness. 12mo . . 1.00
On the Parables. Illustrated. 1.00	Studies of Character. 12mo 1.00
The City and Ragged Schools. 1.00	

WORKS OF THE REV. T. L. CUYLER, D.D.

THE EMPTY CRIB. 24mo, gilt . $1.00	POINTED PAPERS. 12mo . . $1.50
STRAY ARROWS. 18mo 60	FROM THE NILE TO NORWAY.
CEDAR CHRISTIAN 18mo . . .75	12mo 1.50
THOUGHT HIVES. With Portrait. 12mo 1.50	GOD'S LIGHT ON DARK CLOUDS. 18mo 75

*A. L. O. E. LIBRARY. New and very beautiful edition. Complete in 50 volumes. 16mo, crimson cloth. Put up in a neat wooden case. *Net*, $28.00.

 The volumes are sold separately at 80 cents each.

*OLIVE LIBRARY. 40 large 16mo volumes, containing 15,340 pages, in a neat wooden case. *Net* (no discount to S. S. Libraries), $25.00.

INFORMATION AND ILLUSTRATION for Sermons and Addresses. By G. S. BOWES. 12mo. $1.50.

THE PUBLIC MINISTRY AND PASTORAL METHODS OF OUR LORD. By W. G. BLAIKIE, D.D. $1.50.

PHILOSOPHY AND CHRISTIANITY. By Prof. GEORGE S. MORRIS. 12mo. $1.75.

HOW SHALL I GO TO GOD? By HORATIUS BONAR, D.D. 18mo. 40 cents.

THE HUMAN MIND. By EDWARD J. HAMILTON, D.D. 8vo. $3.00.

MOSES AND THE PROPHETS. By Dr. W. H. GREEN. 12mo. $1.00.

THE NEW TESTAMENT SCRIPTURES: Their Claims, History, and Authority. By A. H. CHARTERIS, D.D. 8vo. $2.00.

THE LIFE AND LABORS OF ROBERT MOFFAT, Missionary to Africa. 12mo. $1.25.

ARNOT ON THE PARABLES. New edition. 12mo. $1.75.

FROM YEAR TO YEAR. Hymns and Poems. By the Rev. E. H. Bickersteth. 18mo. $1.25.

FAITH THURSTON'S WORK. By the author of "Win and Wear." 12mo. $1.25.

THROUGH THE NARROWS. By W. W. Everts, D.D. 16mo. 60 cents.

HAUSSER'S PERIOD OF THE REFORMATION. New edition. 12mo. $2.50.

J. M. DRINKWATER CONKLIN'S BOOKS.

Rue's Helps	$1.50	Tessa Wadsworth's Discipline	$1.50
Electa: A Story	1.50	Only Ned	1.25
Fifteen	1.50	Not Bread Alone	1.25
Bek's First Corner	1.50	Fred and Jeanie	1.25
Miss Prudence	1.50		

AGNES GIBERNE'S BOOKS.

Aimee: A Tale of James II.	$1.50	The World's Foundations	$1.50
The Day Star; or, Gospel Stories	1.25	Duties and Duties	1.25
The Curate's Home	1.25	Through the Linn	1.25
Floss Silverthorn	1.25	Sweetbriar	1.50
Coulyng Castle	1.50	Jacob Witherby	.60
Muriel Bertram	1.50	Decima's Promise	1.25
The Sun, Moon, and Stars	1.50	Twilight Talks	.75
		Kathleen	1.50

EMILY SARAH HOLT'S BOOKS.

Isoult Barry	$1.50	Margery's Son	$1.50
Robin Tremayne	1.50	Lady Sybil's Choice	1.50
The Well in the Desert	1.25	The Maiden's Lodge	1.25
Ashcliffe Hall	1.50	Earl Hubert's Daughter	1.50
Verena: A Tale	1.50	Joyce Morrell's Harvest	1.50
The White Rose of Langley	1.50	At ye Grene Griffin	1.00
Imogen	1.50	Red and White	1.50
Clare Avery	1.50	Not for Him	1.25
Lettice Eden	1.50	Wearyholme	1.50
For the Master's Sake	1.00	The Way of the Cross	.60

EMMA MARSHALL'S BOOKS.

Poppies and Pansies . . . $1.50	The Little Peat Cutters . $ .50
Dewdrops and Diamonds . . 1.50	Roger's Apprenticeship . . .50
Rex and Regina 1.50	Katie's Work 50
Dayspring 1.50	Consideration for Others . .50
Ruby and Pearl 1.25	Little Primrose 50
A Chip of the Old Block . .50	The Two Margarets 50
Framilode Hall 50	**Primrose Series.** The above 6 vols., 18mo, in a box . . 3.00
Violet and Lily Series. 6 vols., 16mo, in a box . . 3.00	Between the Cliffs . . . 1.00
Sir Valentine's Victory . . 1.25	Little Brothers and Sisters 1.00
Matthew Frost 1.00	Stories of the Cathedral Cities 1.50
Stellafont Abbey 1.00	

THE EMPEROR'S BOYS. By Ismay Thorn. $1.25.

WILD HYACINTHS. By Lady Hope. $1.50.

MARJORIE'S PROBATION. By J. S. Ranking. $1.25.

THE CAGED LINNET. By Mrs. Stanley Leathes. $1.25.

SUSAN WARNER'S BOOKS.

My Desire $1.75	**A Story of Small Beginnings.** 4 vols., 16mo, in a box $5.00
The End of a Coil 1.75	What She Could 1.25
The Letter of Credit . . 1.75	Opportunities 1.25
Nobody 1.75	The House in Town . . . 1.25
Stephen, M.D. 1.75	Trading 1.25
The Old Helmet 2.25	**The Say and Do Series.** 6 vols., 16mo, in a box . . 7.50
Melbourne House 2.00	Little Camp on Eagle Hill 1.25
Pine Needles 1.25	Willow Brook 1.25
King's People. The. 5 vols., 16mo, in a box 7.00	Sceptres and Crowns . . 1.25
Walks from Eden . . . 1.50	A Flag of Truce 1.25
House of Israel . . . 1.50	Bread and Oranges . . . 1.25
Star Out of Jacob . . . 1.50	Rapids of Niagara . . . 1.25
Kingdom of Judah . . . 1.50	
Broken Walls of Jerusalem 1.25	

ANNA B. WARNER'S BOOKS.

The Blue Flag	$1.25
Tired Church Members	.50
A Bag of Stories	.75
Little Jack's Four Lessons	.50
Stories of Vinegar Hill. 3 vols., 16mo, in a box	3.00
Ellen Montgomery's Book-Shelf. 5 vols., 16mo, in a box	$5.00
Mr. Rutherford's Children	1.00
Sybil and Chryssa	1.00
Hard Maple	1.00
Carl Krinken	1.00
Casper and His Friends	1.00

DR. RICHARD NEWTON'S BOOKS.

The Best Things	$1.25
The King's Highway	1.25
The Safe Compass	1.25
Bible Blessings	1.25
The Great Pilot	1.25
Bible Jewels	1.25
Bible Wonders	1.25
Nature's Wonders	1.25
Leaves from the Tree	1.25
Rills from the Fountain	1.25
The Jewish Tabernacle	$1.25
Giants, and Wonderful Things	1.25
Rays from the Sun of Righteousness	1.25
The King in His Beauty	1.25
Pebbles from the Brook	1.25
Covenant Names and Privileges	1.50

REV. W. W. NEWTON'S BOOKS.

Little and Wise	$1.25
The Wicket Gate	1.25
The Interpreter's House	$1.25
The Palace Beautiful	1.25

BOOKS BY THE AUTHOR OF "WIN AND WEAR."

Win and Wear Series. 6 vols. 16mo	$7.50
The Green Mountain Stories. 5 vols. 16mo	6.00
Ledgeside Series. 6 vols. 16mo	7.50
Faith Thurston's Work	1.25
Highland Series. 6 vols. 16mo	$7.50
Hester Trueworthy's Royalty	1.25
Mabel's Stepmother	1.25
Butterfly's Flights. 3 vols. 18mo	2.25

JULIA MATHEWS' BOOKS.

Drayton Hall Series. 6 vols.	$4.50
Lawrence Bronson's Victory	.75
Christy's Grandson	.75
Allan Haywood	$ .75
Frank Austin's Diamond	.75
Eagle Crag	.75
True to His Flag	.75

JULIA MATHEWS' BOOKS — *Continued.*

Golden Ladder Series. 3 vols. 16mo	$3.00
Dare to Do Right. 5 vols. 16mo	.50
Grandfather's Faith	1.10
Our Four Boys	1.10
Giuseppe's Home	$1.10
Nellie's Stumbling-Block	1.10
Susy's Sacrifice	1.10
Katy and Jim, containing "Little Katy" and "Jolly and Katy"	1.25

JOANNA H. MATHEWS' BOOKS.

Bessie Books. 6 vols., 16mo, in a box	$7.50
At the Seaside	1.25
In the City	1.25
And her Friends	1.25
Among the Mountains	1.25
At School	1.25
On her Travels	1.25
Flowerets. 6 vols., 18mo, in a box	3.60
Little Sunbeams. 6 vols., 16mo., in a box	6.00
Belle Powers' Locket	1.00
Dora's Motto	1.00
Lily Norris' Enemy	1.00
Jessie's Parrot	1.00
Mamie's Watchword	1.00
Nellie's Housekeeping	1.00
Kitty and Lulu Books. 6 vols., 18mo, in a box	$3.60
Miss Ashton's Girls. 6 vols.	7.50
Fanny's Birthday Gift	1.25
The New Scholars	1.25
Rosalie's Pet	1.25
Eleanor's Visit	1.25
Mabel Walton's Experiment	1.25
Elsie's Santa Claus	1.25
Haps and Mishaps. 6 vols.	7.50
Little Friends at Glenwood	1.25
The Broken Mallet	1.25
Blackberry Jam	1.25
Milly's Whims	1.25
Lilies or Thistledown	1.25
Uncle Joe's Thanksgiving	1.25

CATHERINE SHAW'S BOOKS.

The Gabled Farm	$1.25
Nellie Arundel	1.25
In the Sunlight	1.25
Hilda. 12mo	1.25
Only a Cousin	$1.25
Out in the Storm	.50
Alick's Hero	1.25

EMILY BRODIE'S BOOKS.

Jean Lindsay	$1.25
Dora Hamilton's Choice	1.25
Elsie Gordon	1.25
Uncle Fred's Shilling	1.25
Lonely Jack	$1.25
Ruth's Rescue	.50
Nora Clinton	1.25

www.ingramcontent.com/pod-product-compliance
Lightning Source LLC
Chambersburg PA
CBHW020239240426
43672CB00006B/576